ARABIAN
ADVENTURES

ARABIAN ADVENTURES

Ten years of joyful service

JOHN GLUBB

CASSELL
LONDON

CASSELL LTD.
35 Red Lion Square, London WC1R 4SG
and at Sydney, Auckland, Toronto, Johannesburg,
an affiliate of
Macmillan Publishing Co., Inc.,
New York.

First published 1978

The maps have been prepared by Cartographic Enterprises

ISBN 0 304 30171 X

Photoset and printed in Great Britain by
Lowe & Brydone Printers Limited, Thetford, Norfolk

Contents

Maps

Author's Note

In one or two instances, I have drawn somewhat unfavourable pictures of certain individuals. All the persons in question are long since dead, but if I had given their real names, the feelings of their descendants might have been hurt. In these cases, I have given these persons false names.

I would emphasize, however, that all the incidents mentioned are true in every detail. Only, here and there, the real name of one individual may have been changed.

The operations referred to in Chapters 13 and 17, and part of 18, have been more fully described in my book *War in the Desert*. I have, however, inserted summarized versions in the present book, in order to maintain chronological continuity.

I would also like to express my gratitude to Messrs. Hodder and Stoughton, the publishers of *War in the Desert*.

I have made no attempt in this book to spell Arabic names in their classical form, but have used the local colloquial forms of speech. For example, there is no -*ch* sound in Arabic. I have, nevertheless, used the form Beni Huchaim, for example, because this is how it is universally pronounced in Iraq. The correct grammatical form would be Beni Hukaim. There are a few other similar cases.

I vow to thee, my country, all earthly things above,
Entire and whole and perfect, the service of my love;
The love that asks no question, the love that stands the test,
That lays upon the altar, the dearest and the best;
The love that never falters, the love that pays the price,
The love that makes undaunted, the final sacrifice.

And there's another country, I've heard of long ago,
Most dear to them that love her, most great to them that know;
We may not count her armies, we may not see her King;
Her fortress is a faithful heart, her pride is suffering;
And soul by soul and silently, her shining bounds increase,
And her ways are ways of gentleness, and all her paths are peace.

CECIL SPRING-RICE

Introduction

I have always been an inveterate scribbler. All through my life I have written diaries, descriptions of notable events, reports and essays, on anything and everything that happened. If I moved house, I was accompanied by innumerable boxes packed with old papers in faded handwriting.

The incidents described in this book are not, therefore, the memories of an old man, but the vivid impressions of an inexperienced but enthusiastic youth. The views expressed are those held by me in my twenties and early thirties, not necessarily those which I hold today. I have thought it better not to confuse the more or less homogeneous picture of a young officer of fifty years ago by diluting his views with those of an old man in 1978. All that I have done, therefore, is to insert such passages as were necessary to string the various incidents together. The different episodes are almost all copied verbatim from descriptions which I wrote at the time. Passages written later by way of comment have been enclosed within square brackets.

The whole history of Britain's activities in Asia has been the subject of intense political debate and propaganda. Such is the power of modern publicity that it is possible to convince a whole nation of a viewpoint which is, in fact, entirely erroneous. In this manner, the climate of opinion of fifty or sixty years ago has been almost completely lost. It has been my hope, therefore, to write a period piece, in the original words and expressing the thoughts of fifty years ago, to assist the modern reader to appreciate the ideas and the motives of the people of those days.

Whether from error or for the purposes of political propaganda it is a common mistake to refer to the populations of past eras as the rich and the poor, contrasting the extremes of both. This classification is completely misleading, for at any time the majority of the nation belonged to neither extreme.

The officers and officials who manned the British services overseas were financially neither rich nor poor. Often generation after generation followed one another in service in India or the Empire, inspired solely by duty and tradition. Many died young, others endured loneliness and suffering, not for financial gain, but inspired by traditions of duty. My father believed that it was the solemn duty of Britain to control, care for and protect the peoples of the Empire.

In the present materialistic age, Empire is represented as the exploitation of weaker peoples. As a young man, I was unaware of such accusations. The establishment of law and order, the construction of irrigation schemes, the opening of roads and railways seemed to me to be entirely beneficent activities. Some persons may have made money in business. But the Empire and its subsidiaries were operated by a middle class of officials and officers who were far from rich and who led devoted lives, inspired by honour and duty, and by love for the peoples among whom they worked.

Before the First World War the character of Britain's public servants overseas was principally moulded by four factors. First of these was a religious home background. Secondly, by a family tradition of several generations of service overseas. Thirdly, by country life and boyhood sports in Britain, and finally by public schools or grammar schools. Therefore, before telling the story of my service from 1920 to 1930, it seemed to me useful to include a brief history of my boyhood on which was founded my subsequent career among the Arabs.

1
Boyhood Background

My father grew up in very straitened circumstances, his father having died of cholera in India when he was still a baby. In 1871, however, he won a scholarship into Wellington, and thus obtained a public school education. In 1911, I won a scholarship into Cheltenham College, and as a result was educated free of charge. I got through my three years there fairly well. Part of the time was unpleasant, while at other times it was amusing. It was very far from being the happiest time of my life, but public schools in those days served a genuine purpose in making boys tough and self-reliant.

The great joy of my youth was from horses. My father had been something of an amateur jockey in his day and I had inherited his passion. In 1911, when I went to Cheltenham, my father, who was a regular Army officer, was transferred from York to Head Quarters Southern Command at Salisbury. He was entitled to two chargers, and kept a big bay horse which he hunted, called Joe, and a grey Arab called Jumbo, which I used to ride.

The country around Salisbury was not so good for hunting as Yorkshire had been. It consisted of the Wiltshire Downs, bare rolling hills covered with short grass and without hedges, though divided in places by wire fences. This type of country did not suit my father, who liked stiff fences and plenty of jumping with no wire. He consequently preferred to hunt with the South and West Wilts or with the Blackmore Vale. Their countries consisted of a good area of vale country extending round Shaftesbury to Sherborne, with a line of downs to the north.

In Yorkshire the fences had been clean thorn hedges growing out of ground level, with a ditch on one side or the other. In West Wiltshire and Dorset the fields were mostly divided by earth banks with larger ditches, and a thorn fence growing on top of the bank. Most of these obstacles were too big to jump in one. The horse had to jump the ditch and land on the bank, then change his feet on top of the bank and jump over or through the fence which grew on the bank and out into the field beyond. The fields were smaller than in Yorkshire which meant more jumps.

I had for several years ridden the grey Arab pony called Jumbo. He could jump like a stag, but we were a bit anxious at first how he would take to banks. My father's old hunter, Joe, was also new to such country, but both of them learned the art of jumping on to the tops of the banks.

Shaftesbury was too far away to enable us to ride to meets in that area. We used therefore to start early with our two horses and take them by train. It would not have been possible to go by train to cub-hunting meets in September, because they take place soon after dawn. My father rarely had time to come cub-hunting, and kept all his free days for the real hunting season. So I went alone.

My alarm clock would go at half-past one or two in the morning and I would slip into my clothes, tip-toe downstairs in the dark and let myself out of the front door into the night. I would saddle up Jumbo and we would ride through the silent and deserted streets of Salisbury, his hoofs ringing on the metalled pavement. On at a steady jog through Wilton and up those lovely narrow Wiltshire valleys, with their tall trees, narrow lanes and thatched cottages, with the downs on either side showing black against the night sky. The air would be filled with the damp freshness of the English night. As we trotted through the silent village of Burcombe, the first light of dawn would be showing in the eastern sky. At Barford St. Martin it would be daylight, thin columns of smoke would begin to rise from the cottages nestling beneath the downs – soon the first pale rays of sun would glint on the grass, sparkling with diamond dew.

The air is cool and fresh, a joy to breathe. Through the little hamlet of Baverstock and here are the hounds, half a dozen enthusiasts, two men on young horses getting used to hounds and a group of farm workers and children on foot. Hounds move off over a field, leaving a green path across the soaking grass, grey with the heavy dew. Soon the familiar music of the hounds is heard in a nearby wood. At noon the long ride home, through the now busy streets of Wilton and Salisbury, a late breakfast at lunch-time and so to bed, limbs weary, back aching but heart content.

But the serious hunting was in the winter. I remember particularly one great hunt in the 1913-14 Christmas holidays. I was sixteen now and no longer followed my father. He considered that I should be man enough to ride my own line. Jumbo was now an expert in the Wiltshire country and could beat many full-size hunters. This country, which required cleverness as much as strength and speed, gave him extra scope.

We found in a spinney somewhere east of Shaftesbury and our fox made a bee-line due north for the downs. He was obviously an old stager and hounds were quickly away and running so fast that we had to gallop hard to keep in touch. I slipped away from the bulk of the field to a good start and three or four awkward banks and fences soon made even more elbow room. I could see my father riding fifty yards to my right with old Joe striding along, ears-pricked, as if he realized that this was going to be the thing of the season. But the size of the fields grew smaller, so that there was no longer any time to look about. You had scarcely negotiated one fence, when your whole attention was needed to choose your place in the next.

We jumped a small fly-fence in style, then across a field of plough and a scramble and splash through a muddy bottom. Hounds were drawing further ahead, the pace was increasing to that of a steeple-chase and was obviously beginning to tell. On my right, a tall man in a pink coat was galloping on a thoroughbred chestnut horse whose neck and shoulders were already white with a lather of sweat. Poor Jumbo was beginning to blow and I could feel him checking his speed. Worst of all, the country was beginning gradually to rise as we approached the downs, so we were galloping uphill as well as jumping a big fence every few yards.

As we struggled uphill across a small grass paddock, I saw in front of me a fence with a wide ditch and high bank, and on the top of the bank an old straggling thorn fence, perhaps ten or twelve feet high. There was obviously no chance of jumping the fence. The only course was to jump over the ditch on to the bank, crash through the thorn fence and jump off. I rode at a place in front of me which looked just possible.

Jumbo was already blowing and gasping and I should have checked him for a few yards before riding at this ugly place, to let him collect himself. But hounds were nearly out of sight and I was unwilling to allow any of the now rapidly thinning field to gallop past me. He faced up to the fence and we went at it but in the last stride he lost his nerve and planted his four feet. We slid at full speed into the ditch. In this anguished moment Jumbo somehow turned sideways and we crashed into the ditch hitting sideways into the bank beyond. A stray branch knocked in my hat. At some moment in our glissade, my face had bumped violently into Jumbo's neck, I saw stars and my nose poured with blood.

But this was no time to dawdle. We would not miss this hunt! I pulled his head round and kicked him in the flanks as best I could. With a flounder and a heave, he climbed out of the ditch while I clung to his mane. I trotted him twenty yards back and then turned to face our fence again. There was a thinner place ten yards to the right where somebody had already gone through. 'Come on, old man,' I said to him. 'We cannot miss a hunt like this.' I set him at it and gave him my legs as hard as I could at the last two strides – and up on to the bank he jumped and changed his feet, a branch slashed me across the face like a riding-whip, and we were galloping up the next field.

There were only three more fields to the open downs. I could only see five or six other riders in front of me. Hounds had already disappeared over the nearest crest of the downs. Behind us, the country was dotted with pink and black coats, following as best they could. We jumped a low easy bank with no hedge and were out on the open downs.

There were apparently no more fences to jump, but that did not end our troubles for some of these hills were, as the saying goes, as steep as the side of a house. Jumbo fell back – first to a hand canter then to a jog-trot – as he battled up the hill. I leant forward and whispered encouragements in his ear, standing up in my stirrups. Meanwhile my heart burned with frenzy within me. The slope came to a crest at the top of this hill. Fifty yards ahead, should we see the hounds when we topped the crest? Were we left hopelessly behind? My nose must still be bleeding as I could taste the warm blood running into my mouth. 'Come on old man! come on! We must catch up!'

When we topped the rise, hounds were nowhere in sight. A shallow valley in the hills opened in front of us, and about two hundred yards ahead of us was a group of some six or seven horsemen. I kicked Jumbo hard into a gallop. As we rode up, I saw that a long wire fence stretched over the downs to the right and left until it disappeared over the crests of spurs of the downs in both directions. In front of the party of horsemen for a length of about twenty yards the wire fence stopped and was replaced by a high and very solid timber post and rails. There seemed to be no way round the wire fence and no way through. There was nothing for it but to jump

4

the solid oak rails, and it was plain enough that any horse which hit them would turn a somersault. Those rails were not going to break.

As I approached, a tough-looking little man in a black coat rode at the timber fence, cleared it handsomely and galloped away up the slope beyond. It was obvious to me that the rest of the company were secretly afraid, but were pretending that their horses were refusing. A man on a long-tailed grey thoroughbred was using his whip and shouting 'Go on, you brute!' But his horse swerved away to one side. A fat lady with a red face in a great state of excitement was pulling her horse about until she had it almost as nervous as herself. It came plunging towards us half out of control. 'Get out of the way, boy!' shouted the red-faced lady.

Jumbo and I took a look at those oak rails. Then I took him twenty yards back and waited a chance to slip in between all these excited people. A man on a big bay horse galloped away down the wire fence to look for a gate. The grey thoroughbred maddened by the whip, was beginning to rear. The red-faced lady plunged away to the right. Jummy had recovered his wind. 'Come on, old man, we'll show 'em,' I whispered.

'Throw your heart over the fence and your horse will soon follow,' says the old hunting adage. I pressed Jumbo into a canter, gave him all the leg I had for the last three paces, and in less time than it takes to tell, we were galloping up the downs beyond. I believe I heard Jummy laugh as the voice of the man on the grey horse was wafted after us. 'Come on, you damned brute!' he shouted.

About a mile further on as we topped a rise, we came in sight of hounds, crying and jostling round the huntsman, who was holding the dead fox in his hands. 'Who-hoop!' he cried, 'Who-hoop!' as he threw the carcass into the air to be caught and torn by the hounds. There were only five horsemen up. The huntsman and one whip, and three other men. Another galloped up not far behind me. Soon my father appeared on old Joe, who was blowing hard and wagging his tail. He had come up the next valley and through a gate in the wire, without seeing our oak rails.

'Who-hoop!' said Jummy and I in our hearts. 'We did teach them a lesson. What a day! Forty-five minutes at full speed without a check, jumping all the way and a flight of oak rails at the end!' It was the last day's hunting in my life, though I little knew it.

While Jumbo and I were taking our fun across the banks and

rails of Wiltshire and Dorset, the war clouds were piling up in Europe. In July 1914, at the end of the summer term, I went into camp with the Cheltenham contingent of the Officers' Training Corps. We were to stay in camp for ten days. Then Austria declared war on Serbia. On the fifth day of our camp Britain declared war on Germany. The Army was mobilizing and the regular officers who were training us were called away. Before leaving, our company commander, a captain in the 60th, gave us a short address. He told us that the German Army had invaded Belgium, in spite of a treaty signed by Germany guaranteeing Belgian neutrality. This was a moment when every man must do his duty to his country. He ended his little speech with the words 'Perhaps some of you, before this war is over, will enjoy the greatest honour a man can ever gain – that of leading British troops in battle!'

The camp broke up and we had to find our way home as best we could. The train service was disorganized. Long trains loaded with troops were choking the stations and reservists were pouring in to join their units. I arrived home in Salisbury in a milk-cart.

My father had already received his orders. He was to be Chief Engineer of the III Army Corps. The I and II Corps were to cross to France first, so he would not embark for several days. Meanwhile my mother was on holiday in Austria. It was impossible to communicate with her and all Europe was in chaos. My father was in desperate anxiety: on the one hand about the rapid sweep of the German armies into Belgium, on the other about the safety of my mother.

The day after my return home, I went into Salisbury. I was by the County Hotel near the bridge over the river, when I heard a band playing. It was a Territorial battalion of infantry which had been embodied and was marching to the station. People on the pavements cheered and called, 'Good luck!' A white-haired old man standing beside me, held his hat raised above his head until the whole battalion had passed. Tears ran down his face. Perhaps he was an old soldier, a veteran of past campaigns. I was deeply stirred. My company commander in camp had come from the 60th Rifles. It was only yesterday that he had given us his spirited address. I decided to enlist as a soldier in the 60th. To become an officer would take too long. The war might be over before then.

I went home and told my father that I wanted to enlist immediately. He reasoned with me calmly, saying that it would be wasting my experience and training to go as a private soldier. I would serve my country better if I went as an officer and exercised for now a little patience.

At night, when I was going to bed, I suddenly heard a noise downstairs and loud voices in the hall. It was my mother, who had arrived back from Austria. She had crossed Europe undaunted, jumping on odd trains full of soldiers and had caught the last Channel-steamer to cross from Calais to Dover.

A week later, I drove down with my father to Southampton where he was embarking for France with the III Army Corps. We had several hours to wait at Southampton and sat in a bedroom of the South Western Hotel. The hotel, the station and the harbour were packed with troops.

I felt that mixture of fear and the ache of bereavement, which precedes a long parting. Our home in Salisbury was to be broken up and my mother would live in a hotel. My father sat sewing a button on to his field uniform and checking over his kit. What agony he felt in his heart after saying goodbye to my mother and leaving his home, I do not know. He was a man who never showed his emotions, though he was sensitive and felt deeply.

At last I had to go. His ship would not sail till after dark. There were already German submarines in the Channel. 'Goodbye, old boy,' my father said. 'Mind you don't worry. Look after your mother.'

I left the hotel with a sinking heart. As I drove through Southampton, the newspaper hoardings read '*The War to End War* by H. G. Wells'.

A few days later I went up to Burlington Gardens and sat the examination for entrance to the Royal Military Academy at Woolwich. I passed in second. Forty years earlier my father had passed in third. As soon as he heard of my success, he wrote to me, although he was involved day and night in the Battle of the Marne and the operations which followed. His letter reached me the day after I joined at Woolwich.

> My dear old boy,
>
> You will know well how pleased and proud I was when I heard the news of your having passed in second. You beat me. I was only third in my batch. This is a letter of thankfulness, gratitude and rejoicing, but I will add one little word.
>
> You are very nearly a commissioned officer and a man now, dear old boy. See that you are also a gentleman, a simple honest

English gentleman – you cannot be anything better whatever you are. Don't let anything lower your standards, dear old boy.

His life was always as strong an argument as his words, for he himself was just that simple soldier and gentleman which he longed that I should become.

Long before I went to the 'Shop' (as the Woolwich Academy was called), my father had told me stories of the Riding School there and of the jokes retailed by the riding masters. Captain Dann, he told me, had been the Chief Riding Master in his day. It was therefore with some amusement that I discovered that Captain Dann was still the Chief Riding Master – the son of my father's Dann! What is more, the riding masters were still retailing the jokes of the 1870s, which may well have dated from the eighteenth or the seventeenth centuries.

The beginner, when first placed on a horse, often leans forward in a rather painful and ungraceful manner. I have heard this forward bend compared to that of a hen, seeking grains on the floor of the hen-run. But the riding masters had a less genteel word for it – a gibe probably centuries old. 'Sit up, Sir!' Mr. Hance, our riding master would call. 'Sit up! you look like an old lady on a night-commode!'

Mr. Hance had regular groups of jests, which he had doubtless inherited from many generations of riding masters.

'Keep your heels down, sir!' he would shout. 'Unless you keep your heels down, you'll have no more chance than a snowball in Hell!'

He had a particularly telling set of taunts, which he prefaced with the phrase 'You've missed your vocation, Sir!' uttered with every varied intonation of pity or contempt. To a cadet who handled his horse with obvious nervousness, Mr. Hance would remark with withering scorn – 'You've missed your vocation, Sir! You oughtn't to be a soldier! You ought to have been a milkmaid!' I often wondered how many officers who fought at Blenheim or Waterloo had been adjured in the same manner.

When a cadet gave the reins a savage jerk, causing his horse to throw up his head and show his teeth, Mr. Hance made a gesture of extreme despair. Then in a slow and solemn tone he announced: 'You've missed your vocation, Sir! You ought to have been a dentist!'

He was, however, quite capable of producing modern versions of the old jokes. When a cadet, at a jump, flew out of the saddle and landed on the ground on his face several yards away, Mr. Hance remarked briskly: 'You've missed your vocation, Sir! You should have joined the Flying Corps.'

But if some of Hance's jokes were a little lacking in propriety, he was a stickler for the polite conventions before visitors. There was a gallery to the riding school, where spectators, including ladies, sometimes appeared. Mr. Hance had a Bowdlerized version ready for such occasions. The night-commode, for example, disappeared for the duration of the ladies' visit.

'Sit up, Sir! Sit up,' he would call cheerfully. 'You remind me of the proverbial old lady!'

Hance retailed all his quips with such good humour that he was extremely popular with his victims. But Dann, the Chief Riding Master, was of sterner stuff. Sometimes when we were bumping round the indoor riding-school with old Hance, there would be a loud *rat-tat-tat* on the door. An orderly would dash forward, the doors would be flung wide, and Captain Dann would enter *ventre-à-terre*, pulling up his horse on its haunches in the centre of the circle. He would survey us critically for some minutes and then halt the ride. 'Gentlemen,' he would call in stentorian tones, 'when I was out the other day I met the governor' – *The Commandant of the Royal Military Academy was called the "Governor"* – and he said to me – "Dann, how are the gentleman cadets getting on with their riding?"

'And I said to him "Sir!" I said, "There's only one thing wrong with the cadets today."

'"And what's that, Dann?" he said to me.

'"Guts, sir," said I, "They've got no G-U-T-S!" Yes gentlemen, no guts.'

'Ride, cross stirrups! Trot! Trot out!' – and he would keep us bumping round the school with no stirrups until the weaker brethren were slipping and sliding and catching hold of their saddles.

Dann was merciless in his taunts – a man in my batch, called Perry, never could stay on a horse. One day we were going over a jump, when the unhappy Perry fell off. Dann made him remount and go over again, whereupon he again fell off. Once more Dann ordered him to remount and go over the fence. For the third time he fell off, but this time he did not get up. Not that he was hurt, but he was getting tired of falling off and remained lying on the ground on his face. Dann's scorn was biting. 'He's looking for his false teeth in the tan,' he remarked, looking round at the class.

Another Woolwich custom of which my father had told me was that of the morning bath. When I went there in 1914, I found it unchanged since 1870. We slept four in one room, and behind the building was a courtyard, on the far side of which was a long shed full of ordinary domestic baths. All the baths were filled to the brim with water every evening.

As soon as reveille was blown in the morning, you had to get out of bed, take off your pyjamas, seize your sponge but not a towel, run naked across the courtyard and jump into a bath. Scrambling out again, you ran back naked across the courtyard and into your room where you could dry yourself and dress. On a warm day in July the operation was not unpleasant, but in winter a solid layer of ice often covered the bath and had to be broken before you could have your dip. The latter occupied only one second of time and a breathless gasp, as you plunged in and out of the freezing water. Often it was necessary to run back across the court in the snow with bare feet.

There was no supervision as to whether or not you really plunged into your icy tub, yet I cannot remember anyone shirking the ordeal. The freezing bath, like so many other customs at public schools and army colleges in the nineteenth century, was intended to teach young men to endure. Rightly or wrongly, the produce of this system explored or conquered a great part of the world. Their first ambition was to be men, to see active service and to do their duty. I do not think they aspired to earn a large salary – I do not remember such a question ever being discussed, though many of us were poor.

My worst memories of Woolwich are connected with the then prevalent and doubtless ancient custom of 'toshing'. The cadets at Woolwich were organized in three classes, of which the senior class provided Cadet officers and N.C.O.s. The senior class took upon itself to 'put in his place' any cadet in the junior classes whom they considered to be conceited or in other ways to merit being 'taken down a peg'.

The time allotted for 'toshing' was after dinner in the evening, when all cadets were supposed to go to their rooms. The word would be passed round the senior class, who would change into running shorts and assemble outside the library, each armed with a cane. When all were ready the whole pack would set out to find the appointed victim, howling like a host of devils as they went. He would be dragged from his room and chased round the grounds, belaboured with canes should he delay his flight. He would then be taken to the lake, on the shores of which stood an old gun, a trophy from some ancient battle. Forced to stand up on the gun above the heads of his tormentors, he would be ordered to make a speech. The proceedings concluded when the victim was thrown into the lake and the senior class returned to their rooms.

No great injury was ever done to the victims, as far as my experience went. It was the fear of being toshed which was so alarming. I was once in my room on a dark winter evening when I heard the distant baying of the pack. The noise grew louder and louder and louder, it stopped outside the building, it began to ascend the stairs. In a few seconds, a deafening pandemonium was raging outside the door of my room. For several moments, my heart stood still. Then the screaming torrent went on up the stairs to the floor above. The victim taken was in the room immediately above mine. There is something terrifying in an excited crowd which inspires more fear than shells or bullets. I have been involved in various battles since those days, but I doubt if I have ever again been so frightened.

For my last two months at the Shop, I was made a cadet sergeant, and put in command of a Squad. Sergeants at Woolwich in those days wore swords. After church parade on Sundays, we used to march past the Governor, while the Royal Artillery band played *The British Grenadiers*. I can still remember, how bursting I felt with pride as, sword in hand, I passed the saluting-base. The majority of my comrades, who swung with me past that saluting base, were to be killed in the ensuing three years.

On 20 April, 1915, I was commissioned a Second Lieutenant in the Royal Engineers, and on 24 November, 1915, I embarked for France.

I have already stated that it is my ambition in this book to produce a period piece, recording the life and the ideas of a young British officer serving overseas in the 1920s. As my mentality was the result of my upbringing, it seemed to me relevant to include this brief account of my boyhood, of school, my association with horses and of the Shop.

It is intended to be a picture of the times. There is little peculiar to me. Indeed I was the least of such people. The high ideals of my father and grandfather were already weakening in my day, and were being replaced by the ambition to earn a large salary and enjoy a higher standard of material living.

2

Perils by Water

The normal course of training for a young officer in the Royal Engineers was two years in the R.E. Base Depot at Chatham, but owing to the extreme need for officers in 1915, we had been rushed through in a few months. As a result, in February 1919 I was recalled from my unit in France and was posted to Chatham for a Supplementary Course, to complete those parts of my training which had been omitted in 1915.

I had served in France for three years and had been wounded three times,* with the result that I was inclined to look upon myself as something of a soldier. The instructors at Chatham were quick to dispel such illusions. 'All this talk about war is well enough,' they said, 'but now you have got to get down to some real soldiering.'

Part of this process consisted of company drill on the square. Every two young officers held each one end of a fifteen-foot hop-pole between them, representing a platoon of soldiers. With these we wheeled into line, into column, or at the halt, on the left, formed company.

But the greater part of the course consisted of engineering. In the war I had been with a field company, working with sandbags, barbed wire, trenches or light wooden bridges. At Chatham we studied the stresses and strains in steel structures such as the Forth Bridge. One or two highlights were provided by driving a steam traction-engine down a public street and by completely dismantling and re-assembling an internal combustion engine.

The life, however, was monotonous after three years in France and

*See J. B. Glubb: *Into Battle: a Soldier's Diary of the Great War.*

13

Map 1 The Post-War Settlement in the Middle East

NOTES: (1) No boundaries are shown between the rival rulers in the Peninsula of Arabia, because none had been agreed. (2) This map contains an anachronism. Ibn Rasheed had ceased to exist in 1920, before some of the other state boundaries had been fixed.

(3) The boundary agreed at Uqair between Iraq and Ibn Saud was subsequent to the disappearance of Ibn Rasheed.

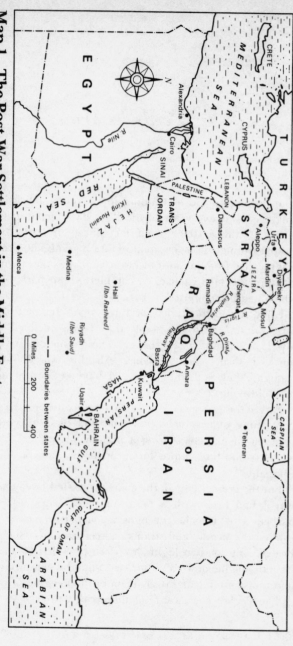

Belgium and I was delighted when, in the summer of 1920, the course came to an end and I was available for posting to a unit.

It so happened that, at this very moment, a tribal rebellion broke out in Iraq, which was still Occupied Enemy Territory, pending the general settlement of peace. There were scarcely any troops in Iraq and nearly all short-service officers had been demobilized. The War Office accordingly issued an appeal for three hundred and fifty regular officer volunteers to go to Iraq forthwith. This seemed to me to be an ideal opportunity to relieve the monotony of Chatham. I applied and was accepted.

All the three hundred and fifty officers embarked on a small and extremely ancient vessel, called appropriately S.S. *Vita*, for she seemed to have lived for ever. She had been used for trooping in the war and the accommodation consisted of tiers of bunks in the hold, which we shared with innumerable rats. A hot steam pipe passed above my bunk, an unnecessary form of 'central heating' when travelling down the Red Sea in midsummer with a following wind.

At length we disembarked at Bombay where, after a few days' delay, we embarked on another ship bound up the Persian Gulf for Basra. Throughout most of the summer life is made reasonable in Basra by a daily cool northerly breeze which, however, ceases in the autumn, making the flaming heat extremely trying. This was before the days of electric fans or of air-conditioning and constituted my first introduction to real heat.

The story was told of a certain Turkish pasha who had been appointed Governor of Basra and arrived in the stifling autumn heat. He complained loudly to the notables of the city of the unbearable temperature. 'This hot spell is useful, your excellency,' pointed out the mayor of the city, 'for it ripens the dates which are nearly due for picking.'

'For Heaven's sake,' retorted the pasha angrily, 'cut down all the date palms. Then we shall not any more have to endure this heat to ripen the dates.'

After sweltering for a few days under the 'date-ripener,' I was posted to Baghdad. The railway from Basra to Baghdad was out of action because the tribes on the Middle Euphrates, through whose territory it passed, were still in rebellion. As a result the only way to reach Baghdad from Basra was up the Tigris.

This was done by means of steam tugs, each of which had a

barge attached to each side of it and towed another astern. As the river was full of sandbanks and was barely deep enough for navigation, many hours every day were spent hauling and heaving and going full speed astern in the attempt to float off a mudbank.

Above Amara, the flat plains on either side of the river were densely covered with low bushes, which were inhabited by immense numbers of black partridge. The O.C. Troops on our vessel was a rather red-faced major, whom I regarded with some awe, being myself a young subaltern of twenty-three. One evening, the major arranged with the captain of our vessel to tie up to the bank for a couple of hours to enable officers to go ashore, stretch their legs and enjoy a little partridge shooting. The proposal caused me some alarm, for the following reasons.

My father had always been fond of shooting – partridges and pheasants – and was an excellent shot. He was anxious that I should enjoy the same pleasure. But, unfortunately, while I was right-handed, my left eye was the stronger and I always missed. My father took me, with the representative of a famous firm of gun-makers, to a clay-pigeon range. Here they fitted me with a special gun with a curved stock, so that, while I placed the butt in my right shoulder, the curved stock put the barrel in front of my left eye. Thus armed, I hit the clay pigeons every time. My father paid a high price for this gun which he gave me when I sailed for Iraq.

Seeing a gun-case in my kit, the officers invited me to join in the shoot. We extended in a line across the flat plain and walked through the scrub. The whole area was crawling with black partridge – running ahead on the ground, flying out right and left, or turning and flying back over our heads. Without any great effort or attention, I put up my gun and fired. Right, left, centre or back over my head, I never missed a bird. Eventually the ship's siren announced that it was time to return on board. I trooped back with the others.

As I entered the saloon, I saw the major sitting at a table on the other side. 'Glubb,' he shouted. 'Glubb. Come over here! What will you have to drink? Where on earth did you learn to shoot like that?' I suddenly found myself the lion of the party, surrounded by a group of such exalted personages as majors and captains.

That was the first and the last time in my life that I ever went out

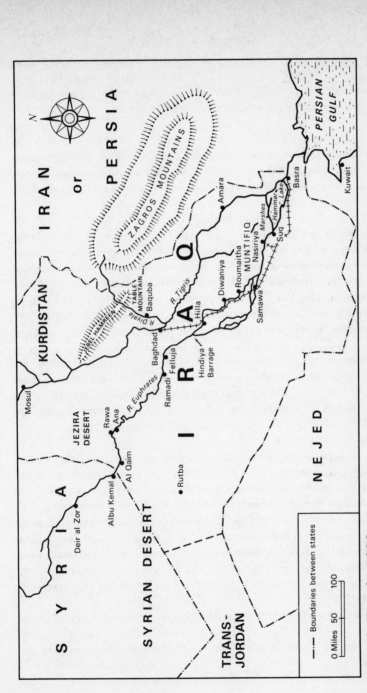

Map 2 Iraq in 1920

Boundaries between states

0 Miles 50 100

shooting. So many things happened after I reached Baghdad that I never thought of the matter again. Somewhere the gun disappeared – probably it was stolen – and all my poor father's trouble and expense went for nothing.

When I arrived in Baghdad, the tribal rebellion was almost at an end, though there was still some fighting in progress in the Roumaitha area of the Middle Euphrates, where indeed it had all begun.

A few miles below Baghdad the Tigris is joined on its left bank by a major tributary river, the Diyala, çoming from the mountains of Persia. When the great snow-covered Persian ranges peter out into the vast alluvial plains of Iraq, the last range of rocky hills is actually inside the Iraqi frontier, being known as the Jebel Hamreen. The Diyala breaks through these rocky foothills in a narrow gorge, before emerging into the great plains. A flat-topped mountain above the gorge had earned the place the name of Table Mountain among the British. (Map 2, page 17)

Here subsidiary canals were taken off the Diyala to irrigate the cultivated land stretching towards Baquba and the Tigris. The British Occupied Enemy Territory Administration – better known as O.E.T.A. – had built regulators and sluices on these canals, to enable the flow of water to be accurately controlled by the Irrigation Department.

It is a curious characteristic of tribes in revolt that they often smash and destroy all the government works within their reach, even if these works have been erected for their own benefit. The local tribes had accordingly damaged the irrigation headworks.

Fighting was over, and the tribes on the Diyala had surrendered. A detachment of one company of the 99th Infantry of the Indian Army had been stationed at Table Mountain, partly to collect fines of rifles imposed on the tribes, and partly to protect a party of Indian coolies who were employed on the repair of the irrigation works.

From Baghdad, I was posted to join this detachment as a solitary engineer officer. Part of the works were on the north and part on the south of the Diyala and there was no bridge. As a result, some means of passing men backwards and forwards across the river was needed. To begin with we stretched a steel cable across, anchored it in the cliffs on either bank, and constructed a box, like the basket usually hung beneath a balloon. This box, which held three men, was then hauled backwards and forwards across the river on a pulley.

Later, as this three-man car proved too slow, we obtained a ferry-boat, passed another steel cable across the river at water level, and hauled the boat backwards and forwards, loaded with men. This arrangement seemed adequate.

The company of the 99th Infantry at Table Mountain was commanded by a young British officer. A third British member of our little mess was a middle-aged man, Captain and Quartermaster Williams, whose duty it was to organize the supplies and rations for our detachment from Baghdad to Table Mountain.

Captain Williams had risen from the ranks and had passed all his life in the army, during which prolonged period he had acquired a strong addiction to whisky. During the day he was a pleasant companion, but at sunset he would take his seat at our improvised mess table with a bottle of whisky. Unbuckling his belt and unbuttoning his jacket, he would place his cap on the table beside him and settle down silently to the business of the evening.

After drinking for some time in silence, he would begin to recite the regiments of the British Army. 'The First of Foot is the Royal Scots. The Second of Foot . . . ' and so on until he reached the twenty-seventh. Then he would pause, button up his jacket, buckle his belt, put his cap on his head, stand up stiffly to attention and bring his right hand to his cap in a rigid salute. Then looking straight in front of him as if standing on a ceremonial parade, he would announce in a loud voice, full of joy and pride:

'And the twenty-eighth is the Old Braggs.'

For perhaps half a minute, he would remain standing stiffly at the salute, fired by the proud memories of his old regiment. Then suddenly he would slump into his chair, undo his belt and his jacket, and reach for the bottle. Sometimes the same ceremonial would be repeated three or four times in the evening until he fell exhausted on his bed.

We two young officers suspected that he must have been sent to our remote outpost to get him out of Baghdad. Eventually, by private representations, we succeeded in having him withdrawn to

19

Baghdad once more. But I shall never forget the pathos of that poor, broken old man, standing rigidly at the salute and announcing in tones vibrant with military pride – 'The twenty-eighth is the Old Braggs.'

The mighty Tigris and Euphrates take their sources from the Taurus Mountains in Asia Minor and from the snow-covered ranges along the southern shores of the Black Sea. After leaving Turkish soil they receive virtually no tributaries. When the snows melt in the spring on the mountains of Asia Minor, both great rivers pour down in flood, often bursting their banks and flooding wide areas of the alluvial plains of Iraq. In winter, however, rain in Iraq itself makes no difference to the level of water in the Tigris and Euphrates. The Diyala, on the other hand, took its source from the Persian mountains, only some one hundred miles east of our camp at Table Mountain. A heavy fall of rain in that area could cause the river to rise in spate almost overnight, a fact of which we were blissfully ignorant.

One night we were woken in the small hours by an ever increasing and alarming roar. Peering out in the darkness, we could dimly see the swollen river racing past, but as our camp was on high ground we returned to our beds undismayed.

The next morning our cable ferry boat duly set out to transport across the river a party of Indian coolies who were to work on the north bank. It is not quite clear what happened, but the boat was soon in difficulties. With a struggle, however, the crew succeeded in bringing it back to shore but, in the confusion, one coolie fell overboard and was swept away.

I was sitting in our mess after breakfast when I suddenly heard a wild burst of shouting and screaming. Running out to the river bank, I heard excited voices calling that the ferry had overturned and that a man had been carried away by the river. Many men came running down the bank pointing to the water, as though they could see the drowning man in the swift flowing stream. Hastily throwing off my jacket, I threw myself into the river, which was roaring past like a mill-race.

This was not an act of courage, but of sudden emotion, perhaps hysteria, performed without thought. I had no idea where the drowning man was and the river was racing by in waves, whirlpools and spray. I had imagined that I could swim, but the instant I entered the water I was swept away, utterly helpless, like any fragment of flotsam. Most of the time I was sucked underneath and was swept along under water, but occasionally I was brought to the surface for a few seconds and then sucked down once more.

I have no idea how long this process continued, but as the river flowed out into the plain, it gradually widened, the rapids became less violent and I was able to swim enough to get my head above water. I was travelling downstream at a high speed, but was no longer constantly sucked under.

A long way downstream I saw an island. I could make no impression at all by swimming against such a current, but I swam desperately across the stream, in order to place myself upstream of the island. As I raced past it in the current, I was able to clutch hold of a bush and to haul myself utterly exhausted on to the shore, where I lay panting.

Providentially, an Arab on the river bank had seen me. Living beside the river, these people had evolved a way of crossing it by inflating a goat skin with air. Then, lying on these primitive water-wings, they would swim across the river. Inflating such a skin, the man ran as fast as he could upstream, then entered the water. Drifting rapidly downstream, he had judged the speed accurately and landed close to me on the island. After allowing me a short time to recover, he placed me on the goatskin and, swimming beside me, launched us together into the stream.

We were, of course, immediately swept away by the current, but, swimming steadily, we reached the south bank of the river, perhaps a mile further down. My rescuer escorted me back to camp, and then vanished. I was never able to reward or even to thank him. The body of the drowned coolie was never recovered.

In April 1921 I was transferred to Ramadi, the headquarters of the Dulaim Division on the Euphrates. As I was walking down the street of Felluja on my way to Ramadi, I approached the dyke which formed the bank of the Euphrates, which, at the time, was running in its full spring flood. Suddenly arose the same chorus of yells and screams, as I had heard on that winter morning on the Diyala.

For a second I was seized with a wild panic desire to turn and run. Was I now to find myself jumping into the mighty Euphrates to rescue another drowning man? With a desperate effort of self-control, I walked terrified to the river bank. It was a small empty boat which had slipped its moorings, and was being carried away rapidly downstream on the flood!

In Ramadi, my principal task was to maintain a frail floating bridge over the Euphrates, the only bridge spanning the great river on the two-hundred-and-fifty-mile stretch from the Syrian border to the Hindiya Barrage. From the military point of view, therefore, this single bridge was of considerable importance. Near either bank, the roadway was carried on some five or six fairly stout wooden boats. But the centre portion of the bridge was supported by frail boats made of reeds and daubed all over with bitumen, of which there were natural springs a few miles away.

The technique was an ancient one. Noah had daubed his ark within and without with pitch (Genesis VI, 14). The mother of Moses had constructed for him a small boat made of bulrushes and 'had daubed it with slime and with pitch' (Exodus II, 3). The technique was, therefore, one which must have been several thousand years old. Considering the materials available, reeds and bitumen, the construction of such boats involved considerable skill.

At Chatham I had not been taught to build boats with bulrushes and bitumen and was glad to leave the technicalities of their maintenance to my Arab crew, with whom I could with difficulty exchange a few words of broken Arabic.

The Euphrates, at the time, was running at its full spring flood and it was with some surprise and alarm that I arrived on the site one morning to find that my bridge was no longer there. With some difficulty I eventually discovered from the Arab gang that it was they themselves who had cut it. It appeared that the central part of the bridge, that carried on the reed and bitumen boats, was unable to stand up to the tremendous pressure of the river in flood. As a result, the crew had cut the cables. The sections near the bank, carried on strong wooden boats, had merely swung back against the bank. The central portion, in rafts of four or five boats together, had floated off down the river.

'But where is the bridge now?' I asked the Arabs in bewilderment. 'That's for you to find out,' they answered with a grin. In due course we collected the several sections of our bridge which had become caught up in bushes on the bank at the various bends of the river. As the light reed-and-bitumen boats had merely drifted down the river on the surface, none of them was damaged. When the flood subsided, we duly towed them back and reconstructed our bridge as though nothing had happened. From the Forth Bridge to that of Ramadi, engineering assumes many different forms.

There was not much work to do in Ramadi, so I bought a pony and took to visiting neighbouring villages, the homes of members of my bridge gang. The duty of maintaining the bridge compelled me to make serious attempts to acquire colloquial Arabic, a process further assisted by my visits to the villages. Soon I was able to make myself understood in simple conversations. The humour of the members of the bridge crew and the warm but simple hospitality of their homes first enamoured me of the Arab world.

3

Air Control

The Arab Rebellion of 1920 in Iraq originated in a variety of different causes. As the British-Indian Army advanced slowly up the Tigris and Euphrates from 1915 to 1918 it left behind it a lengthening and increasingly precarious line of communications up the two rivers. The country on both sides of the rivers was inhabited by wild and warlike tribes over which the Ottoman Government had never succeeded in establishing adequate control.

To prevent the tribes from interfering with the communications of the Army, a primitive form of administration had to be established. For this purpose, 'political officers' were recruited from the Army and were put in control of districts and sub-districts with the duty of keeping the country quiet and of ensuring that nothing interfered with the prosecution of the military operations.

Many enthusiastic young political officers, anxious to secure the allegiance of the Arab tribes, had painted vivid word-pictures to the shaikhs of the prosperity introduced all over the world by British administration.

[Nowadays, in 1978, the memory of the benefits conferred by British rule on backward countries has been largely forgotten, owing to the stream of hostile propaganda directed against 'colonialism'. This change in public opinion has been partly due to the benefits themselves. The poor and primitive countries have so far advanced that they are now in a position to govern themselves. When the children are grown up, they rarely remember with gratitude the old nurse who directed their infant footsteps. In 1916, however, these benefits were still generally appreciated.]

The example of the wealth acquired by Egypt under British administration still received widespread recognition and was held up as prophetic of the future of Iraq. Moreover, the liberal subsidies distributed by the British and the large profits which could be made in war time, grew to be regarded by the Arabs as a normal accompaniment of British control.

The tribesmen, and many who should have known better, omitted to consider the fact that great irrigation works, dams and canals, such as had brought prosperity to Egypt, had required nearly forty years to construct.

In wartime, high salaries were paid to tribal chiefs, with little or no demand for the payment of taxes. Tribesmen had no conception of the fact that governments must balance their budgets. Many of them, hearing that rupees were stamped in the Indian Mint, had a vague idea that governments manufactured money and that their principal rôle was to distribute it to all and sundry.

Government appeared to the tribal Arabs to be a vast and mysterious power, quite apart from the people. Western conceptions, that the government is merely the people organized, and that officials are individuals deputed by the people to rule in order to save the man in the street from the trouble of doing so, were quite incomprehensible to them. Both the Turkish and the British Governments were vague and distant despots, but they differed in one important essential – whereas the Turks had formerly demanded money, the British gave money away.

But with the close of the war came sudden and unpleasant disillusionment. The British began collecting revenue also, and by methods much more stringent than those employed by the Turks. It was less easy to bribe their officials, and their greater energy and efficiency made it more difficult for a man to conceal his real income.

Old Jacob's prophecy over his son Reuben applied to the Arab tribes – 'Unstable as water Thou shalt not excel.' Any new régime is liable to be acclaimed by them with jubilation. A few years later the same system is denounced by them as an unspeakable tyranny and salvation is proclaimed to lie in some other arrangement. In 1920 the pendulum was ready to swing. External factors only added momentum.

Perhaps one of the main causes of unrest in lower Iraq, however, was the adoption by the British of an unfortunate policy in dealing with the tribes. The country had formerly been divided into a small number of Arab principalities. Khazal, Zubaid and especially the Sadoon, for example, were autonomous Arab princes who submitted with reluctance to pay tribute to the Turkish government, but who were almost entirely free of interference in their dealings with their own tribesmen.

During the latter half of the nineteenth century and the early years of the twentieth, however, the Turks had made strenuous efforts to modernize their empire in imitation of the nations of Europe. With this object in view, they determined to destroy the tribal system and to bring the people of the country under their direct control. With the tragic, negative characteristic of impatient reformers, they set themselves to destroy the existing social structure of the country, instead of, by wise and positive leadership, transforming it into something better with the consent and co-operation of the people.

The first objective of the Ottoman administration had been the overthrow of the Arab princely houses, the power of which was too great to enable them to live peaceably within the framework of a modern government. The Ottomans succeeded in destroying the princes by intrigue, by nominating a junior member of the ruling family to be paramount ruler and supporting him with funds, thereby stirring up a family civil war.

The result was that the tribes, having lost their traditional rulers, were soon torn by bitter internal feuds. The tribes were splintered to fragments and reduced to innumerable chaotic little sections, but the central government was not strong enough itself to assume direct control. The petty chiefs, released from the authority of their patriarchal princes, fought, murdered and robbed one another with impunity.

It was at this stage that the British Army arrived during the First World War. Tribes numbering many thousands of fighting men, released from the authority of their traditional princes, were found to be split up between tens, or even hundreds, of petty warring chiefs. Each had his own village or villages, his war-tower and his private feuds and rivalries.

It is a common feature of human nature that we hate our neighbours and our competitors, whom we meet every day, more than we do the distant political enemies of our country. Some of these tiny potentates ruled over no more than twenty or thirty followers. In the Muntifiq many lived in the recesses of the marshes, inaccessible to troops or police.

It was the improvised British 'political officers' who were expected to bring order out of this chaos. Few of them were concerned to look many years ahead; the immediate task was to win the war. This necessitated the prevention of major tribal wars and the protection of the lines of communication, detachments of troops and isolated convoys from Arab attack. This objective was almost unattainable, owing to the impossibility of fixing the responsibility for any outrage. Even were the offenders known to belong to a certain tribe, the innumerable little chiefs foisted the blame upon one another, while many of them were so elusive or so inaccessible that it was impossible to bring them to book. An obvious, though perhaps short-sighted remedy was therefore almost everywhere adopted – it was decided to appoint a single shaikh over each tribe.

The system worked fairly satisfactorily during the remainder of the war. The government shaikhs received considerable financial subsidies, and if necessary the backing of government armed forces. On the other hand, they were responsible for all crimes committed by their tribesmen. By this means, the immediate object of keeping the lines of communication safe, during the continuance of the war, was achieved; perhaps no other method could have been adopted.

Two factors, however, contributed to the tribal discontent which broke out in 1920. The first of these was that the little chiefs, having tasted the sweets of independence during the Turkish period of anarchy, would not again willingly consent to be subordinated to greater shaikhs. The second factor was that the greater shaikhs were more untrustworthy than had been thought possible.

These government shaikhs took little thought for the future. Their view was limited to the continuance of the then existing régime, under which they found themselves rich and almost despotic. Their first step was often to wreak dire vengeance on such of the smaller shaikhs as had opposed them in Turkish times. Having thus established their power without dispute, they commenced to oppress their followers, extorting bribes and seizing land and women. It must be admitted that there were honourable exceptions, but it is probably true to say that the tribal rebellion in 1920 was directed more against the petty tyranny of the government shaikhs than against the central government.

To coincide with this tribal dissatisfaction, a political cause arose. On the other side of the Arabian Peninsula, an Arab force under the Ameer Faisal had been operating with Allenby's army against the Turks. This military co-operation had resulted from an agreement, signed in December 1915, between the British High

Commissioner in Egypt and the Sherif Husain of Mecca. In this document, Britain had vaguely promised to support the creation of an independent Arab state at the end of the First World War, covering the northern Arab countries with a few minor exceptions. Lebanon was excluded from this pledge, because France had been promised a special position there.

To implement this undertaking, the British Government after the war had installed the Ameer Faisal in Damascus, where he formed an Arab government for Syria. But Faisal's supporters resented the presence of the French in Lebanon, frontier skirmishes took place and eventually the French marched on Damascus, drove out Faisal, overthrew the Syrian Government and took over the direct rule of Syria themselves. This action was contrary to Britain's pledges to the Arabs, and the British Government protested but finally relapsed into silence.

A part of the Ameer Faisal's army had been recruited from Turkish prisoners of war of Arab race, including a number of officers. Many Iraqis had served in the Turkish Army and several of these had been captured by the British and had then joined Faisal's Arab Army and subsequently the Damascus government.

When the French overthrew the latter, the Iraqi officers escaped to Aleppo and the Upper Euphrates, and thence to Mesopotamia. Embittered by the failure of their hopes of an Arab government in Syria and claiming that the Allies had betrayed their promises to the Arabs, they did all they could to raise discontent and revolt against the British administration in Iraq.

Technically Iraq (Mesopotamia) was still Occupied Enemy Territory until a peace treaty could be concluded with Turkey. Only then could an Arab state be officially proclaimed. The Sherifian officers, however, who had seen their hopes fade already in Syria, suspected that a new breach of faith was contemplated in Iraq. The British Acting High Commissioner, Sir Arnold Wilson, cabled London urging an unequivocal statement of policy, but the British Government were preoccupied with treaty-making at Versailles. This political independence movement, represented by the officers of Faisal's army, happened to coincide with tribal dissatisfaction to produce rebellion.

The causes of the 1920 outbreak were therefore threefold:

(1) The disillusionment amongst the tribesmen, who had

expected one wave of the British wand to transform Iraq into a second Egypt.

(2) The revolt of the tribes against the tyrannical rule of the shaikhs whom the British Military Occupation had imposed upon them.

Neither of these causes had any connection with politics or Arab nationalism. Indeed they were retrograde, the desire of the tribes to return to the chaos to which they had become accustomed under the Turks. In this direction, the British Occupation represented progress, law and order, and a modern administration.

(3) The disillusionment of the educated Arabs, mostly army officers, who witnessed (or anticipated) the evaporation of their dreams of Arab independence. Their suspicions were fostered by the endless delays of the peacemakers in Versailles, and the inability or neglect of the British Government to issue an unequivocal pledge to set up an Arab government in Iraq, although such was in fact their intention.

The rebellion was suppressed and was followed by the granting of a generous measure of self-government. Arab ministers formed a government and Arab governors appeared in each division or province – in Arabic *liwah* – with the title of mutasarrifs. In sub-districts, or *qadhas*, qaimaqams took the place of the former assistant political officers. The chiefs who had played a leading part in the rebellion received an amnesty and settled down to live quietly at their homes.

Nevertheless the after-effects of the fighting could not be immediately eradicated. The shaikhs who had not rebelled looked forward to favoured treatment under a British administration. Those who had rebelled looked forward to the future with anxiety, fearing that they had compromised their position with the British authorities.

The establishment of an Arab administration, however, gave new hope to the late rebel chiefs. Perhaps, they thought, they could atone for their past errors by making friends with the new Arab officials. They accordingly loudly declared themselves to be patriots, ready to die for the cause of a purely Arab administration with no British interference.

The shaikhs who had not rebelled were alarmed. They had imagined that their futures under a British administration were assured. But now they saw their rivals, the former rebels, making friends with the new Arab administration. The more important shaikhs, especially on the Middle Euphrates, divided into two camps. Those who had not rebelled proclaimed their determination to support the continuance of British administration, while the former rebels declared for an Arab government.

In fact, neither group of shaikhs was inspired by nationalist or political ideals, which had not penetrated to the tribal mentality. Each group was merely anxious to support the type of administration from which they expected to receive favour.

The line of cleavage between the two groups of tribes on the Euphrates became strongly marked. These tribes had indeed constantly fought one another in Turkish times. Now, however, instead of invoking, in their threats and war-dances the names of their ancestors or their tribal war-cries, they fought one another in the alleged cause of 'Independence' or of 'British Protection'.

Under the new government, each division of the country had an Arab mutasarrif, but the whole country was still in confusion and the new Iraq Government had no forces with which to maintain order. Several years would be needed to raise an efficient Iraq army and police force. During this period, British forces would be obliged to keep order.

To ensure the necessary liaison between the Arab administration and the British forces supporting it, a British adviser was appointed to assist the mutasarrif of every division. First entitled the Divisional Adviser, his title was subsequently changed to that of Administrative Inspector. The executive authority in each division, however, rested with the mutasarrif.

However sincerely the mutasarrif and his British colleague endeavoured to co-operate, their task was rendered much more difficult by the division of the tribes into two groups, one of which declared itself loyal to the mutasarrif and the other to the adviser.

All these troubles and schisms had been basically due to the peace-makers in Versailles. Firstly, to the French seizure of Syria contrary to the pledges given by Britain during the war. And secondly to the long delays in the adoption of a decision and in the issue of a categorical statement by the British Government. Britain never intended to reduce Iraq to a colonial administration, but never issued a public statement to that effect.

In March 1921 a conference was held in Cairo, under the chairmanship of Mr. Winston Churchill, to endeavour to produce some form of order from the chaos resulting from the war, and the confused and sometimes contradictory promises made by the British Government. Two and a half years had elapsed since the armistice in 1918, during which the negotiators in Paris had been engaged in endless bargaining, largely concerned with the Great Powers and the major world issues. Meanwhile, the Arab countries had remained in a state of uncertainty under temporary quasi-military occupations. The Cairo Conference endeavoured, not without success, to tie up the many loose ends.

Iraq was proclaimed an independent state, though under a British League of Nations Mandate, the Ameer Faisal being shortly afterwards elected king. His brother, the Ameer Abdulla, became the ruler of the new state of Trans-Jordan. As a junior Army officer, I was little concerned in these affairs of state, but another of the conference decisions was immediately to change my whole career.

Iraq was a large country, some five hundred miles long by three hundred wide, completely devoid of roads. Large parts of it were occupied by rivers, canals and marshes, by waterless deserts or by the high rocky mountains of Kurdistan. The whole country was inhabited by armed and warlike tribes, most of them in a state of chaos, largely engaged in fighting one another.

Iraq had been declared an independent country, with an elected parliament, a cabinet and a constitutional king on the British model – but it had no army. There was considerable political opposition in Britain to the maintenance of a British army in Iraq, 'pouring money into the sands of the desert'. Yet without armed forces, the new Iraqi Government would never be able to set up an administration.

In this situation, the Cairo Conference produced a new and startling proposal – air control. In the event of tribal rebellion (and such rebellions were virtually endemic), the despatch of a military punitive column would occupy weeks or months – not owing to the military opposition likely to be encountered, but due to the great distances involved, the large rivers, marshes and deserts, and the ponderous organization needed to construct roads and bridges and to maintain long lines of communication through tribal country.

The recently formed Royal Air Force was anxious to prove its value and offered to replace the Army as the peace-keeping force in Iraq, until that country could raise its own army. If the tribes rose in rebellion several hundred miles from Baghdad, it was argued, a military expedition might take many weeks and cost millions of pounds.

But if the R.A.F. was in control, aircraft could take off after breakfast from Baghdad, bomb the insurgents and be back in Baghdad for lunch. The cost of such an operation would be negligible. The idea sounded plausible – even a stroke of genius – and was adopted. An Air Officer Commanding was appointed to succeed the military G.O.C., and the take-over of responsibility began.

The proposal (in Cairo at least) seemed to provide a perfect solution. But as soon as aircraft began to fly over Iraq a problem arose. The vast plains of that country were covered by innumerable villages or encampments, each looking from the air exactly like all the others.

The tribal organization was in a state of disintegration. It was not possible to demarcate on a map tribal areas, everything inside which could be considered hostile. It was more than likely that, if one section of a tribe were in revolt, another section of the same tribe would be supporting the government. How was the ordinary operational R.A.F. pilot to distinguish the friendly from the hostile? This problem suddenly threatened to make the whole plan of air control impracticable.

The solution adopted was to appoint a number of intelligence officers, known as Special Service Officers, or S.S.O.s. Each of these was assigned an area of country with which it was his duty thoroughly to familiarize himself on the ground. In the event of a sudden uprising in his area, this officer would then be available to fly in the leading aircraft and point out to the pilot which villages or encampments were hostile and which friendly.

This sounded well enough, but at the immediate time of the R.A.F. take-over no such officers were available and, once appointed, it would obviously take each one many months, if not years, to become completely familiar with the tribes and villages of his area. The organization of the S.S.O.s was, therefore, a matter of some urgency.

My interest in learning Arabic and in visiting the local villages, while I was in Ramadi, was known in Headquarters. If the Army were evacuating Iraq, I would obviously go with it. Meanwhile, however, I had acquired an intense interest in the country. The two factors coincided. Air Headquarters invited me to be seconded to the R.A.F. and to become an S.S.O. I still regarded myself as a soldier, and asked if I could be attached, rather than seconded. To this, both the Army and the R.A.F. agreed. I accordingly reported to the Air Staff Intelligence in Baghdad and my engineering career came to an end.

4

The Shaikh of Shaikhs

In May 1922 I was posted as Special Service Officer – that is to say, R.A.F. Intelligence Officer – to the Muntifiq Division in Southern Iraq. This division or province represented fairly accurately the former dominions of the Sadoon, one of the great princely families between whom Iraq had formerly been divided. The story of how the Ottoman Empire destroyed the Sadoon is more or less typical and briefly to explain it will set the scene for the narrative of my own experiences in the marshes of the Lower Euphrates.

Before 1914, the Arabs had lived for centuries in nominal political subjection to the Sultan of Turkey. The Turks had maintained large garrisons in the major cities such as Baghdad, Basra and Damascus, but made little or no attempt to enforce their authority in tribal areas. It was normally impossible to travel from one city to another without paying tribute to tribal chiefs for permission to pass through their territories.

Periodically when some tribal group or other had exceeded what even the Ottoman authorities could endure, a military force was collected, a punitive expedition was undertaken, villages were burnt, flocks driven off and battles fought with the tribes. Almost as often as not the column was defeated and destroyed, or retired discomfited to the city on which it was based. Communications were so slow that news of such incidents took weeks to penetrate to the Sublime Porte in Istanbul and, even when it did so, probably evoked only a passing interest in the distant imperial capital, which was normally more immediately concerned with its wars in Europe.

Meanwhile the Arabs had evolved a system of stability, combined with a complete lack of public security. The stability lay in the fact that all and sundry regarded the remote Sultan and Khalif – or Caliph – as the Ruler of the World and the God-appointed Prince of all

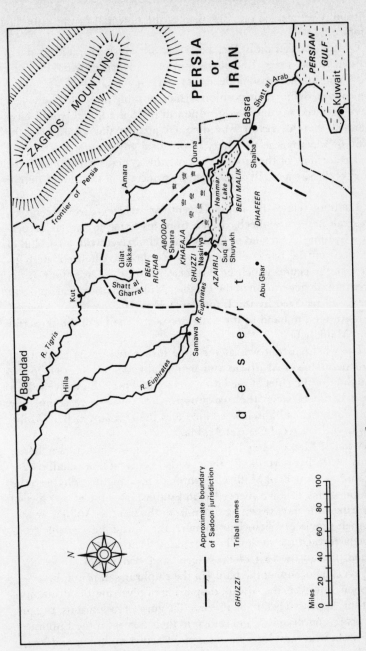

Map 3 Dominions of the Sadoon

35

faithful Muslims. No one dreamed of the downfall of the Ottoman Empire.

On the level of daily life, however, all who were able to do so refused to pay taxes. Rebellions and pitched battles with the army were considered reasonable enough. If any Arab had attempted logically to define their position (which possibly none did) he would have declared his undying devotion to the Sultan, and would have claimed that his revolt was directed against the tyranny of the Wali or Viceroy, the treachery of the local governor or the excesses and extortions of the troops. Against this general background, the story of the rise and fall of the Sadoon princes is not without interest.

Tradition relates that in the sixteenth or early seventeenth century, an Arab named Shabeeb, driven from his home in the Hejaz perhaps by some blood feud or family quarrel, arrived with a handful of relations on the banks of the Lower Euphrates. Shabeeb, perhaps through the claims which he put forward to be a descendant in the twenty-sixth generation of the Prophet Muhammad, appears to have been well received by the Euphrates tribes. His son Mana received in marriage the hand of the daughter of the shaikh of the powerful Beni Malik tribe.

The whole district was at the time torn between the rival tribal confederations of Al Ajwad and Beni Malik. Mana, married to the daughter of the chief of the latter, soon found himself involved. In a great battle between the two groups, the Ajwad were completely victorious, Mana himself was killed and the remnant of Beni Malik fled to the deserts of Central Arabia.

A son of Mana, named Shabeeb like his grandfather, was borne away with Beni Malik in their exile, being still a small child. Grandson of the Beni Malik chief through his daughter, Shabeeb the second seems to have succeeded in establishing himself as chief of the tribe. One day, sweeping down from the Central Arabian wastes on their previously victorious enemies, the Ajwad, he was able completely to turn the tables. The remnants of the Ajwad, finally defeated, fled to the east of the Tigris, and Beni Malik under their Hejazi chief occupied the banks of the Euphrates in triumph.

Soon, however, the Ajwad, despairing of reversing the decision of fortune, appeared before Shabeeb in the guise of supplicants, begging for peace and permission to return to their homes on the Euphrates. Shabeeb, who must have been a man of wider ambition and longer foresight than most tribal chiefs, forgave the slayers of his father and welcomed back his enemies without imposing any fine or indemnity. The sole condition that he laid down was that they, in common with Beni Malik, should acknowledge him as their paramount Lord and that all who entered his presence should kiss his hand.

The name of Muntifiq, though now more often spelt locally Muntifik with a *k*, was probably derived from the Arabic root *wafaqa*, 'to agree together'. It was doubtless adopted to celebrate Shabeeb's treaty of peace, which put an end to the blood-soaked wars of mutual extermination between the Ajwad and Beni Malik. These two tribal groups and a number of others who joined the new alliance had been settled for centuries in southern Iraq and had been converted to the Shiite sect of Islam. The descendants of Shabeeb, arriving hundreds of years later, were Sunnites. From the first they established themselves as an exclusive aristocracy in the midst of their Shiite subjects, assuming the title of the Shaikh of Shaikhs.

The great traditions of the ancient Arabs, their poetry and their literature, were inextricably bound up with the nomad life, the tent and the camel. The Ajwad and Beni Malik, however, had largely abandoned these things in favour of the more profitable pursuits of agriculture, the cutting of reeds, fishing and buffalo keeping in the marshes. The descendants of Shabeeb regarded such occupations with undisguised contempt and for more than three hundred years they refused to take any part in them, though they profited by them indirectly by taxing their cultivator subjects.

These exclusive aristocrats, with few exceptions, still remained faithful to their tents and their camels in the 1920s. Constantly moving their tented courts, they scorned to take part in any baser occupations than hunting and war. The breeding of thoroughbred horses, or the training of falcons and greyhounds, filled their leisure hours. Though still almost as simple in their habits as the desert bedouins, they were as socially exclusive as any aristocracy in Europe, nor would they ever give their daughters in marriage to the surrounding tribes.

It is difficult for Europeans today to appreciate the tremendous prestige enjoyed in ancient Arabia by the black tent, which even in 1922 still persisted. Many local tribes which centuries earlier had abandoned nomadism still preferred to retain their social status by living in black tents.

To the peoples of the Western world, long brought up on the Old

Testament, the Muntifiq story is of interest, because it resembles so closely the history of the Children of Israel in Palestine. They too arrived, a few thousand strong, from the desert, and established themselves as a minority ruling caste over the numerous population of Palestine. The Children of Israel, as an aristocracy, continued to live in their black tents.

The conquest of the Land of Canaan by Joshua took place about 1222 B.C. After the death of Solomon in 927 B.C., the Israelite hegemony began to disintegrate, that is to say after a period of three hundred years. They were, however, still living in tents, though the Palestinians lived in towns and villages. The death of Solomon was followed by a rebellion, during which the rebels cried out, 'To your tents, O Israel'. Like the Muntifiq princes in 1922, the Israelites were still living in their black tents after three hundred years of aristocratic domination of the cultivating tribes. Let us, however, now return to the history of the princes of the Muntifiq.

In 1694, Mana ibn Mughamis, the then Prince of the Muntifiq, captured the city of Basra itself. He rapidly extended his power from the deserts of Arabia to the Persian hills and for a short time ruled as a despot over all lower Iraq. But in 1697, rival tribal groups drove him out of Basra, back to the Lower Euphrates.

The Muntifiq domains thereafter consisted of a varying area of the Arabian deserts, the Euphrates valley from below Samawa to the vicinity of Basra, and the Shatt al Gharraf area. The latter was a river which branched from the Tigris at Kut, flowed past the towns of Qilat Sikkar and Shatra and disappeared into the marshes of the Lower Euphrates. Altogether, the Muntifiq probably covered an area of some eight thousand five hundred square miles, including cultivation, marsh and desert – an area possibly larger than England and Wales. (Map 3, page 35.) During the eighteenth century, other Arab principalities appeared – such as the Khazal on the Middle Euphrates, and Zubaid south of Baghdad – but none attained to the power and prestige of the Muntifiq.

Early in the eighteenth century the ruling prince was Sadoon ibn Muhammad, whose name has since then been applied to the whole ruling family, superseding that of Shabeeb. Sadoon blockaded Basra, made war on the surrounding tribes, was taken prisoner, imprisoned in Baghdad, released, rebelled, fought, was defeated and killed. The fact that, after him, the whole family adopted the name of Sadoon is an eloquent tribute to the impact of his turbulent personality on his contemporaries.

Meanwhile about 1750 an extremist religious revival had commenced in Central Arabia, supported in arms by a certain Muhammad ibn Saud of the tribe of Anaiza. By 1770, the Wahhabis, as the new sect was called, had established their dominion over all Central Arabia as the result of a passionate outbreak of religious enthusiasm. Between 1793 and 1795 several attacks were made on Kuwait.

The Ottoman Empire at the time seemed to be on the verge of collapse. Wars with Russia, Napoleon's invasion of Egypt, and the repeated mutinies of her regular army, the Janissaries, made it impossible for the Porte to send troops to Iraq.

In February 1797, the Wali, or Viceroy, accordingly nominated Thuwaini ibn Abdulla ibn Sadoon, the ruling Muntifiq prince at the time, to be governor of the province of Basra, on condition that he led a tribal army to conquer the Wahhabis in Arabia. In 1801, he advanced with a large force of tribesmen but, when somewhere south of Kuwait, Thuwaini was murdered by one of his own slaves, and his army fled in confusion.

The Muntifiq, though prepared to pay lip-service to the Sultan – and occasionally even gifts or tribute – were frequently in a state of rebellion. In 1813, the then Pasha of Baghdad, Abdulla Tutunchi, marched against them with a military force, but he was totally defeated by the Muntifiq prince, Hamood ibn Thamir. The Pasha himself was put to death by the Arabs, in revenge for the death of Burghash, the son of Hamood ibn Thamir, who had died of wounds received in the battle. Hamood reigned over the Muntifiq for forty years, during twenty of which he was blind in both eyes.

A long list of the endless battles and expeditions led by or against the Muntifiq princes is of little interest to the general reader. The above incidents have merely been related to illustrate the degree of power and influence to which the Sadoon princes had attained.

In the second half of the nineteenth century, however, a new era opened. An ill-formulated desire for progress had appeared in the rulers of Istanbul, who pressed the Baghdad authorities to assume a more aggressive attitude towards the Sadoon.

The Ottoman administration set about the task of destroying the Sadoon in a manner typical of their government. Instead of extending their rule by conquest and then reconciling the defeated by the justice of their administration (a course which they had neither the power nor the will to adopt), they set themselves to destroy the power of the prince by infiltration.

In 1863, the Wali of Baghdad endeavoured to regularize the position of the Muntifiq chief, whose power he was unable to overthrow, by appointing him to the Ottoman Civil Service with the rank of qaimaqam, or deputy governor. The next step was to appoint a Turkish revenue official to maintain his accounts! Mansoor, the ruling prince, rose in rebellion and the Wali was obliged to cancel his instructions.

A more subtle policy was then adopted. Mansoor being in rebellion, the Ottoman authorities made approaches to his younger brother, Nasir, whom they won over to the government by flattery and by awarding him the Turkish title of Pasha. Nasir fell into the trap and was appointed Prince of the Muntifiq, in succession to his elder brother Mansoor, who took refuge in the desert with the bedouin tribe of the Dhafeer.

[Pasha was a Turkish title somewhat similar to knighthood in Britain. It was normally bestowed on government servants, such as cabinet ministers, provincial governors, or generals. Occasionally it was awarded to distinguished notables for political reasons, as in the case of Nasir ibn Sadoon.]

In 1869, Midhat Pasha, a conscientious if often misguided reformer, became Wali of Baghdad, and conceived of a new method of bribing the Sadoon princes. The latter had hitherto maintained their position by collecting taxes from the towns and the agricultural tribes. Midhat Pasha offered to apportion all the lands cultivated by the Shiite tribes between the Sadoon family and to give them valid Turkish title deeds of ownership.

For three hundred years, the tribes had remained loyal to the Muntifiq princes, because they had repulsed the intervention of the Turks. No sooner, however, did the tribesmen realize that Nasir (now Nasir Pasha) had become a Turkish tool, than they rose in rebellion against him and his government masters alike. But Nasir had gone too far to draw back. The town of Nasiriya, flatteringly named after him by the Ottomans, was founded on the Euphrates and a Turkish garrison was installed. For the first time Ottoman officials had actually penetrated the Muntifiq.

The tribes of the whole province were divided by the bitterness of the feud between the brothers, Mansoor and Nasir. Mani al Menna and his brother Jarrar, shaikhs of the Ajwad, had formerly supported Mansoor. They were seized in Nasiriya by Nasir and his black slaves and dragged into the street where, drawing their swords, the slaves literally hacked Mani to pieces. Jarrar, seeing his brother's fate, threw himself into the Euphrates, though his feet were shackled. Although pursued, he succeeded in alternately diving and swimming till the current carried him far down stream, where he crawled out on the bank and escaped.

In 1872, Nasir Pasha with a force of Muntifiq tribesmen assisted the Turks to conquer the Hasa province on the Persian Gulf, from Ibn Saud and his Wahhabis. In 1875, Nasir Pasha was appointed Wali of the province of Basra, in addition to being Prince of the Muntifiq. But Nasir experienced the fate which has so often overtaken the favourites of arbitrary governments. He was adjudged to have grown too powerful and, in 1877, he was disgraced, arrested and exiled to Istanbul, where he passed the rest of his life.

For a short time, the Turks endeavoured to administer the province themselves, but fresh troubles broke out following the dis-appearance of Nasir. The tribes vehemently resisted the joint demands for rent put forward by the Ottoman Government and their satellite Sadoons, on the basis of Midhat Pasha's land distribution. Meanwhile the rebellious Mansoor, elder brother of Nasir, had died and been succeeded by his no less turbulent son, Sadoon.

At their wit's end, the Turks installed Falih, the son of Nasir, gave him the rank of Pasha and requested him to continue his father's work of Ottomanization. The Muntifiq were now divided into two tribal confederations – that under Falih Pasha ibn Nasir with official Turkish backing, and that under Sadoon ibn Mansoor, whose watchword was 'no Turkish interference'. In 1900, Sadoon allied himself with Mubarak ibn Sobah, the Shaikh of Kuwait, who was also apprehensive of Turkish encroachment on his principality.

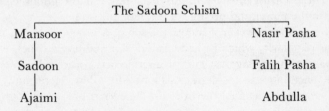

The Sadoon Schism

Mansoor   Nasir Pasha

Sadoon   Falih Pasha

Ajaimi   Abdulla

In 1903, Sadoon, the son of Mansoor, descended upon the Shatra tribes to raise contributions from them. He was still popular with the cultivating tribes, being regarded as the nucleus of the tribal party, bitterly opposed to Turkish encroachment. He was joined by the Beni Zaid and Khafaja, and sent letters up the Shatt al Gharraf, calling for help from the Beni Richab and Al Humaid. The Abooda tribe, however, resisted, and appealed to Falih Pasha ibn Nasir and to the Turks.

A Turkish column, commanded by a colonel, Muhammad Azlam Beg, set out for Shatra and battle was joined between Sadoon and his tribal supporters on the one hand, and the Turkish troops and the Abooda on the other. At the height of the struggle, reinforcements reached Sadoon from Beni Richab. The government force was annihilated, Colonel Muhammad Azlam being killed. Sadoon, thereupon, withdrew from Shatra, recrossed the Euphrates above Nasiriya, and moved out to a fort which he had built himself in the desert at Abu Ghar. (Map 3, page 35)

In spite, however, of all these outrages and of the slaughter of Colonel Muhammad Azlam and his column, Sadoon shortly afterwards succeeded in winning the favour of the Wali of Basra, much to the fury and jealousy of his cousin and bitter rival, Falih Pasha ibn Nasir. Accompanied instead of pursued by a Turkish military force, Sadoon returned to Shatra – such were the unforeseeable vicissitudes of Turkish rule.

Thereupon Falih Pasha ibn Nasir, enraged by the favour shown by the Turks to Sadoon, sent his own son Abdulla to fight the latter. The Khafaja tribe joined Sadoon, the Abooda rallied to Abdulla, and furious fighting raged in the streets of Shatra. It appears that the Wali of Baghdad supported Falih Pasha ibn Nasir while the Wali of Basra favoured Sadoon, the rivalries of the Ottoman governors adding fuel to the fire of the internal Sadoon feuds. The ensuing insane anarchy resulted in the death of many officers and men of the Turkish army involved in this bedlam, but it also put an end for ever to the power and prestige of the Sadoon family.

Meanwhile, however, Sadoon, the son of Mansoor, had lost most of the popularity which he had formerly enjoyed in the tribes, when he was their leader against Turkish interference. He accordingly withdrew once more to his desert castle at Abu Ghar. Here, however, his arrogance alienated the bedouin Dhafeer tribe, which had first welcomed him as an enemy of the Turks. Nejed, or Central Arabia, was at the time divided between two rival princes, Ibn Saud and Ibn Rasheed. Before long, Sadoon was engaged in battles with the Dhafeer and the nomads of the Muntifiq, as well as with Ibn Saud and Ibn Rasheed.

At last the old bandit baron had reached the end of his resources. He wandered almost alone through the Azairij and Hachcham tribes. Eventually he was enticed into surrender to the Turkish authorities, who immediately seized him and exiled him to Aleppo, where shortly afterwards he died a premature death. His eldest son, Ajaimi, remained in the Muntifiq, where he already showed signs of becoming no less ill-omened a stormy petrel than his father.

When the British landed at Basra in the First World War, the Turks called upon the Euphrates tribes to raise a force to drive out the invaders, just as they had more than once called upon the Muntifiq to fight Ibn Saud in the past. But the Ottoman Government had destroyed the princes who used to lead these tribal armies. They could not have it both ways. The tribes were defeated by the British army at the battle of Shaiba, outside Basra.

Ajaimi, the son of Sadoon, declared for the Turks, but he was unable to play any important role in the operations, because he had no tribal following. At the end of the First World War, he retired with the Turkish army and settled down in Turkey. During the war, the British Occupied Enemy Territory Administration dealt direct with the tribes. The Sadoon family no longer played any political role in what had once been their dominions. The Ottomans, having first destroyed the Sadoon, were destroyed themselves.

Nevertheless much of the prestige of past centuries still survived. Even in 1922 I remember Abdulla ibn Falih Pasha walking down the street in Nasiriya, and men pushing forward to kiss his hand, as Shabeeb had insisted that all the Muntifiq must do, more than three centuries before.

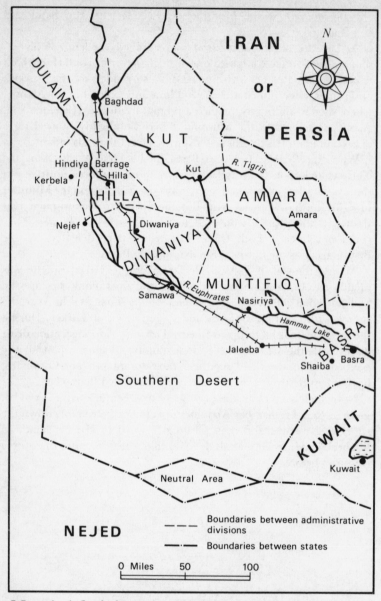

Map 4 Administrative Divisions of Southern Iraq

5

Marsh Men

I have described in some detail the former glory and prestige of the Sadoon family to explain the background of treachery, violence and anarchy to which the local tribes had grown accustomed. With the disappearance of their former princes tribal chaos and confusion reigned supreme in the Muntifiq.

The day after my arrival as Special Service Officer in the area in May 1922, I paid a courtesy call on the mutasarrif and on his British colleague, the Divisional Adviser, and found them together in the office of the former. Just as I was introducing myself, a violent scuffle was heard outside the door and an indignant Arab burst into the office. It appeared that aircraft had been sent to drop bombs on some dissident tribal group, but had by mistake dropped them on this man's village, a shaikh who had always been scrupulously loyal to the authorities. An old woman and a cow had been killed.

Only very small twenty-pound bombs had been used, which did virtually no damage. Nevertheless, this seemed to be an excellent example of how air control should NOT be exercised. Fortunately I had not yet assumed responsibility. I retired modestly into a corner of the office and said nothing.

The Euphrates flows in one mighty stream from the Syrian border to the Hindiya Barrage, where it divides into innumerable channels and irrigates an area some hundred and fifty miles long by forty miles wide, covered with crops of wheat, barley and rice, and with gardens of date palms. This area is known as the Middle Euphrates.

At Samawa, however, the river unites once more into a single bed, and continues as such to a point some ten miles below Nasiriya. Here it splits into numerous channels, leading first through dense gardens of date palms, then into marshes full of reeds and into a vast expanse of open water, known as the Hammar Lake.

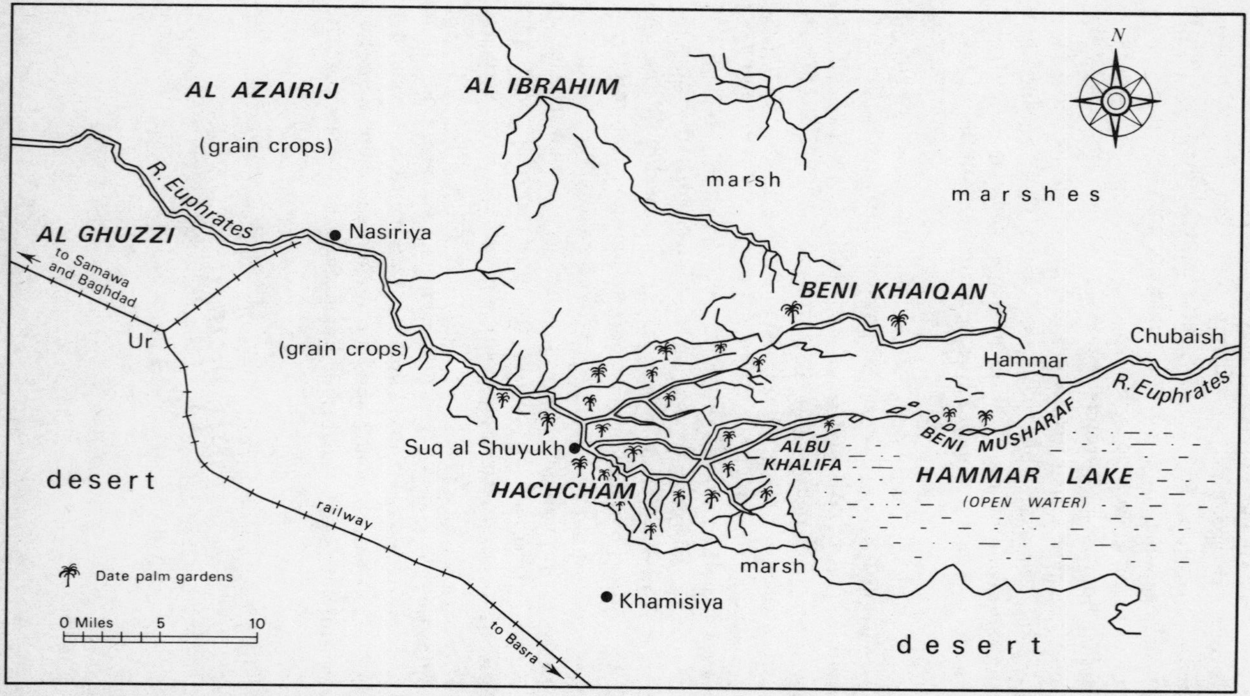

Map 5 The Suq al Shuykukh Area

The marsh tribes below Nasiriya were largely out of control. Not that they showed any signs of opposing the government in arms, but the many small chiefs in the marshes were bitterly hostile to one another. The banks of the innumerable rivers and water channels and the fringes of the marshes were covered with dense gardens of date palms, in the clearings between which were grown crops of rice, maize or barley.

In these clearings the tribesmen built their war-towers round which clustered the reed-huts of the village. A battle was an almost daily, or at least a weekly occurrence. The life of the whole area depended on irrigation and a frequent cause of fighting was the closing of a canal by one party to secure more water for themselves at the expense of their neighbours.

A more delicate jest was to sally forth at night at harvest time and to endeavour silently to reap some of the crops of a neighbouring village, carrying the booty back to the war-tower before dawn. When the victims came into their fields in the morning, the fruits of months of labour had vanished in the night. The cause was not far to seek for the triumphant enemy was already dancing a war-dance round his tower. Quickly the alarm was given, war-banners emerged from the date gardens, the lilt of other war-chants approached and soon the date gardens echoed with the crackle of rifle-fire.

In an hour or two, by which time four or five men had been killed, a saiyid would appear between the hostile lines and a truce would be arranged. A saiyid was a reputed descendant of the Prophet Muhammad, and was a sacred character among the tribes, a fact which enabled him to arbitrate between the combatants. The police would then arrive on the scene. Too weak to intervene by force, they would invite the rival leaders to come in to the government, where the incident could be investigated.

A few days after my arrival in Nasiriya, a telegram was received from the neighbouring sub-district of Suq al Shuyukh: 'heavy fighting in the Beni Khaiqan. Twenty-five killed.'

The Beni Khaiqan feud, a typical case of its kind, may perhaps be worth an explanation. Farhood al Mughashghash had, before the First World War, been one of the most influential chiefs of a vague group of tribes called the Beni Khaiqan, though he possessed no authority except over his immediate followers.

When the British Army arrived in the area, they found it impossible to fix the responsibility for any murder or highway robbery under such a chaotic system. They accordingly appointed Farhood sole chief of the Beni Khaiqan, with a government salary, apparently assuming him to be a man of honour.

He, however, soon imprisoned his rivals, while he himself and his relatives acquired great wealth. When the Beni Khaiqan joined the 1920 rebellion, the erstwhile dictator of the tribe was compelled to seek refuge with the government military forces in Nasiriya.

After the rebellion, times had changed. Insistent demands for economy had put an end to shaikhly subsidies. When public security was restored, Farhood was obliged to sneak home to his village as a private individual.

Meanwhile another family, the Ifreet, had taken the lead of the party opposed to Farhood. The rival war-towers of the two chiefs, separated by the placid waters of a branch of the Euphrates, peered at one another over the tops of the surrounding palm groves. Causes of conflict were not long wanting.

As soon as the telegram was received reporting the Beni Khaiqan battle, the mutasarrif sent an official down the river to ascertain the situation. I obtained permission to accompany him. Below Nasiriya, the cultivation of grain crops came to an end and, on both banks of the river, the date gardens became almost continuous. The many irrigation channels made it impossible to ride along the bank and no roads existed in the whole area. The Euphrates was, therefore, the only highway.

We set off down the river in the small government motor launch, early in the morning, while the air was still fresh before the midday heat. The vast silvery surface of the river glided along between steep muddy banks some eight or ten feet high. Just above the water level, innumerable turtles lay in the mud, hastily plopping into the river with a splash as the motor boat approached.

Some miles below Nasiriya lay the little town of Suq al Shuyukh – Market of the Shaikhs – which had once been the Muntifiq capital, in the great days of the Sadoon princes, before the Turkish or the British Governments interfered with tribal affairs. It was now the headquarters of a sub-district of the administration. Here we ascertained the following details of the incident.

The banks of the Euphrates were always liable to burst in flood time and the Government accordingly endeavoured to collect working parties from the tribes to strengthen the dykes. On this occasion, Hajji Atshan al Ifreet arrived with his merry men and noticed an enemy of his standing on top of the river bank. Turning his back on this hated rival, Hajji Atshan placed his rifle over his shoulder, while he stood apparently talking to a friend.

Suddenly he pressed the trigger and shot his enemy dead over his shoulder, apparently without looking round – a feat of marksmanship which I have never known equalled elsewhere. The ensuing battle gave rise to the deaths of twenty-five men.

The Government was too weak to use force against the tribesmen. All it could do was to mediate a truce and to call upon both sides to sign undertakings to keep the peace – till next time. Feelings were running high after the loss of twenty-five killed – *forat al dem*, the boiling of blood, the Arabs called this period of excitement.

We accordingly thought it advisable to take Hajji Atshan back to Nasiriya with us in the motor launch. All the way up the river, he sat with two policemen and the motor launch crew telling good stories, roaring with laughter and smacking his thighs with delight. I could scarcely believe that a man who had just committed a murder and taken part in a battle with twenty-five killed could seem so jovial and carefree. The marshmen used perhaps to be the most ruffianly blackguards, but they all had a humorous twinkle in their eyes.

Six days later, both sides of the Beni Khaiqan signed a truce and an undertaking henceforward to keep the peace. Matters having been thus arranged and the boiling of blood it was assumed, having subsided, Hajji Atshan was allowed to return home. Five days later he was murdered. Such was life in 1922 in the marshes of the Muntifiq.

A few miles from the war-towers of the Ifreet and Mughashghash lived another tribe called the Hachcham. It also was divided against itself. Two chiefs, Farhood al Fandi and Hajji Yasir al Nasir, were allied to the Ifreet, while their rival, Gassid al Nahi, had sworn a treaty with the Mughashghash.

Gassid was a remarkable personality. About fifty-five years of age, blind in one eye, with a beard dyed bright red with henna, unlimited assurance and a ready sense of humour, even at his own expense, he was certainly a most jovial scoundrel. I forget how many men he claimed to have killed – I think between twenty and thirty.

But his rival, Hajji Yasir al Nasir, was even more deadly. The First World War having been fought foot by foot from Basra to Baghdad, every marshman had seized the opportunity to provide himself with a rifle by fair means or (more likely) by foul. But Hajji Yasir had gone one better – he had obtained a German automatic pistol. Not only so, but he had somehow procured sufficient ammunition to enable him to practise. He became not only a first-class shot, but so quick on the draw that his enemies never succeeded in firing at all – in fact they never knew what hit them.

He followed the good old custom of cutting a nick in the butt of his pistol for every enemy he despatched to a better world. When I arrived in the Muntifiq, the score stood at thirty-eight. A few weeks later, the worthy old pilgrim scored his thirty-ninth victory. But perhaps success had made him careless. One day he was walking along a path through the palm gardens, when an enemy fired at him with a rifle from behind a tree. Hajji Yasir set out on the long pilgrimage without knowing what had happened.

After the death of Hajji Yasir, a movement was set on foot for the reconciliation of the two sections of the Hachcham. Husain al Nasir, the brother of the late Hajji Yasir, invited his rival, Gassid al Nahi, to a feast to celebrate the inauguration of peace. Sheep were slaughtered wholesale and, heaped upon vast platters of rice, were greedily consumed by the tribesmen, squatting on the ground in circles.

Old Gassid, hairy, one-eyed, jovial and full of mutton and rice, must have relaxed his customary vigilance. The time for coffee had come and Gassid was sitting with his back to the reed wall of the hut. The mat covering of the wall had been raised to admit a cool breeze. A negro retainer of Husain al Nasir shot their guest in the back from outside the hut.

These few sketches must suffice to illustrate the conditions under which I served my apprenticeship with the marsh Arabs. Five years later, in 1927, nothing but the memory of these 'good old days' survives. It is now several years since the *hosa*, the deep-voiced war chant, has rung through the date palm gardens outside Suq al Shuyukh. The war-banners are rolled up in the villages, or are unfurled only on feast days.

Much has been heard of alleged British colonialism, or of the extremism of Arab nationalism, but the public has never been told of how a handful of Iraqi and British civil officials, working as close colleagues, introduced law and order in these remote and wild areas, by patience, persistence and fair dealing, almost without any backing of force.

Yet the nature of the marshman seemed entirely different from that of other Arabs. All other tribesmen, from camel bedouin to shepherds and cultivators, affected to despise the marshmen, who seem, indeed, to have cast away almost all the Arab traditions. Husain al Nasir seemed to be little criticized for murdering Gassid al Nahi, when he was a guest in his own hut and had just eaten his bread and salt, a crime detestable beyond words among other tribes and in other places.

Such then was the marshman of the Lower Euphrates. Wild, bearded, paddling about all day half naked in his canoe, unscrupulous, hot-headed, courageous, little more moral than an animal, but jovial, undignified, confessing, and laughing at his own worst enormities – he is far from being so repulsive a savage as a list of his crimes would cause the uninitiated to believe.

Many a pleasant day has he afforded me, pushing blindly in a canoe through the reeds, gliding silently down the mirror-like canals between the date groves, filled in the morning with the cooing of doves, or paddling ankle deep in the waving ricefields.

At times, I used to wonder how men could bear to live with death awaiting them round every corner. But one becomes accustomed to everything. I thought of the humour displayed by British troops in the trenches, when their chances of survival were probably even less than those of Hachcham or Beni Khaiqan. Perhaps the American Wild West, where every man carried his gun, was a not dissimilar way of life.

Those who passed on below Suq al Shuyukh, down one of the many channels of the Euphrates, emerged unexpectedly in a short time from the forest of date palms on to a vast expanse of water, known as the Hammar Lake. If the traveller looked straight on ahead, the great expanse of water extended to the very horizon. On the right, the first low gravelly foothills of the desert danced above the heat haze.

On the left, that is to the north, almost on the horizon, the tops of palm trees seemed to float on air above the water. These belonged to a chain of islands planted with palms, which skirted the northern fringe of the lake.

I once visited these islands across the lake, travelling in a *mashhoof*, the marshmen's canoe. The tribesmen on the islands were poor but hospitable and, after a savoury meal of chicken and rice, I lay down to sleep, tired out by a long journey. Soon I awoke in pain and irritation. The guest hut was empty but a hurricane lantern, turned low, had been left on the floor beside me. I turned up the wick and jumped to my feet.

Looking down my legs, I could see a swarm of black dots ascending them, like the columns of ants, which come and go to an ant-heap. I brushed at them with my hand – the column dispersed, hopping here and there and landing all over me. They were black processions of myriads of marching fleas.

There was, of course, no furniture in the little reed hut – only reed mats spread on the floor. I tore off my clothes and shook them. I rolled up the mat on which I had been lying and threw it across the hut. Nothing was of any use. I put on my clothes again and went out. A few yards from the hut, the tiny waves of the lake lapped the shore.

Between the reed huts of the village, the figures of tribesmen, wrapped in their light worsted cloaks, lay sleeping silently. A dog barked. The clear Iraqi moon shone from a crystal clear sky, irradiating with a silver radiance the mirror-like surface of the lake and the motionless palms. I spent the rest of the night standing up, walking a few paces, sitting down and dozing, then waking again. In the morning, I appeared to have scarlet fever.

Presumably the blood of the marshmen has developed some anti-dote, which either makes it distasteful to fleas, or which makes the men immune to the irritation of the bites. While I was enduring my night of agony, the silent figures of sleeping Arabs lay all around in undisturbed slumbers.

Some Arabs in Iraq, I was told, were in the habit of using large muslin bags, like laundry bags, in which they customarily slept. The user would hastily throw off his clothes, slip naked into this sack and tie it up with a string above his head – or, better still, get someone else to tie it for him. If the neck of the sack were securely tied, it was possible to get a good night's sleep, even with columns of fleas marching up and down outside. But if an enemy should arrive, the nude warrior tied up inside his muslin bag might well be at something of a tactical disadvantage.

North of the Hammar Lake lay fifty miles of reed marshes, reaching to the Tigris at Amara. Doubtless many centuries ago, the whole of this area was covered by villages and fields, irrigated from the Tigris or the Euphrates. The water is almost everywhere quite shallow and the marsh boats are propelled, for mile after mile, by poling. Here and there, a low ridge rises from the water, probably the remains of some ancient town of Babylonian days.

To explore these vast marshes (which few are sufficiently enterprising to do), it was necessary to take a *mashhoof*, or marsh canoe, with two marshmen, one of whom stood in the bow and the other in the stern. Armed with long poles cut from the reeds of the marsh, they propelled the canoe along by punting.

Leaving the vast expanse of the Hammar Lake, we pushed northwards into a narrow channel, shut in by a wall of reeds on each side, perhaps six or eight feet high. Sometimes the channel would narrow down to only a few feet wide, sometimes the boatmen would thrust their way into an apparently solid wall of reeds.

The boat pushed slowly through this dense forest of reeds which scraped past down either side of the canoe, their leafy tops almost shutting out the sun. At other times we emerged into an open lake, bounded all round by walls of tall reeds, the sun blazing overhead and the little waves dancing to a cool northerly breeze. In some places, the reeds would be twenty feet high or more, an apparently impenetrable wall.

Here and there, in the heart of marshes, low mounds rose a foot or two above the surface of the water. On these low muddy hillocks a few huts made of reed mats were dotted. The grey soil round the hovels was foul with buffalo droppings and excreta. The whole community, human beings, buffaloes and dogs, was confined on a tiny island of two or three acres.

Lean dogs yapped at the approaching stranger, baring their fangs, the bristles standing erect on their necks. Girls in threadbare black robes reaching to the ground glided from hut to hut, their faces marked with indigo tattooing and little gold rings in their noses. In their arms they carried dirty babies, flies clustered round their eyes and blue beads sewn into little skull caps, to ward off the evil eye.

Although the women were dressed in flowing garments from their chins to their very toes, the marshmen went half naked most of the day, with perhaps a cloak twisted round their middles, leaving their muscular torsos bare – and even stark naked when they worked in the marshes.

The world is familiar with the Arab tribesman, but it associates him with the desert, the camel and the black tent. Here in the marshes were groups of nomadic families, living always in the forests of reeds, in hovels made of reed mats and moving by canoe. They subsisted on the produce of their watery world – by milking their water buffaloes or by spearing fish with a three-pronged harpoon.

A stranger who saw one of these almost completely isolated settlements for the first time, might well vote them to be one of the lowest manifestations of humanity, but he would be grievously mistaken. These men were full of humour, simple people adhering to their own codes, hospitable, generous and cheerful.

Nearly all Arabs are acutely conscious of personal dignity. They dread to be vulgar or ridiculous in public. Even if clad in rags, they walk with the slow dignity of princes. They will not laugh uproariously or play the buffoon in public. But the marshman was the Cockney of the Arab world, always ready with a joke or an antic. Always near death, he would disregard it in a tribal fight, or, even more, in seeking revenge in a blood feud.

In many respects, the marshmen seem so different from other Arabs, that it is difficult to believe that they can be of the same race. There is, indeed, a story that one of the early Arab khalifs imported large numbers of water buffaloes from India, together with sufficient Indians to look after them. Whatever their ethnic origins may be, they constitute a most remarkable community. Other Arabs affect to regard the marshmen with contempt. I have not lived with them since 1922, but I shall always remember them with affection.

6

Down to the Grass-Roots

In December 1922, I was transferred from the Muntifiq Division to Ramadi, the headquarters of the Dulaim Division, where I had previously been in charge of the Euphrates bridge in the days when I was still a Royal Engineer.

It may be as well at this stage to explain that the modern state of Iraq is divided into approximately three main areas. Of these the eastern and north-eastern areas are mountainous and largely inhabited by Kurds.

The valley of the Tigris and Euphrates is divided into two sections by a line approximately drawn east and west through Baghdad. North of this line, the country consists of gravelly undulating hills and the desert extends across the Euphrates as far east as, and in places beyond, the Tigris. The desert between the Euphrates and the Tigris north of Baghdad is called Jezira. There is no cultivation in this area except by irrigation.

Approximately from Baghdad to the south, the valley of the Tigris and Euphrates consists of alluvial soil which, having been deposited by water, is dead flat. Presumably the Persian Gulf once extended up to Baghdad, but has been filled up by the silt deposited by the rivers in the course of thousands of years. Originally the name of Iraq belonged to this alluvial area alone.

The population is divided into two portions on the same lines as the soil. The riverine cultivators and the marsh-dwellers below Baghdad belong to the Shiite division of Islam. Those north of Baghdad are Sunnites. It is not necessary to embark on a theological explanation of the difference between Shiites and Sunnites, but the reader may perhaps liken them to the difference between Protestants and Catholics.

Of Iraq's neighbours, Iran – or Persia – is Shiite, while the

Kurds, the Turks and the peoples of the Arabian Peninsula are Sunnites.

Four years after the 1918 armistice, the nations of the world were still wrangling over the peace terms. Turkey was laying claim to the Mosul Division, which had meanwhile been incorporated in Iraq. Relations were so strained that an armed Turkish invasion of the Mosul area was feared. As a result of the establishment of Air Control, there were no ground troops in the country, the Iraq Army not yet being operational.

Although the Ottoman Empire had suffered a disastrous defeat in the First World War, the clumsy actions of the Allied Powers who were in occupation of Istanbul and an ill-timed Greek invasion of Anatolia had, after the armistice, roused a new spirit of Turkish national resistance.

The Nationalists, led by Mustafa Kemal Pasha – later called Ataturk – agreed to self-determination for the Arab provinces of their former empire, but demanded that Turkey retain all territories inhabited by a majority of non-Arab Muslims. This demand meant that the Mosul area would remain Turkish, although the Iraq Government had already occupied the province.

There was not a Turkish majority in the Mosul area, but there was a non-Arab Muslim majority, the difference being due to the presence of the Kurds who, however, had not been consulted by anyone. The fact that there were believed to be large underground reserves of oil in the Mosul area may have had something to do with Turkey's insistence.

On 24 July, 1923, a peace treaty was ultimately signed between Turkey and the Western Allies. The former secured most of the demands put forward by the Nationalists, but the question of the province of Mosul was postponed for direct negotiations between Britain and Turkey at a later day.

On 19 May, 1924, a conference assembled in Istanbul (Constantinople) to negotiate over the ownership of Mosul, but failed to reach agreement. As a result, the problem was referred to the League of Nations which decided, on 16 December, 1925, that Mosul should belong to Iraq, thereby finally putting an end to four years of international tension.

Throughout this period the possibility of war between Britain and Turkey was freely discussed. The latter could only invade Iraq by occupying Mosul and marching down the Tigris to Baghdad. The valley of the Euphrates might, geographically, have provided an alternative line of advance from Anatolia (Asia Minor) into Iraq, but could not be used by the Turkish army as a strip of Syria, under French Mandate, extending from the Euphrates almost to Mosul, intervened between Iraq and Turkey. (Map 1, page 14)

In spite, however, of the presence of the French in Syria, the Dulaim district did possess a certain significance in connection with the possibility of hostilities with Turkey, and that for two reasons.

Firstly, there was a fair amount of traffic coming and going up and down the Euphrates between Baghdad and Aleppo. Reports of troop movements in southern Turkey in the Urfa-Diyarbekr-Mardin area could at times be obtained through travellers from Aleppo.

Secondly, the Jezira, the desert area between the Tigris and Euphrates, was full of wild and partly uncontrolled Arab tribes, principally Shammar. There were rumours that, if the Turks were to attack Mosul, these tribes would be stirred up by them to cut the long line of communications between Baghdad and Mosul, possibly between Samarra and Sherqat.

Apart from the possibility of a war with Turkey, the upper reaches of the Euphrates enjoyed a secondary importance owing to the friction between Iraq and Syria, resulting from trans-frontier tribal raiding. Such was the situation when, in December 1922, I arrived at the headquarters of the Dulaim Division in Ramadi.

From east of Aleppo to the Hindiya Barrage, a distance of over seven hundred miles (twice the distance from London to Edinburgh), the Euphrates flows in a narrow bed, with rolling gravelly desert hills on both sides. Throughout the greater part of this distance, the valley of the river is less than a mile wide between rocky desert hills. Where a narrow space intervenes between the river and the gravelly surface of the desert, little patches of cultivation exist, sometimes only a hundred yards wide, sometimes – especially at a bend in the river – widening out into a little plain. (Map 2, page 17)

In the 1920s, these patches of cultivation were watered by *kerids*, or horse-operated water lifts. The cultivators lived in black tents like the bedouin, both from custom and because the river in spring often overflowed its banks and the inhabitants barely found time to remove their tents and families to the nearest spurs of the desert hills.

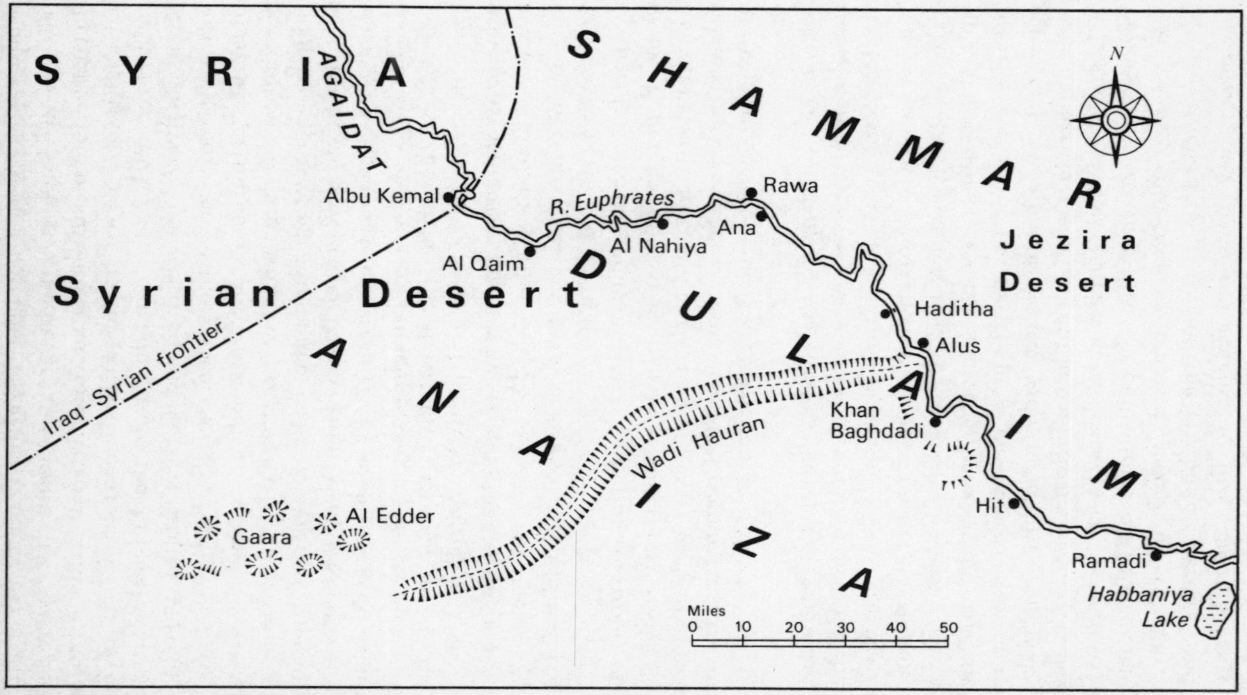

Map 6 The Dulaim Division

58

From Deir al Zor to Felluja, the Euphrates was inhabited by only two tribes, the Agaidat from Deir al Zor to Albu Kemal and the Dulaim from Albu Kemal to Felluja. Both tribes were in the same stage of development.

From Hit to a little below Felluja, the majority of the Dulaim were cultivators, growing wheat and barley which they irrigated with water lifts from the river. Here and there a few gardens of date palms stood on the river bank. In winter and spring, however, when the rains caused the desert to be covered with a pale shade of green grass, the sheep would be moved a few miles away from the river, donkeys being used to carry the supplies and the small black tents required by the shepherds and their families.

North of Hit, however, the Euphrates flowed through a narrow bed between desert cliffs and there was no space for cultivation on its banks. Here were entirely nomadic sections of Dulaim, owning no cultivated land. These sections differed from the bedouins proper in that their principal wealth was in sheep and their beasts of burden were donkeys not camels. The humble donkey forms a better travelling companion for sheep than does the long-striding camel.

The Agaidat, strung along the river banks from Deir al Zor to Albu Kemal, lived, like the Dulaim, in black tents, cultivated on the river banks and allowed their sheep to wander a few miles into the desert in spring. Both tribes, in those days, possessed considerable numbers of horses, which were their only means of transport and were also needed to work the water lifts. [Today the bus has largely replaced the horse for personal transport, and the mechanical pump has done away with the water-lift.]

Across the rolling desert hills, on either side of the Euphrates, wandered portions of two of the largest bedouin tribes of Arabia – Anaiza on the west and Shammar on the east. In Turkish times the bedouins presented a formidable problem to the government. In the desert, the camel was the only means of transport, where water was too scarce to permit the use of horsed cavalry. The camel, however, cannot live in health under settled or civilized conditions. Consequently camels were not used by the government. As a result, to all but the bedouin tribes, the desert was completely impassable.

The bedouins could wander behind the pale blue horizons of the desert, out of sight of the settled area, until they chose their objective. Then, appearing unexpectedly from the blue, they could descend upon some unsuspecting village and loot it, vanishing once more before the men of neighbouring villages (much less the government forces) could rally to their rescue. As neither the government nor the villagers owned camels, pursuit was out of the question.

To secure immunity from such attacks, nearly all villages and agricultural tribes paid regular tribute to the bedouins. In addition, the latter exacted fees from commercial caravans travelling along the verge of the desert, in return for their protection. These sums, extorted from farmers, merchants or travellers, were euphemistically known as *khawa*, or brotherhood.

The system was complicated and elaborate. The brotherhood of different communities was divided up between various nomadic chiefs. One shaikh of Anaiza might be entitled to take the *khawa* of the Agaidat, another that of the merchants of Baghdad and a third that of the merchants of Aleppo.

Thus, before embarking on the desert with a commercial caravan, a merchant would communicate with his 'brother', say a shaikh of Anaiza, pay the dues of brotherhood, and receive a bedouin escort who was obliged to protect him from interference by any other members of his tribe. The system was normally honourably observed. Once the dues had been paid, the bedouin escort would risk his life to protect his 'brother'. For centuries, indeed probably for thousands of years, the bedouins had held a great part of the Middle East to ransom in this manner.

Anaiza are an immense group of tribes, extending from the Hejaz to the Euphrates and the borders of Turkey. That portion of the tribe which occupied the desert immediately west of the Euphrates was called the Amarat and its paramount chief was Fahad ibn Hadhdhal.

Fahad had been a friend of the famous Colonel Leachman and was given a subsidy by the British Occupied Enemy Territory Administration. He was also a wise old patriarch – a little wizened old man, who seemed to live on cigarettes and coffee. His benignity was almost sublime, though infinitely gentle.

The British O.E.T.A. in 1918 could not countenance bedouin raids on villages or the collection of tribute by one class of its subjects from another. Fahad acquiesced in the abandonment of his claims to brotherhood, especially as the subsidy which he received from the British considerably exceeded the 'dues' which he used to collect.

The Agaidat, however, were not contented with their new immunity from bedouin domination, perhaps even oppression. Realizing that Anaiza were no longer able to hit back, they proceeded to raid outlying bedouin camps, to waylay travellers, and to become themselves the oppressors where but lately they had been the oppressed.

The Agaidat were reputed to be of ignoble birth and other tribes refused to marry their daughters. Perhaps this bar sinister on their escutcheon gave them a feeling of inferiority which they burned to efface. From a despised and ignoble community they became the tyrants of the countryside, constantly on horseback, raiding the bedouins, cutting the roads, attacking the Dulaim or robbing merchant caravans.

Divide and rule – or rather divide and avoid being ruled – was regarded by the Arabs as an axiom of politics. The postwar frontier between Syria and Iraq coincided with the boundary between the Agaidat and the Dulaim.

In the Middle East, Britain and France – allies elsewhere – were, as a result of the confused pledges given during the war, jealous and suspicious of one another. The Agaidat were quick to appreciate the situation and to carry out their depredations in Iraq, while at the same time loudly complaining to the French that the British and Iraqi Governments were urging their tribes to raid Syria. Such was the general situation in the Dulaim district, which I found on my arrival at Ramadi in December 1922.

My duties as an intelligence officer at Ramadi were not onerous. An occasional report on troop movements in the Urfa-Diyarbekr area, or a note on the tribal situation seemed to satisfy Air Headquarters in Baghdad. This, however, was not the limit of my duties. Should war break out with Turkey, or the tribal situation get out of hand, I might suddenly be called upon to produce quantities of information or to lead an air sortie or a column of ground troops. I accordingly set myself to know equally thoroughly both the people and the geography of my new district.

I bought for myself a strongly-built Arab liver-chestnut stallion, whom I named Al Feel, or The Elephant, in reference to his stout build and powerful hindquarters. The money having run rather low, I acquired for my servant, Ali al Yunis, a rather weedy chestnut, whose feebleness in contrast to the elephantine proportions of his stable companion earned him the title of The Rat.

Accompanied by Ali on the Rat, while I bestrode the Elephant, and wrapped in our Arab cloaks, our faces swathed in Arab head-dress leaving only our eyes visible, we tiptupped out of Ramadi at a hand canter, bent on exploration and adventure.

I was not without that youthful passion for romance and adventure, which, in those days at least, so easily beset the young Englishman in the east. To ride out alone into unknown country full of armed tribesmen and to mix with them as one of themselves – what more could I have hoped for in my wildest dreams?

As we emerged from the last garden of date palms, out on to the clean, gravelly surface of the desert, I gave a shout, clapped my legs to the Elephant's flanks, and raced away at full speed to the north-west. The Elephant, entering into the spirit of adventure, bucked high into the air like a bronco. Ali, not to be outdone, drove his heels into the Rat who, in spite of his weediness, proved to possess a turn of speed. Poising his riding cane in his right hand like a javelin, Ali raced after me, shouting in stentorian tones, 'Surrender, O horseman! Your neck will be spared if you hand over your mount!'

We proposed to ride to the Syrian frontier at Al Qaim, a distance of one hundred and fifty miles as the crow flies, and doubtless much more when following the bends of the Euphrates. The good nature of tribal warfare is illustrated by the fact that we were travelling through Dulaim country, whereas Ali was from the Agaidat, a tribe at feud with the Dulaim. It is true that the Government was at that time respected by the latter tribe and I was in no great danger. But it might well have been thought that my companion might have received some sour looks. In fact, however, nothing of the kind took place.

A number of little towns and villages were scattered up the Euphrates north of Ramadi. The first was Hit, a very ancient village, perched on a mound. There were many date palm gardens on the river above and below Hit, the most northerly place in which dates flourish. The local people claim that Hit was the home of Job, whose tomb is shown on the edge of the town, though perhaps more expert antiquarians claim that he lived at Tebuk, in the northern Hejaz.

The state of public security in Job's day might indeed equally have described conditions on the Euphrates, if not in 1923, at least until 1920. 'And there came a messenger to Job and said; The oxen were ploughing and the asses feeding beside them: and the Sabaeans fell upon them and took them away. . . . And while he was yet speaking there came also another and said: The Chaldeans made out three bands and fell upon the camels, and have carried them away' (Job I, 14-17).

Hit is also said to be the Ahava mentioned in the book of Ezra, where the Jews of the Captivity collected before setting out from Babylonia to rebuild Jerusalem.

It was down this same Euphrates valley that Xenophon marched with the ten thousand Greeks to fight the King of Persia in the plains of Iraq in 401 B.C. They must have presented an imposing spectacle with their brazen helmets, scarlet tunics, greaves and polished shields.

They marched down the east bank of the river, which is flatter country, the west bank being constantly intersected by rocky spurs and water-courses coming down from the Syrian Desert. Xenophon describes the Jezira as a region where the ground was utterly flat, as level as the sea. It was covered with small shrubs, all of which were as fragrant and odoriferous as perfume – but there were no trees (Xenophon, *Anabasis*).

A soldier campaigning in the desert would be quick to notice the perfume of the shrubs, for it is when they are cut and piled upon the camp fire that this quality of fragrance is most noticeable – now, as it was more than two thousand years ago. Many an evening, sitting round the camp fire, have I enjoyed, like old Xenophon, this desert incense.

Above Hit, two or three little Arab hamlets, ten or fifteen miles apart, cling precariously to small rocky islands in the middle of the great river. The bare, gravelly desert hills drop in steep slopes and rocky cliffs to the very edge of the lapping wavelets of the great Euphrates.

From time immemorial raiding parties had roamed over these yellow hills and had scrambled down these stony slopes to water their horses and camels at the river. But these tiny settled communities had clung tenaciously to their little rocky islands, protected on either side from the predatory nomads, partly by their own poverty and partly by the fact that half the Euphrates flowed past them on either side.

It was already dark when we reached the river bank opposite the little island of Haditha. The river was low and the water was shallow between the island and the west bank, where stood a few houses, encouraged in their exposed position by the presence of a government post and a few mounted police.

Stiff and tired, we slid from the backs of our horses by the water's edge. The river roared and babbled past the shingly beach. A man came out of a house, shedding a beam of lamplight from the open front door over the dark foreshore and the white dancing waters. '*Marhaba, ya walad* – welcome, my lad,' we shouted. 'Two welcomes to you,' he called back cheerfully, and, coming towards us, inquired who we were.

We told him we were travellers and asked where we could spend the night. 'The headman, Abdul Rezzaq, will welcome you as guests,' the man replied. 'I will guide you.' We forded the river to the island, stumbling up a narrow stony path. Suddenly we heard voices and saw figures advancing towards us, carrying a lantern. 'God welcome these guests,' called the cheerful voice of Abdul Rezzaq. He pushed open a rough wooden door and showed us into his (and indeed the village's) guestroom.

It was about thirty feet long by twelve feet wide, dimly lit by a lantern set on a stool. In the centre of the floor was an open hearth, on which glowed a fire of hot, red embers. There was no chimney, and the roof and walls were black with smoke. The floor was of beaten earth, but spread round it were long strips of threadbare carpet on which sat a number of men with their backs to the wall.

We paused at the door to say 'Peace be upon you,' at which all rose to their feet, replying, 'And on you be peace.' We sat down on the strips of carpet with our backs to the wall amongst the others.

Our host sat down at the hearth, called for tea and sugar and pushed a blackened kettle into the red embers. Soon we were drinking hot, sweet tea, without milk, in little glasses about two inches high. Comfort is relative. After a long day on horseback in the sun, my back ached and my eyes were tired and sore. Then to find hot, sweet tea, a fire of glowing embers, a wall against which

to lean my back and the pleasant company of simple, friendly men –
all these things made my heart glow with happiness.

The company was mixed. There were three or four villagers of
Haditha, two tribesmen who seemed to be Dulaimis, and an
obvious bedouin. Although the Dulaimis and the Anaizi (for such he
proved to be) were all tribesmen, there was little resemblance
between them. The semi-settled Dulaimis were bigger men, appeared
better nourished and were wearing more clothes. On their heads
they wore heavy black silk scarves, ornamented with many tassels
and gold thread – a product of Syria, locally called *mugronis*. On
their feet, they wore European shoes.

The Anaizi was a smaller and frailer man of much lighter build.
He was dressed only in a white cotton shirt reaching from his
throat to his feet, while on his head he wore a white cotton
cloth, badly in need of the laundry. Yet there was about him an
indefinable air of aristocracy, as compared with the Dulaimi yokels.

The Anaizi, it appeared, was the partner of Abdul Rezzaq, our
host, in the ownership of a mare. The curious custom of owning
part of a mare was very common among Arabs. This did not mean
that the joint-owners rode her alternately. It was concerned with
her pedigree and offspring. If a man owned a thoroughbred mare
which he did not need for daily use or could not afford to keep
up, he sold half of her. The purchaser looked after the mare and
rode her, but the original owner was entitled to receive the first
filly to which she gave birth, or perhaps the first two fillies.

The car and the motor road have destroyed the patriarchal system
of administration which existed in many countries in the nineteenth
century. Patriarchy is, nowadays, commonly referred to with
contempt, like feudalism, but it had many advantages. Basically
it was a system of rule founded on the mutual love of the governor
and the governed.

In this respect, the tribe is an easier unit than the government
district, for the shaikh is, in theory at least, the ancestor of the
tribe, and every member is his 'cousin'. Before the advent of
mechanized transport, the governor or district commissioner was
obliged to tour his area on horseback, spending the night in the
villages and mixing with the people, thus inevitably becoming
familiar with their way of life and their problems.

But now that the car has succeeded the horse, the governor can visit the subordinate towns of his province in an hour or two. He calls at the office of the deputy-governor, his subordinate, joins him for lunch and is back home for tea. If he is conscientious, he may see a few local notables in the government office. But in an office interviews must be brief and all parties are reserved. Only in his own village, round the camp fire or in the guest hall, would the Arab villager relax, be natural and talk freely to an official. Thus the car has severed the bonds of mutual affection, which often united the administrator to the rural population of his province.

The telegraph, the post office and the telephone have completed the disappearance of the old patriarchy. For now higher authority can interfere in everything. The great number of monthly reports, returns and statistics required by the central government has reduced the district governor to an office man. He no longer has time to go round his area, meeting the people and listening to their problems. Instead of discussing their hopes and fears round the evening coffee fires, he is obliged to ascertain his facts by summoning the embarrassed village head-men to an interview in his office.

But yet another, and perhaps an even worse factor soon arose, at least in Iraq. The vast increase in paper work had been accompanied by the inauguration of 'democracy'. This had involved the formation of political parties in Baghdad, which had before long begun to interfere in rural districts, trying to create disaffection, or using political patronage to distort administrative decisions for political ends. I myself, a few years later, was to become an administrator and to suffer from these changes, as this narrative will show.

But even in the old days, the district governor was obliged to tour with some ceremony, in the interests of government prestige. He probably had a police escort, grooms and servants, and perhaps his private tent. The car had at least the advantage that he could arrive at a village with only one policeman and a driver.

In my case, however, no question of government prestige was involved. I was not connected with the civil government. My brief was just to get to know the people and the country perfectly. If all remained calm, I had scarcely any routine duties. But if an emergency should arise, or war break out with Turkey, my familiarity with the area would be of inestimable value to the general staff, to lead air strikes or ground columns, or to influence the tribal chiefs.

I was, for the moment, a nobody, and could fraternize alike with tribesmen or villagers, shaikhs or herdsmen, officials or constables. Nobody was impressed by two young men on ponies, drifting around the countryside, and consequently everyone was natural and friendly. I can never be sufficiently grateful for these early years, when I was able to live inconspicuously among the people of Iraq, from the poorest bedouin to the administrative officials. I thus enjoyed an almost unique opportunity to start at the grass roots.

7

Dogs and Animals

We set off early the following morning from Haditha after taking an affectionate farewell of our kind hosts and rode some forty miles up the west bank of the Euphrates to the town of Ana. The latter must be one of the most remarkable townships in the world, being several miles long but only some three hundred yards wide.

The reason for this exotic shape is that it lies on a narrow shelf between the steep, yellow desert hills and the bank of the mighty Euphrates. Not that the houses are continuous throughout its length. It consists of dispersed and ramshackle houses, courtyards where a horse or some donkeys are tied up and hens scratch the dusty soil, then a patch of date palms, an abandoned ruin, a couple of tiny mudbrick shops, some more date palms, and so on for mile after mile. The swift Euphrates flows past, behind the houses and gardens.

Ana was a sub-district of the Dulaim Division and was the head-quarters of a qaimaqam, which we may translate as a deputy-governor.

The qaimaqam of Ana, Hameed Beg, was a man of small stature, with a sallow complexion, slit eyes, a slightly flattened nose and a wide mouth. In brief, although he was a native of Baghdad, he seemed a living embodiment of a Mongol. It was easy to imagine him, astride a rough-haired Tartar pony, following Jenghiz Khan or Tamerlane, sacking, burning and slaughtering. 'Scratch a Turk and you will find a Tartar', the old proverb used to say – but in the case of Hameed Beg no scratching was necessary.

Far, however, from acknowledging any connection with his savage ancestors, he professed to be extremely enlightened and never tired of denouncing in scathing terms the ignorance, the idleness and the worthlessness of the poor people of Ana.

In the last chapter, we discussed two varieties of administration the patriarchal and the bureaucratic. Hameed Beg represented a third, which we may call the Old Ottoman. He was typical of a certain type of Turkish official who, while professing supreme contempt for the ignorant people of the country, was himself bursting with character and energy. It was such men who, when (as often occurred) the Ottoman Empire was in utter weakness and disorganization, nevertheless maintained a considerable degree of authority by sheer strength of character and aggressive bluff.

Hameed Beg welcomed me with apparent enthusiasm and I was given a small room in the government office building in which to sleep. This was something of a privilege, for the seat of government in Ana was little more than a rather ramshackle cottage.

The qaimaqam entertained me to dinner in a small room of his house, the walls of which had been roughly plastered with mud and then whitewashed. The furniture consisted of a rough wooden table covered with a piece of oil-cloth, and five wooden chairs.

The custom of bringing in different kinds of food in successive courses is apparently of European origin and presumably presupposes the presence of servants to fetch and carry. In an Arab household the food was prepared by the women who, however, were unable to be present at the meal if there were male guests. As a result, all the food was placed on the table in advance, meat, vegetables, sweets and fruit. The ladies then withdrew and the host invited the male guests to enter.

Many varieties of food were often to be found on the table, such as chickens, bowls of meat stew or of vegetables in gravy, tomatoes, aubergines or beans. Iraq is a rice-producing country and rice was the foundation of every meal.

On this occasion the party consisted of three others and myself. Hameed Beg was the host and directed operations, the other guests being the qadhi, or judge, of Ana, and the government treasurer. Each of us was armed with a dessert spoon and scooped a heap of rice from a large central dish on to his plate. He then helped himself to meat, vegetables and sauces, which he placed on top of the pile of rice on his plate. When he had eaten this first instalment, he would refill his plate once more – firstly by helping himself to more rice, and then foraging round the other dishes still using the dessert spoon from which he had been eating. (In Stuart England much the same procedure was followed, each man bringing his own spoon.)

The qaimaqam was bubbling over with talk and energy. He

repeatedly referred to the people of Ana as dogs and animals and urged me never to speak to one of them. In fact he strongly counselled me never to leave the government building as long as I remained in Ana.

In spite, however, of his injunctions, I set out early the next morning to explore. Ana in the 1920s still maintained the ancient standards of Arab hospitality. No shop in the town sold food for consumption, nor was there any such thing as an inn or a restaurant. Every respectable family kept open house. As soon as any stranger appeared, he was immediately invited to be a guest by the first householder whom he met. All down the long straggling street the doors of the guestrooms stood open to welcome all and sundry who passed by.

Of course, the people of Ana were merchants, who bought and sold from the tribes. But their customers, while these transactions were taking place, stayed with the men of Ana as guests.

It was not long before one of the good men of Ana saw me walking down the street and pressed me to enter his house for coffee. Very soon the room was filled with those 'dogs and animals' against whom Hameed Beg had warned me. It was soon obvious that the antipathy expressed by him for the people of Ana was amply reciprocated.

As the day wore on, however, I heard a number of other viewpoints. A year before, it appeared, in the days of the previous qaimaqam, no man left his house in Ana unless he were carrying his rifle and two bandoliers full of ammunition. Since Hameed Beg had assumed control, no one ventured to carry so much as a walking stick anywhere in Ana – let alone a rifle.

The citizens of these little towns in the desert, like Hit, Haditha and Ana, lived by buying sheep, wool and animal oil from the tribes and reselling these articles in the larger towns. With the price of these sales they bought clothing and other simple requirements and sold them to the tribes.

The state of security on the desert tracks and the possibility of the plundering of caravans interested them deeply. In this connection they could not but pay a rather grudging tribute to the qaimaqam.

Some weeks earlier a raiding party of Shammar bedouin had waylaid a number of cars on the track between Ana and Al Qaim and had robbed the passengers. On receipt of this report, Hameed Beg had snorted with rage, like a warhorse scenting the battle. With only a handful of police under his command, it was out of the question for him to pursue the raiders.

But Ana was a market town, where tribesmen were frequent visitors. The qaimaqam declared war on all Shammar. The first haul was two tribesmen who rode into the town on horses. They were unceremoniously seized by the police, one of them thrown into prison, and the two horses confiscated. The other man was told to walk home and to tell the tribe that the prisoner and the two horses would be held until the property looted from the cars was returned.

Shammar were too numerous and their camps were too widely scattered for news of Hameed Beg's declaration of war to reach them quickly. Within ten days there were nine Shammaris in prison in Ana, and the miscellaneous proceeds of the hostilities now amounted to three horses, five camels, two rifles and a sack of dates.

The qaimaqam gave us a spirited account of these operations. He rapped the table in front of him and cried, 'Ha, ha! Sons of the dog! I will fix them!' He grinned right and left at the company, his wide mouth splitting his slant-eyed Mongol face.

A useful by-product of Hameed Beg's war with Shammar arose from the fact that the former was engaged in building himself a new house. The addition of nine unskilled workers without wages made it possible to expedite the work without additional cost.

Three weeks after the robbery, a bedouin arrived in Ana with a letter from Wadi ibn Ali, a Shammar shaikh, together with sixty-nine Turkish gold liras. One of the nine prisoners, a follower of Ibn Ali, was released. Shortly afterwards, another seventy-three liras arrived. The exact value of the articles taken was difficult to fix, but it seemed probable that the value of virtually all the loot had now been returned. This being the case, and the qaimaqam having completed the building of his house, the prisoners were released. No further robberies by bedouin raiders occurred for some time to come.

As I was walking along Ana's rough and stony lane in the evening dusk, an Arab sidled up to me and pulled my sleeve. 'Beware!' he whispered hotly in my ear. 'Hameed Beg is a traitor. He has written to the Turks and has invited them to come and capture Ana.'

I daresay it was true. In such unstable and uncertain days a wise little Tartar would naturally wish to re-insure by protesting his devoted loyalty to both sides. On the other hand, many people in Ana were tired of their qaimaqam and to denounce him to the government was a natural reaction on the part of the dogs and animals who constituted his unwilling subjects. Only Allah knows the truth!

The qaimaqam was slightly over-addicted to arrack, a fiery spirit distilled from dates in Iraq. Courtesy compelled me to join him – though cautiously – in his potations. The qadhi, being a man of religion, was obliged to confine himself to tea, but the police inspector drank enough for two, thereby levelling up the average.

After several glasses the qaimaqam became not a little exhilarated. We sat on the veranda of the ramshackle government building, looking out at the plumed date palms, the swiftly flowing Euphrates and the outline of the desert hills beyond, dim in the fading evening light. Hameed Beg banged the table, making the glasses rattle. 'Dogs!' he shouted. 'Animals! I'll show them!'

Sitting on the floor on my unrolled bedding that evening, and writing by the dim light of a hurricane lantern, I made the following entry in my diary:

> Like many government officials, Hameed Beg has the education of a junior clerk; that is to say that he is sufficiently educated to cause him to imagine that he belongs to a different world from the mere Arabs, who cumber the face of the Iraqi soil. Were his mind a little broader, he would see that European clothes, a smattering of French, drinking arrack, and having once been to Istanbul do not necessarily raise him to such an immeasurable height above mere mortals.
>
> The Ottoman system appears to have been based on the principle that the people are made for the government, and no one seems to question the theory that the interests of the two are essentially opposed. The government is at present on top in Ana, owing to the energetic measures of Hameed Beg, but the last people whom he desires to benefit by this new public security are the inhabitants of the town. Indeed he frequently expresses a pious wish that he could massacre the lot, in the good old Johnny Turk style.

These words were written, in a cheerful, careless mood, one evening in Ana in April 1923. Since then, Turkey has become a 'modern democracy'. A whole new generation of Arabs now holds positions of authority, who were not even born in Ottoman days. But amazing as the changes have been, the heritage of the old Turkish days still profoundly affects the northern Arab countries of today. The diary continues:

The moral and mental atmosphere of nations has been built up for centuries, not to say millennia. Yet, with effect from Woodrow Wilson, the West has continued to demand that the nations of Asia and Africa should make a clean cut with their past, and, at one fell stroke, adopt the mentality and traditions of the Western democracies. The British press, and often politicians also, continue to pour contempt on any country, which does not appear on the surface to have organized its political life on lines identical with those followed in Britain and the United States.

Would it not be more practical, as well as more polite, if we left these nations to govern themselves in their own way? We seem to be no less narrow minded than Hameed Beg, who was convinced that a European suit and a smattering of French placed him in a different world from the good people of Ana.

On 10 April, 1923, three days after my arrival in Ana, a remarkably daring, and equally incompetent, raid took place.

Some 450 sheep and twenty donkeys, belonging to the people of Ana, were grazing in the desert two miles west of the town when they were attacked by six men on foot, armed only with sticks. The robbers took the shepherds with them to prevent their raising the alarm, and drove off the sheep and donkeys. At six o'clock the next morning the shepherds, who had been released, gave the alarm at the Nahiya police post.

A desert police force, enlisted entirely from bedouins, held posts at Al Qaim, Nahiya and Ana and sent out parties of camelmen and horsemen to seek the raiders. None of the posts had wireless or telephones, but a car from Ana had been sent to warn them.

The robbers, as it proved, were six boys of the Agaidat, all in their early teens, who, with boyish enthusiasm, were anxious to prove their manhood. Being riverine cultivators, they were entirely ignorant of the desert country, yet they set out without food or water, and completely unarmed. In this condition they had walked a hundred miles and had seized the sheep and driven them off, intending to return by the same route.

Having rounded up the sheep at two o'clock in the afternoon, they walked the rest of that day and all the night and the following morning, by which time they had covered sixty miles of the return journey and were south-east of the Al Qaim post. They were almost exhausted, as also were the sheep which refused to be driven any further. The boys consequently abandoned the sheep and mounted the donkeys. Weak from starvation and giddy from thirst they struggled on. Before sunset they began falling off the donkeys from sheer exhaustion and lack of sleep. Abandoning the donkeys, they crawled into the shade of a group of rocks and lay down to die. There, an hour later, they were captured by the Desert Force.

It was an amateurish effort indeed, but, as a feat of courage and endurance, their performance seemed almost incredible for boys of fourteen or fifteen. They had walked a hundred and sixty miles across undulating stony desert, without food or water, in a day temperature of 95° Fahrenheit, without any pause for sleep until they all collapsed from exhaustion.

The Desert Force returned to Ana in triumph with the prisoners. One of them escaped during the night – a boy of fifteen – but was found twenty-four hours later, lying in the desert, delirious and unconscious.

The tribes, although they raided one another, had their own code of rules. If the Agaidat boys had been captured by the Dulaim they would have been treated as guests, allowed to rest for a day or two in the tents of their enemies and then provided with food and water for the journey home. It so happened, however, that they had been captured by the Government, which was intent on introducing civilization to these benighted savages.

The arrival of the raiders in Ana, driven along – their hands tied behind their backs – by police on horses, was the signal for an orgy of savagery. The police and the townspeople turned out en masse and fell upon them. Surrounded by the crowd, bewildered and exhausted by days of walking, thirst and starvation, the prisoners were already more dead than alive. In this state they were beaten, knocked down, kicked and scoffed at. The police sergeant-major of Ana appeared with a long stick and thrashed each of them in turn till his arm ached, whereupon the crowd followed his example. At last they were mercifully thrown into prison.

Next morning, before a concourse of about a hundred people whom Hameed Beg had summoned to the government building, the victims were dragged out once again. Stripped to the waist, they were thrown to the ground face downwards, two policemen being detailed to hold each one down. The qaimaqam then urged the civilian spectators to try their hand at flogging. The good people of Ana, though they were by no means enamoured of Hameed Beg, were anxious to discourage the Agaidat from raiding their sheep, and were ready enough to strike a blow in defence of their property. Soon great welts appeared across the backs of the victims, but still volunteers came forward, some of them government officials in European suits.

Meanwhile, as the blows fell, Hameed Beg stooped down by the head of each victim. A leering grin split his face as he shouted triumphantly:

'Dogs! Animals! Ha! Ha! So you would raid sheep? Take that! Take that! Hit harder, policeman! Sons of a dog! I will show you!'

Throughout the whole performance, until the victims – mere slender children – were half dragged and half carried back to the prison, not a sob or a cry escaped their lips.

I felt utterly sickened by this orgy. How unexpectedly complicated the world appeared to be. It had all seemed so simple when I first became interested in Iraq. What greater service could a man render than to help to put an end to fighting and robbery and to lead these wild tribesmen to be law-abiding and enlightened citizens. Yet here was a party of young robbers behaving with the stoicism of heroes while the representatives of civilization were taking a sadistic delight in torturing them. Moreover, if these boys had been captured by other 'savage' tribesmen, they would have been forgiven and sent home by their good-natured captors.

Yet Hameed Beg's efforts had indeed resulted in an improvement in public security, of which all were fully aware – not least Hameed Beg himself. These results confirmed him, and most of the police and officials, in their belief in the manifest rightness of his actions. The qaimaqam's reaction had been in line with those of the Ottoman administration for centuries. The tribes did not obey the government and, therefore, they must be destroyed. The interests of the tribes and the government were diametrically opposed. Loyalty to the government meant hostility to the tribes.

Hameed Beg was undoubtedly an extremely capable official, but his outlook was one of contempt for the people in his district (they could not speak French and had never been to Istanbul). He was determined to rule, and indeed he did so, but it was the hated rule of violence. Lying in my sleeping bag on the hard floor of my little room, I pondered on these apparently insoluble problems.

The factor which emerged most clearly in my mind was that the Ottomans and their immediate Arab successors (most of whom had previously served under them) had lacked a positive outlook. The tribes were disorderly and, therefore, their power must be forcibly destroyed. Nobody had ever thought of converting the tribes from their lawless ways and leading them to a better way of life. This would have required sympathetic and positive leadership, which had hitherto been totally lacking. The policy had always been limited to smashing all opposition.

[In 1923, the West still seemed to be in a position to advocate positive leadership and an easing of coercion. But more than fifty years later it is doubtful if we can still do so. For, in the intervening period, indiscriminate violence has everywhere gained ground. Not only have governments resorted to Fascism or Communism, but every extremist party and faction has learned to indulge increasingly in indiscriminate violence. Even Hameed Beg, or the Agaidat, would have condemned time-bombs left in public places with the intention of killing the maximum number of human beings, regardless of age, sex, race, religion or political views.

Perhaps violence is always the result of the lack of positive leadership. Our democracy, alas, produces only politicians, not statesmen.]

Hearing one day that a nomadic sheep-breeding section of the Dulaim were camped in the desert a few miles west of Ana, Ali al Yunis and I rode out one afternoon to visit them and to spend the night with them. We found, also staying with them as guests, a small party of derwishes, from a community in Syria on the Khabur river, who called themselves the Sons of Shaikh Isa.

After dinner they commenced a *dhikr*, beating on drums and chanting. Commencing quietly, the pace and the loudness gradually increased and the tension and excitement mounted. When everyone was thoroughly thrilled, one of them stood up, holding in his hand a kind of polished steel skewer, perhaps some four feet long.

Opening the front of his shirt, he felt his stomach carefully until he seemed to find the right spot. He then placed the point of the skewer carefully on this place, holding it so that it stuck out horizontally in front of him. Meanwhile the drumming and the chanting had risen to a passionate frenzy of excitement.

76

Suddenly the man plunged forward, so that the other end of the skewer struck the ground. The man's weight coming thus on the skewer forced it through his body until it protruded perhaps six inches behind his back. We were all sitting round the camp fire and the man was only four or five feet from me. I am absolutely convinced that the skewer had passed through his body and I could see it projecting from his back.

He then straightened himself up, with the skewer protruding in front of his body and out of his back, horizontally. At this stage, an assistant stepped forward. The man himself placed both his hands on his stomach, pressing with his fingers on either side of the skewer. The assistant began gradually to pull out the skewer. The man himself directed him, saying – 'Right! Go on! Easy! Stop a second! All right' – until the skewer had been very gradually and gently withdrawn from his body. He then sat down by the fire, about four feet from me. I noticed that his hands were trembling. He sat still, then drank some coffee and gradually recovered himself. Personally I was convinced that the skewer had passed through his body.

We slept the night with the Dulaim shepherds. Next morning, as we were riding back to Ana, I asked Ali if the skewer had actually gone through the man's body. He replied very positively that it had.

'Can you push it through your body anywhere?' I asked. 'Or is there a special place.'?

'There is only one special place,' he answered.

Then, opening the front of his shirt, 'I lived with the Sons of Shaikh Isa myself for a time when I was a boy,' he said. 'I wanted to be a derwish and I also learned to pierce myself. You can still see here the scar on my stomach.'

I never again saw, or heard of, derwishes of this kind in any Arab country.

A few miles above Ana, and on the opposite bank of the Euphrates, lay the little town of Rawa. The Rawis differed a good deal in character from the people of Ana. The caravan track from Baghdad to Aleppo has passed through Ana for four thousand years, a fact which has perhaps rendered the people of the town more cosmopolitan in their outlook. Many Anis worked as merchants and caravaners, and had visited the cities of Iraq and Syria alike.

The people of Rawa lived on the east bank of the Euphrates, in a backwater cut off from the great world and from the commerce of cities. They gained their livelihood by trading with the wilder tribes of the Jezira Desert, particularly Shammar. They were, there-fore, themselves wilder, more virile and more primitive than the people of Ana.

Rawa was also the headquarters of a colony of Muslim holy men, under the spiritual leadership of a little old man called Shaikh Muhsin. I paid a visit one day to the venerable Shaikh in his guestroom in a narrow street, beside the rushing babbling Euphrates, which is here wide and shallow with many rapids. The holy man, like every other notable citizen of Rawa, kept open house. The door of his guest room was open day and night, and all and sundry walked in and out as they wished. Coffee pots simmered on the hearth, and ragged mats were laid round the floor at the foot of the walls.

But Shaikh Muhsin had renounced the world and owned nothing. The hospitality dispensed in his guest room was supplied by the gifts of the pious. Even as I sat there, a tribesman came in with half a sack of flour which he left as an offering. Half an hour later a poor carpenter of Rawa brought a small bag of coffee.

The shaikh himself came and sat with us for a short time, though he scarcely spoke. He appeared to be very old, thin and frail, with a dry parchment-like skin of deathlike whiteness. In spite of his age, he still bathed in the Euphrates every morning at dawn, even on the coldest winter mornings. Moreover the river came from the snow-clad mountains of Asia minor and its waters often felt icy.

Perhaps the early Christian hermits of the desert were like this frail old Muslim saint. Those who have completely abandoned the world to give themselves to God are of one fraternity, no matter the details of the creed which they profess. Shaikh Muhsin smiled upon us a gentle smile – an Arab poverello on the rocky desert shore of the swift Euphrates.

Having thus, to some extent at least, explored the Dulaim Division from Ramadi to the Syrian frontier, I thought that I should also make a reconnaissance of the Southern sections of the Dulaim between Ramadi and Felluja. Mounted on the Elephant and the

Rat, Ali and I accordingly set out to ride down the Euphrates below Ramadi. In the evening we reached the great black tent of Habeeb al Shallal, the shaikh of the Muhamda section of the Dulaim. After a large meal of rice and boiled mutton, we sat talking pleasantly in the tent by the flickering light of the coffee fire. I hazarded a question about the history of the Dulaim tribe, whereupon the shaikh called upon a white-bearded old man to tell us a story of old times. The old man sat down opposite to me, amid the wide circle of bearded faces and began his narrative; the Romance of Mauza the Beautiful.

In the old days, when the great tribe of Zubaid occupied its ancient territory in Central Arabia or Nejed, there dwelt among them a shaikh whose name was Jabreen. He had three daughters, but the eldest, who was called Mauza, was of a beauty beyond all compare. And the sons of her uncles, who had the first claim on her hand, began to quarrel among themselves as to who should marry her – the sons of Thamir, of Jubber and of Jannab, her uncles.

And Jabreen spoke to his wife one evening in his tent, saying, 'What shall we do with our daughter Mauza, whose beauty is beyond compare? For to whichever of the sons of her uncles we give her in marriage, the others have sworn to kill him. Then our family will be torn by internal blood feuds.' Then his wife said to him, 'This shall we do. Do you order our tent to be struck tomorrow and we will slip away and escape and go to a distant area, with a strange tribe and in a far country. Then whoever of the lovers follows us up shall be the one who deserves the hand of Mauza, whose beauty is without compare.'

Accordingly the next morning Jabreen's wife struck the tent and packed it on the camels and made ready to move. But the men of the tribe came up to Jabreen and said, 'O Jabreen, where are you moving to?' And Jabreen answered, 'I have found a valley behind that hill over there in which there are plentiful green herbs on which my camels can graze, and I am moving my tent to camp in it,' and they said, 'In the safe keeping of God.' But when they got behind the hill, they marched on and on and on. For many days they went on until they came to the banks of the Euphrates, to the camp of the tribe of Mrai. And they pitched their tent near the tent of the shaikh.

The shaikh of the Mrai, looking from his tent, saw a strange tent pitched. And he called an old woman of his household and told her to go and visit the tent and enquire who these strangers were who had camped under his protection.

Now Mauza was sitting on the floor of the tent in the women's apartment, and in front of her was the Holy Quran on a reading stool. And she sat upright on the ground and read (for she was literate), and the long plaits of her hair hung down to the ground. And when the old woman entered the tent, she saw Mauza sitting upon the floor and the long plaits of her hair hanging down to the ground. And she ran back to the shaikh and said, 'By Allah, there is in that tent a maiden whose beauty is beyond compare.'

The next day, the shaikhs of the Mrai paid a visit to Jabreen in the men's portion of his tent. And he provided coffee and served them, and they drank and departed.

And the second day they again visited Jabreen, and he slaughtered a young camel and set before them a feast. And after feasting the shaikh said, 'O Jabreen,' and he said, 'Yes.' And the shaikh said, 'I want your daughter in marriage, and I will pay you for her a handsome dowry. Name any sum of money you like and you shall have it, but give me the hand of your daughter in marriage. And it is no use for you to refuse for you are but one tent and the Mrai camped all around you are many thousands, and you alone cannot fight a tribe. And if you would attempt to escape, I can saddle a hundred mares and overtake you.'

But Jabreen said, 'It cannot be. For the sons of her uncles of the tribe of Zubaid desire her hand in marriage, and I cannot wed her to a stranger.' But the shaikh replied, 'By Allah the Almighty, nothing will serve but that I marry her.' And Jabreen said, 'Give me three days to consider,' and the shaikh said, 'Good.'

Then Jabreen consulted with his wife what to do. And his wife said, 'Give the girl to him and take the money, for we cannot fight against a tribe neither can we run away.' But he answered, 'By Allah it shall not be, but I will fight them.' And on the third day, Jabreen buckled on his breastplate and took his lance and mounted his mare and he said, 'I have chosen war against the tribe of Mrai.'

In those days they fought one by one by challenge, not in great numbers and from afar as they do now. So they marked out a field, and Jabreen tilted against the leaders of the Mrai, one by one, with his lance. And he overthrew eight of them. But the ninth pierced

Jabreen through the body with his lance, and he fell from his mare and died.

Then the shaikhs of the Mrai were gathered in the tent of the great shaikh and they drank coffee. And Mauza covered her face with her cloak and approached the tent. And she said, 'Peace be upon you,' and they replied, 'And on you be peace.' 'I make a request, O shaikh,' she cried, and he answered, 'Say on.' Then she said, 'Suffer us to mourn forty days for our father, and then do as you please.' He replied, 'On my head, it shall be so.'

Then Mauza returned to the tent and sat down, and wrote letters to Thamir and Jubber and Jannab her uncles, the shaikhs of the tribe of Zubaid and set forth all that had occurred. She told them how Jabreen her father had been killed and that she had only forty days respite before she would be married to the shaikh of the Mrai.

Then she went to her own riding camel – her name was Naina – and cut off her hair in patches and rubbed black oil into her skin until she appeared all ragged and blotchy like a camel with the mange. And she bound the letters she had written under the camel saddle and turned her free. And Naina set off to the south, longing for her old home in the country of the tribe of Zubaid, following the same route by which Jabreen had brought them.

But whenever she drew near to any tribe or camp or well in the desert, that she might drink and rest, they all cried out 'She is mangy! Do not let her approach our herds!', and they drove her off with sticks and stones, so that she fled on towards the south.

One day the shaikhs of Zubaid were standing by a desert well, in the glow of the sunset, watching the slaves and the herdsmen drawing up water in leather buckets and sloshing it into the troughs. The camel herds were collected a short distance away, ready to drink as soon as the troughs were filled. Naina knew the well, for she had reached her own home district, and she drew near toiling across the desert. But as soon as the men saw her they cried, 'She is mangy! she is mangy! Keep her off!'

But Thamir saw her and noticed that she was weary and exhausted, though he did not at first recognize her. 'It is a sin to deny her water,' he cried. 'Let her drink but keep her away from the herds.' So they allowed her to come to the troughs. Then Naina drank and drank deep and again, for she had travelled without tasting water since she left the camp of the Mrai. Her belly filled with water and when she had drunk her fill, she heaved a great sigh. Then the girths burst, the saddle fell off and the letters were scattered on the ground. Thamir and Jubber read the letters and found that they were from Mauza. In them she told all that had happened, how Jabreen was dead and that she had only forty days' reprieve and then must marry the shaikh of the Mrai. So they called out the banners and rallied their men and set out.

Naina went in front of them and showed them the way. Every night they hobbled her in the centre of the camp lest she should escape and they be deprived of their guide. After many days they arrived on the bank of the Euphrates. Thamir that night could not sleep, and as he sat awake he noticed Naina. She kept struggling to rise, but the knee-hobbles prevented her from standing up. Then Thamir thought to himself, 'the place must be near. For Naina thinks she can reach it tonight, and she will not wait for another day's march'.

So he wakened his own men and loosed Naina and followed her, leaving the others still asleep. They then followed Naina through the darkness of the night. Presently they heard a barking of dogs, and Thamir caused his men to lie down, while he went on alone with Naina, and before long he saw the dark forms of innumerable tents. Then Naina led him to one tent which was pitched a little apart from the others and she knelt down. Mauza was standing before the tent weeping with her hand upon the tent rope, gazing to the south. For this was the fortieth night and next day she was to be married to the shaikh of the Mrai.

Then Thamir returned and roused his men and brought them quietly to the tent of Mauza. And she pointed out to him the tent of the great shaikh and the tents of the lesser shaikhs and Thamir and his men fell upon the Mrai in the night when they were sleeping and slew them with a great slaughter.

Next morning when Jubber and his brother, Jannab, awoke, Naina was gone and Thamir and his men were not to be found. So they quickly took up their arms and followed. And they came to the camp of the Mrai, and saw Thamir pounding the coffee in a huge mortar in the tent of the great shaikh of the Mrai. Thamir was the ancestor of the Dulaim, and his brothers, Jubber and Jannab, were the ancestors of the Juboor and the Jannabiyeen, who still live on the Euphrates further south.

The old man's voice fell silent. During the narration, not a sound was to be heard in the large tent full of men. When the story was ended, the voice of our host broke the silence. 'Pour out more coffee,' he cried. 'Put wood on the fire. We have no need to sleep on this blessed night.'

8

Authorized Raiding

The Turkish administration had never made any attempt to control the nomadic tribes in the desert, for it possessed no camels, the sole means of transport. Only if bedouin depredations in the cultivated area became unendurable did the Ottoman Government attempt reprisals against any members of the offending tribe who approached the settled area.

Thus left to themselves, the great bedouin tribes behaved like small independent nations. They declared war on one another, or concluded peace, without regard to the outside world. The bedouin tribesman's loyalty was solely to his tribe, regardless of the Ottoman Empire, the British, the French or the Iraq Government. His attitude to these powers was similar to that of the citizens of France or Britain to the League of Nations. They might at times be useful, but the tribesman owed them no personal loyalty.

Merchants, travellers and farmers were regarded by the free nomads as inferior types, who could be made to pay dues to the bedouins, if they wished to make use of the desert, which the nomads regarded as their own land – in the same manner as a landlord collects rent from his tenant farmers.

Between themselves, however, such bedouin tribes as Anaiza or Shammar regarded one another as equals, the aristocrats in a plebeian world. Anaiza in general camped in the Syrian Desert west of the Euphrates and Shammar east of the river in the Jezira. Fahad ibn Hadhdhal was the chief shaikh of Anaiza in the area, but Shammar had no single chief. They were also in the happy position of having half their grazing area in Iraq and half in Syria, there being no extradition treaty between the two governments. Thus any man, or section, which incurred the displeasure of one government had only to move its tents a few miles across the boundary (which was not demarcated on the ground) in order to secure immunity from punishment. (Map 6, page 58)

Anaiza on the whole were richer than Shammar and their shaikh, Ibn Hadhdhal, was an old man fond of peace. The result was that Anaiza usually played a defensive, and Shammar an offensive rôle.

The Dulaim Division possessed a Desert Force mounted on camels, and recruited entirely from bedouins, but it was only sixty strong, extended in small posts along the Euphrates from Al Qaim, on the Syrian frontier, to Nahiya, Ana and Khan Baghdadi. So numerous were the Shammar raiding parties which almost daily crossed the Euphrates and so weak the camel police, that I found on my visit in April 1923 that an unofficial working arrangement existed between the two. The Desert Force did not attempt to arrest raiders, on condition that they did not molest non-bedouins, farmers or travellers.

In summer, the Euphrates was fordable at several places and raiders could come and go. But in winter and spring, incidents would arise when the raiders demanded boats to ferry them across.

The problem of bedouin raiding became a bone of contention in the Ministry of the Interior. Iraqi officials in general regarded nomadic tribes with aversion and were well satisfied that they should fight one another – some day perhaps they would exterminate one another, and decent citizens could live in peace without them. Unfortunately, this idea had occurred to the bedouins also, and fatal casualties in their battles were remarkably few. They realized that the sport could not continue if all the players were dead.

A number of British officials in the Ministry, however, adopted a more sporting standpoint. Raiding, they said, was the bedouin's national sport, like league football or county cricket. Watching sheep or camels eat shrubs, or the thin desert grass, was an extremely monotonous way of life, like a repetitive job on an industrial production line. Psychologically the desert dwellers were starved of excitement and romance – a deficiency supplied by the glory and excitement of raiding.

Eventually, the officials of the Ministry of the Interior produced a remarkable solution. All agreed that the bedouins should be free to fight one another, but only on condition that they did not molest non-bedouins, cultivators, travellers, merchants or townspeople. Already cars were crossing the Syrian Desert from Baghdad to Damascus, while the R.A.F. was flying air mails over the desert from Cairo and Amman to Baghdad.

Agreement having thus been reached, the officials prepared a booklet of *Rules for Raiders* which constituted a masterpiece of bureaucratic draftmanship. Divided into an Introduction and several parts, the paragraphs and sub-paragraphs were marked *a,b,c*, and 1, 2, 3, and 4. Every foreseeable situation was included, and the raider was informed in detail what action he should take on each occasion. Large numbers of the booklet were printed in Arabic and the R.A.F. was asked to fly all over the desert and drop bundles of the leaflets on every nomad camp.

Raiders were also instructed to report at a police post where possible, and to give full details of their enterprise and its objective. The police post at Al Qaim which, although on the banks of the Euphrates, was almost surrounded by desert, opened a special register for raiders. Columns were ruled on each page for date, number of raiders, name of leader, tribe and objective. The last column was for the result of the expedition. I spent several days in the desert police post at Al Qaim at various times, and saw a number of raid leaders report and register. Alas! The best laid plans of mice and men gang oft agley. The Ministry had overlooked one point, namely that no bedouins could read! In the vast expanse of the Syrian Desert – five hundred miles by four hundred – there were probably only two men who could read and write, the clerks employed respectively by the great shaikhs, Ibn Hadhdhal of the Amarat Anaiza, and Ibn Shaalan of the Ruwalla Anaiza.

The R.A.F. carried out its task with precision. Flying for monotonous hours over the desert, they conscientiously dropped a bundle of leaflets on every group of tents they saw. The bedouins were alarmed by these operations. Most groups on which a bundle of leaflets was dropped hastily struck camp and moved away to a safe distance, leaving the dangerous-looking package lying on the dusty face of the desert. It was altogether a remarkable example of the genius of bureaucracy.

Copies, however, had also been sent to the civil officials and police and the news gradually leaked out, even reaching some of the bedouins in a more or less garbled form.

One day I was sitting in the tent of the commander of the Desert Force at Al Qaim, when a camel policeman came in and reported that a raiding party was crossing the Euphrates about two miles from the post. An N.C.O. and two men were sent out to bring in the leader, who proved to be a dirty, ragged bedouin with his kerchief drawn across his face, concealing all his features except for a pair of deep-set piercing eyes. He strolled up to us, then paused to greet us in stentorian tones with a deep-voiced, *Al Salaam alaikum*. 'And on you peace,' we replied politely, inviting him to sit down.

Every bedouin is a *grand seigneur* in rags and is perfectly at ease whether he be talking to a king or to a shepherd. Our bearded warrior gave his name as Bunaiyan al Shallal of the Jerba Shammar, and he declared his intention of raiding Anaiza. The commandant, thereupon, made an entry in the ledger in which raids were daily recorded, and then warned Bunaiyan not to interfere with travellers or farmers, but to confine his attention to Anaiza. After a cup of coffee, he took his leave amid great cordiality.

Ten days later, a couple of camel riders called at the post. The police, many of whom were themselves of Shammar, were anxious to hear the news. '*Min ain jayyetkum*! *Allah hayyakum*,' they called cheerfully to the weary-looking riders. 'Where have you come from? May God give you life.' From Bunaiyan's raiding party they answered – a bedouin gives his news slowly, bit by bit, so that his hearers may relish each morsel as it is extracted.

They had found the camels of Murdhi al Rufidi of Anaiza (Murdhi was a little man with a twinkle in his eye. I always thought of him as an Irishman, but perhaps that was due to the resemblance between Rufidi and Rafferty). The camels had been grazing at a distance from the tents. The Shammaris had charged down upon the herds in the afternoon and had driven off about sixty head.

Anaiza had given chase mounted on horses, placing the Shammaris at a disadvantage, for they were all on camels, their homes being too far away for them to have come on horses. The raiders were hard-pressed by the horsemen, who fired from the saddle as they galloped. They accordingly abandoned twenty camels in order to delay their pursuers, but they made away with forty head under cover of darkness, having suffered two men killed and three of their riding camels killed. All these details were carefully entered in the police register. The two exhausted raiders were regaled by the desert police to a large meal of mutton and rice in the guest tent. Then they quietly mounted their camels and bade us goodbye. 'Goodbye – in the safe keeping of God,' replied the police heartily, and the two bandits faded from sight into the vast darkness of the wilderness.

In June 1923, a section of Anaiza was foolish enough to encamp some ten miles west of the Al Qaim post. About an equal distance away to the north-east, on the other bank of the Euphrates, lay the camp of Abdulla al Daham of Shammar. Bedouins have two methods of seeking loot from their enemies. The raid proper consists of mounted men, whether horse or camelmen, who normally operate by day under a tribal leader. But many young men are too poor to possess either a horse or a riding camel. These adopt the tactics of the *hanshooli* or foot-robber.

A young man of this kind, either alone or with one or two companions and armed only with a club or dagger, will often cover long distances on foot across the desert until he finds an enemy camp. He will then lie concealed until nightfall when, creeping into the camp where the camels lie couched in front of the tents, he will coax one or two camels to their feet and lead them stealthily out of the camp. Then, mounting one of them and driving the other before him, he will make off as fast as possible through the night.

But the enterprise is precarious. The camp is full of dogs which might start to bark. The tent owner might wake up, take his rifle and prowl around to seek a possible robber. If the boy ran for it, the owner of the camels might take a shot at him. But there was no ill-feeling. If he came suddenly on the would-be thief, crouching among the camels, he would quite probably bring him into the tent, keep him next day to rest and then send him home with food for the journey.

Sometimes the foot-robber would fail the first night, the camp being restless and the watchdogs all barking. Then, at dawn, the thief would retire, lie up all day in the hills and try again the following night until his food and water were exhausted. Then he could either set off to walk home empty-handed, or slip into a tent. No bedouin would kill a guest in his tent and if he asked the boy whence he came, the latter would reply – 'To steal one of your camels, but God gave me no success.'

At Al Qaim in June 1923, with an Anaiza and a Shammar camp each ten miles away, all day long groups of foot-robbers, clad in rags with wooden clubs in their hands, would file past the police post. The police gave up the task of writing down all their names as they did with raiders, but a few of the desert constables would spend part of the day laughing and talking with the passing robbers.

'God strengthen you, O boys! Where are you from?'

'From Ibn Daham's camp.'

'Where are you going?'

'Perhaps,' they would reply, 'God will provide us with the means of livelihood from the camp in front of us.'

'If God wills,' the police would ejaculate piously. 'May God be with you.'

As a result of these human relationships, a remarkable spirit of friendliness had grown up between the Al Qaim post and the bedouins, particularly Shammar. About this time, a pair of American commercial travellers were driving one day in a Ford car, up the track from Ana to Al Qaim. Suddenly, topping a spur of the hills, they found themselves in the midst of a large Shammar raiding party, led by one Mitab al Sadi. The wild-looking, gaunt, dirty and ragged men, each with his rifle across the saddle in front of him, looked anything but friendly. All had their kerchiefs tied across their faces, leaving only their eyes visible, as mysterious and as terrifying as the Ku Klux Klan.

But as the car drove up, the bedouins made way and, mistaking the occupants for British, saluted and grinned calling out '*Marhaba*! Welcome!' The businessmen, who had expected to have their throats cut, were unable to account for the remarkable behaviour of these friendly bandits. Things never worked out that way in the movies. In fact the raiders were on their way to report to the police post at Al Qaim before proceeding to attack Anaiza.

Occasionally, however, Shammar seemed to misinterpret the spirit of authorized raiding. One Ajil al Yawar had been appointed by the government as shaikh of all the Shammar in Iraq and was allotted a handsome salary for his services in keeping the tribe quiet – a duty which he was unable to perform.

One day, his own brother appeared opposite Al Qaim post with a large raiding party, with a view to attacking Anaiza. The river was in flood and unfordable, so the brother of the great Ajil sent a message to the Desert Force post at Al Qaim to the following effect:

'We are your fellow soldiers, being in receipt of government pay, just as you are. Please, therefore, provide boats to ferry our raiding party across the river, as we are going to attack Anaiza.'

The desert police were somewhat piqued by this message. It was all right sometimes to turn a blind eye, but it was too much to be treated by the bandits as equals. If you give some fellows an inch, they want to take an ell.

Unfortunately these harmonious relations with raiders were soon afterwards disturbed because Shammar broke the rules of the game. One day a Shammar raiding party held up several Ford cars on the track between Ana and Al Qaim. A Syrian dancing-girl was deprived of her jewellery which she was carrying, together with her best frock, wrapped up in a cotton scarf and held in her lap. An Arab merchant was relieved of a hundred Turkish liras in gold. The robbers made away, but were identified as Shammar.

This was quite contrary to the rules which prescribed that bedouins were to confine their robberies to their own social circle. The police were highly indignant and refused to play cops and robbers with Shammar any longer. Even the romantic British officials in the Ministry of the Interior, who had argued that raiding was a bedouin national sport, were outraged by such unsportsmanlike actions. They were obliged to admit that robbing a dancing-girl was not cricket. This regrettable incident dimmed the first enthusiasm which had been roused by the idea of Authorized Raiding.

In fact, in addition to their illiteracy, one other quality of the bedouins had been overlooked by the Ministry of the Interior. This peculiarity was that they observed their honourable and chivalrous rules only in raids against one another. In dealing with non-bedouins, the rule of honour did not apply, and in such cases raiders could be rough and overbearing. Armed raiders, therefore, although their principal object was to loot camels from a rival tribe, were not always too particular regarding whom they robbed on the way.

Interference with non-bedouins had, of course, been forbidden in the booklet of the rules but, as already explained, the tribes had only heard garbled versions of the regulations, being themselves unable to read.

Another problem arose owing to the fact that the Peace Treaties after the First World War had divided northern Arabia into 'countries'. The borders between these countries were drawn on a map on the scale of one-over-a-million. Even a trained surveyor, equipped with such maps, if he found himself in the midst of the vast distances of the desert, would be unable to decide which side of the line he was standing, unless he fixed his position by the stars.

To those nomads whose ancestors had wandered untrammelled

over these rolling steppes for generations, these imaginary lines on maps were completely unknown. It is true that the *Rules for Raiders* stipulated that no raids were to leave Iraq territory and enter neighbouring states, but inevitably the injunction was chiefly honoured in the breach. Authorized raiding in Iraq soon provoked a chorus of protests from her neighbours.

Eventually the supporters of the League Football school of thought found themselves discredited. *Rules for Raiders* was withdrawn, authorized raiding was pronounced a failure, and soon the fiat was to go forth – 'tribal raiding must cease'.

9

Visit to a Gentleman

By the end of June 1923, I had made myself reasonably familiar with
the Euphrates from Ramadi to the Syrian frontier, having covered
it all, several times over, on horseback and stayed for a meal or a
night at many villages and camps. But the river formed only a
narrow ribbon crossing the wide expanse of the Dulaim Division: I
began to consider the exploration of the desert on either side.

I use the word explore in a limited sense. The overland mail
route from Ramadi to Damascus was not yet established at that time.
Yet a number of preliminary expeditions by car had been made,
chiefly by Major Holt, an officer employed by the Iraq Railways.
Proposals had been mooted for a railway from Damascus or Amman
to Baghdad.

The great areas on either side of these routes had also been
crossed by Colonel Leachman, the lion of the Syrian Desert, who
had been assassinated in 1920, but he had left no written records
on paper. As a result there was little topographical information,
except along the line of Major Holt's route. My object, however,
was not basically topographical but human. I wanted to meet and to
know these famous bedouin tribes, whom some admired and some
detested, but who might play an important rôle in the event of war
with Turkey.

In June 1923, Fahad ibn Hadhdhal, the great shaikh of the
Amarat division of Anaiza, was said to be camped in the Ga'ara
area. I decided to pay him a visit. Through the kindness of the
desert police post at Al Qaim, I was enabled to hire two riding
camels, one for myself and one for my servant, Ali al Yunis, and
to obtain the services of two bedouin constables of the desert
police, one from Anaiza and one from Shammar. (Map 6, page 58)

The Iraq Government, at that time, exercised no control in the
desert, except in the roundabout manner of bringing pressure on

the principal shaikhs. The only system to follow, enabling a non-bedouin to travel with at least partial safety in the desert, was that of *wajh*, or 'face'. The intending traveller engages, for a sum of money, the services of one man from each of the bedouin tribes through the area of which he proposes to pass, or the raiding parties of which he might meet. This man is bound to protect him and his property, if necessary with his own life, from all aggression by members of his own tribe – a service which is usually faithfully performed. Moreover, the would-be robber will normally stay his hand if he finds his intended victim to be under the protection of a man of his own tribe.

In the old days, a tribal protector of this kind was a safer escort than at present. The long lance was then the bedouin's chief weapon and, combats being hand-to-hand, the protector was able to ride forward to meet a raiding party and call out – for example – 'O Shammar! O war party! I am Chaab al Rizni and this townsman is in my face.'

Since the war, however, the knightly lance had been replaced by the rifle. No man could afford to approach a potential enemy to enquire his identity. The bedouins now shot first and asked questions afterwards. Thus it was now possible to be killed at long range by a tribe, although a member of that tribe was actually accompanying the party as their protector.

Our party, myself, Ali al Yunis, Matr, an Anaizi, and Ghannam, a Shammari, left al Qaim at 8 p.m., in order to obtain full advantage from the cool night for travelling. The desert at such times has a charm of its own. The sparkling cleanness of the stars, unknown in European atmospheres, the fresh cool air after the heat and dust of the day, the outlines of the vast rolling steppes, dimly seen in the dark, the deathlike silence broken only by the soft padding of the camels' feet – all combine to form an unforgettable experience.

As we leave boyhood behind, the moments of really vivid joy in experience grow rarer and rarer. The commencement of a desert journey can still make my heart leap with the same joy as it did fifteen years ago, when I was on the way home from boarding school for the holidays.

I say advisedly the commencement of a desert journey, for the task of the desert traveller, who journeys as a bedouin among bedouins, is by no means a light one. (I do not include those European explorers who travel with a private caravan and servants, nor indeed our latest class of desert tourists in six-cylinder cars.)

To the first intoxication of cool night breezes and great open spaces succeed the long days of glaring heat and dust, the backache and the exhaustion, the hunger and thirst, the dirt and the lice, until one curses that mad fever of exploration which impelled him to leave comfort and security to embark on such foolish ventures. How sweet are the pleasures of civilisation when one at last returns in safety to a hot bath, a clean meal and a tune on the gramophone.

And yet once more, after a month or two of town and office, the fever returns. Out comes the still incomplete map, guides are engaged, camels purchased, and with the same enthusiasm as before, one devotes himself to the details of preparation. The water skins are tested, the rope and leather bucket for drawing water, the hatchet, the rifles, the prismatic compass and the sheepskin cloak.

The bedouin on camelback is well nigh inexhaustible. On this my first night of real desert travel, we rode from 8 p.m. until 2 a.m. without a halt. Inexperienced as I was, I had left everything to the two desert soldiers, and devoted all my energies to sticking it out.

At 2 a.m., Matr (pronounced like the English word *martyr*) tapped his camel on the neck with his cane to make it kneel, and looking round said, '*nabghi namrih* – we want to sleep.' Scarcely, however, as it seemed to me, had I stretched myself on the gravelly soil and fallen asleep than I was shaken by the arm. It was 4 a.m. The camels were waiting, already reloaded, and a spot of white dust on the tip of Matr's nose showed that he had already prostrated his face to the ground while saying his morning prayers. My mouth was dry, my back ached and I felt considerably worse than I did before sleeping.

We rode from 4 a.m. to 2 p.m. By nine o'clock, the sun was flaming down, and that morning was one long torture of headache, backache and the struggle against sleep.

Matr and Ghannam tapped their camels into a trot and broke into a loud bedouin song, keeping time with the paces of their camels. The bedouin, silent, dignified and reserved before company, breaks away like a schoolboy when he emerges into the open desert, singing, shouting and laughing, at least when he can see the horizon and knows that no enemy is within earshot.

We put up a hare which Ghannam, slipping off his camel and tucking up his long cotton shirt, proceeded to stalk while we rode on. After a few minutes he came running after us, rifle in hand, and

VISIT TO A GENTLEMAN

catching hold of the saddle-tree swung himself back on to the camel's back. 'It escaped – may God curse it,' he called out laughing.

At two o'clock in the afternoon, as a concession to my being a townsman, we halted for one hour and the bedouins arranged a cloak, supported on a cane pushed into the ground, to keep the sun off my face, for there was, of course, no shade within fifty miles.

At three o'clock we set out once more, when Matr calmly announced that we had used all our water. Asked when we should find some more, he replied that we should reach Hassian al Edder – the Edder water-holes – the same night, but that they were often dry in summer. Should they contain no water, we should have to travel another eight hours to the next well. Half a day with no water, when the temperature stands at 120° Fahrenheit, seemed to me a serious proposition. We, therefore, trotted on at our best pace, eventually reaching the Edder water-holes at eight o'clock in the evening.

The water-holes were situated in a deep depression, surrounded by cliffs, loose boulders and rocks. Ghannam and Matr raced on ahead and, as I reached the rim of the depression, I could see them far below as they hobbled their camels and ran forward to look for water. I slipped off my camel to lead it down the zigzag stony path, which wound round the cliff face.

I had not previously realized that I was tired, though I had suffered severely from backache, headache, soreness and the weary monotony of it. I seemed, however, to have become accustomed to the saddle and felt as if I could have ridden on for a week without dismounting.

But no sooner did my feet touch the ground, than my knees gave way. I felt like a man who, after a long illness, first gets out of bed, and tries to walk across the room. Half way down the cliff path, I met Matr running up towards me with a brimming bowl, shouting '*Ma! Ma!*' They had found water.

I was almost exhausted when we sat down to eat at the Hassian al Edder. We had covered ninety miles in twenty-four hours, with two and a half hours sleep and twenty-one and a half hours in the saddle. To avoid waste of time by dismounting, we had eaten nothing for twenty-four hours.

Perhaps this was an unnecessarily drastic first camel ride. The fault was my own and I did not fail to profit by the experience. The moral was that bedouins are very careless and unreliable. We could easily have carried water for three days and have travelled at our leisure, but the bedouins were too casual to work it all out and too indifferent to hardship to suffer. A hundred miles across the desert without food or water was to them no more than an evening stroll.

After a hasty meal, we travelled on through the night. Bedouins are ill at ease sitting near a well, where raiding parties will frequently call to replenish their water-skins under .cover of darkness. I felt much better after a meal and I think that hunger and thirst, more than the physical exhaustion, were the real causes of my collapse. We eventually found the camp of Fahad ibn Hadhdhal the next morning.

The bedouin, though he will shout, sing and laugh when in the open desert, assumes an air of the strictest decorum when he approaches a camp. As we advanced towards the tents, the Arabs adjusted their cloaks and kerchiefs and, forming up knee to knee, we rode in discreet silence up to the great guest tent. Simultaneously we tapped our camels on the neck with our canes, giving vent to a guttural *akh-akh*, until, with a groan, they fell upon their knees.

Slipping from our saddles, we advanced at the slowest of walks to the great black booth, for nothing, amongst Arabs, can be more undignified than haste. Pausing in front of the tent, we gave the greeting of peace, '*Al Salaam alaikum.*' '*We alaikum al salaam*' returned twenty or thirty deep voices, and the circle of wild bearded figures rose to their feet to make room for the guests.

A negro hastened to spread a carpet, on which he placed a camel saddle for me to lean on, and we seated ourselves, still in a dignified silence, while the coffee man blew up the embers of the fire to make tea and coffee.

Matr was here among his own tribe and the usual unending solemn Arab greetings ensued. From the other side of the huge tent, a bearded figure would call – '*Salaam, ya Matr.*'

The man opposite and Matr would both rise, step out into the middle of the circle and kiss each other solemnly several times on both cheeks and then on the left shoulder.

Then standing back a pace apart, each with his right hand on his breast, they embarked on the usual greetings.

'*Chaif ent?* How are you?'

'God bless you. How are you? May God prolong your life.'

'May God preserve you.'

'Good health.'

'May God give you health.'

'May God bless that face.'

'May God preserve you from the fire [of Hell].'

Scarcely had the two friends seated themselves again, than another deep voice came from the other side of the tent.

'God give you strength, O Matr' – and the whole process would be repeated once more.

Fahad ibn Hadhdhal was one of the most important bedouin shaikhs in Arabia. During the second half of the war, he had declared for the British, and the final victory of the Allies had added to his prestige.

Today the old patriarch was ill and besought me to obtain a doctor for him, which I did on my return. He always addressed me as *Ya Walaidi*, my little boy, although I was twenty-six.

I spent three very pleasant days in the camp in the large Ga'ara Depression. There can be no doubt of the beauty and attraction of the desert to those who live in it. Our hopeful reformers, who aspired to teach the bedouins to settle down and grow tomatoes, were unaware of the beauties of the high desert or of the freedom of the nomadic life.

The old shaikh ordered a special tent to be pitched for me and detailed two of his negro slaves to serve me constantly with tea and coffee. Here I had my own little sitting room where, seated on a brightly coloured rug and leaning against a camel saddle, I could gaze across the wide Ga'ara basin, with its grazing flocks of camels, sheep and horses, to the jagged hills and rocks to the north. Meanwhile the lesser shaikhs would call upon me, drink coffee, recount their raiding exploits or argue over the speed of a greyhound or a mare. Raiding, hawking and coursing seem to be the only three occupations worthy of a bedouin gentleman.

The inevitable bedouin poet was always at hand to recite, over the dull glow of the evening camp fire, long sonorous hexameters celebrating the warlike deeds of the tribe. The tribesmen, to whom poetry is almost the breath of life, take infinite delight in these performances, repeating aloud the last word of each line after the reciter.

Fahad himself was too ill to leave his tent, but I spent several hours by his bedside while the old man lamented the passing of the good old days. It was impossible to listen to the words of this old aristocrat without an overwhelming sense of the smallness of the world and the sameness of human nature.

97

With a few changes in names and localities, his words might have been used by any old English landowner of a generation or two ago. The upstart Agaidat came in for a good deal of his opprobrium. These people were all right in their place, he said, but they were not gentlemen. Government was undercutting the roots of the old society, by strengthening the lower classes and by sacrificing the noble.

He and his ancestors had ruled the desert for centuries. Now any baseborn sheepman could insult him with impunity. The country was sacrificing its natural leaders and was promoting individuals who were motivated only by a desire for gain, not by honour or pride of race.

Our return journey, though better organized, nearly proved even more exciting than the outward trip. I had purchased an additional water-skin, while Fahad provided a whole cooked sheep as a haversack ration. We were thus able to travel at a leisurely pace, halting for food and sleep on the way. We covered the hundred odd miles in about thirty-three hours without fatigue.

On our way, however, we halted again for an hour at the Edder water-holes to water our camels, fill our water-skins and eat some food. To halt at a well is contrary to every custom of bedouin travel, for, particularly in summer when water is scarce, the few watering-places are the constant resort of passing raiding parties. When we had drunk, eaten and watered our camels at the Edder, we moved on and reached Al Qaim in due course in safety.

It was only some weeks later that we discovered the risks which we had run. A few hours after we left the water-holes, a raiding party of the Dhafeer, under Hazza ibn Aqab, had attacked the flocks grazing near Fahad's camp and, after killing two herdsmen, had driven off fifty camels. Anaiza had pursued for a day and a half without succeeding in overtaking the raiders, and had then given up the pursuit.

Many years before, Hazza ibn Aqab had quarrelled with the shaikh of his own tribe, Ibn Suwait. Abandoning his tribe, the Dhafeer, he had taken refuge with Ibn Hadhdhal, besought his protection and camped with him. A few years later, having become reconciled with Ibn Suwait, he bade farewell to his kind Anaiza hosts and returned to the Dhafeer.

Now, looking over the fifty camels he had just looted from Anaiza, he noticed that some of them bore the private brand mark of Ibn Hadhdhal, his one-time friend and protector. Separating these from the remainder, he returned two days journey to Fahad's camp and handed them back to their owner. Although four days before, he had raided them and had killed two Anaiza herdsmen, Hazza was hospitably welcomed. Sitting round the coffee pots on the fire, they amicably discussed the incidents of the raid, as bridge players will discuss a hand of bridge.

'We lay up in the rocks above the Edder water-holes,' Hazza remarked, 'while our scouts were locating your flocks. We saw four camelmen, watering at the wells, and were about to rush them, when our scouts came back, having located your flocks. We decided to let the four go unhurt, for fear they might shoot if attacked and give the alarm to your herds. Who were the four camelmen?'

The Anaizas laughed. 'That must have been the sahib,' they said. 'What,' exclaimed Hazza, 'an Englishman! Just my luck! He was probably carrying a treasure chest of gold!'

10

Beni Huchaim

In the summer of 1923, I was moved back from Ramadi to the Muntifiq Division once more, the threat of war with Turkey having faded. On the Lower Euphrates, however, the situation was precarious.

Some sixty miles upstream from Nasiriya on the Euphrates lay the little township of Samawa, which was the market town for the surrounding countryside. The tribes which lived and cultivated in the district were collectively known as Beni Huchaim.

The tribes of the Samawa district, in common with nearly all those inhabiting the Middle and Lower Euphrates, were notoriously wild and unsubjugated in Turkish times. Among them, Beni Huchaim at one time had played a considerable rôle in tribal politics. As in the case of the Muntifiq, however, the partial establishment of Turkish control had resulted in the break-up of the Beni Huchaim confederation, under the leadership of the Al Muhsin family, but without establishing a government strong enough to replace the great tribal chiefs.

Chaos had followed, with many years of continual tribal fighting and periodical Turkish military punitive operations, never strong enough or efficient enough to establish permanent government control. As soon as the troops withdrew, the original chaotic conditions returned.

During the years 1917 to 1920, the presence of strong British military forces in Iraq temporarily overawed these poor but turbulent tribes. In 1920, however, they rose in rebellion once more and played a leading part in the disturbances of that year.

The Samawa district was a peculiarly difficult one for military operations. Roads were, of course, completely non-existent, while the country was intersected by the many branches into which the Euphrates was here split up. Many of these rivers and canals constituted serious military obstacles to ground troops. In the winter and spring,

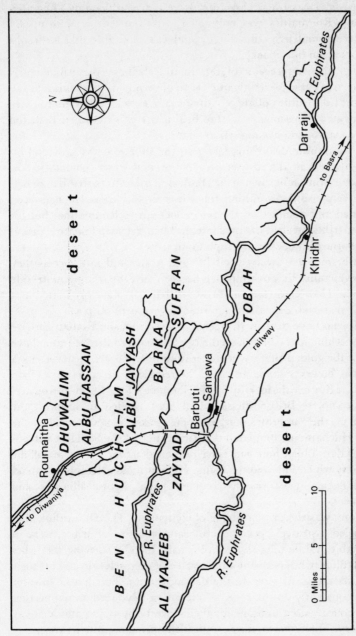

Map 7 The Samawa Sub-district, to show Tribes of Beni Huchaim

moreover, large tracts of country were liable to flooding. The area around Roumaitha was cultivated with rice crops, split up by numerous small irrigation ditches, and was impossible alike for troops on foot or on horseback.

After the suppression of the 1920 Rebellion, the tribal chiefs in the area surrendered themselves to government, but owing to the physical difficulties of the country the area was never thoroughly subjugated. No sooner were the British troops withdrawn than the district subsided once more into anarchy.

A continuing disturbing factor in the situation was provided by the presence in the district of a clever and unscrupulous shaikh, Shaalan albu Chon, chief of the Dhuwalim tribe. In 1920 this man had been responsible for raising the tribes in the area. He had been arrested and detained in the police lock-up in Roumaitha, but his armed tribesmen had irrupted into the town, released him from prison and borne him back in triumph to his tribe.

Tribesmen are always excitable and fickle, and any success they achieve against the government is liable to raise the whole countryside in arms. How many long and costly tribal wars have originated in a petty 'regrettable incident' against a government outpost.

All who have dealt with warlike tribes, from the Roman Empire on the Rhine to the British on the North-West Frontier of India, have learnt the golden rule – when operating in tribal areas, never risk a reverse, however small. In 1920, the release of Shaalan albu Chon from the Roumaitha lock-up by his tribesmen set the Euphrates on fire.

A complete British division had been needed to suppress the rising on the Euphrates, but, for some reason, it never reached the Beni Huchaim or completed the pacification of the Samawa tribes.

Shaalan albu Chon had been pardoned under the terms of the amnesty which followed the rising. His continual attempts to extend his influence gave rise to frequent tribal fights, alliances and intrigues.

Water was the primary bone of contention. The Dhuwalim, who occupied a strategic position upstream of the other tribes, were in the habit of damming rivers and canals, thereby starving the tribes below them, while ensuring ample water for themselves to irrigate their rich rice crops. As a result, the Barkat, Sufran, Tobah and Juwabir were constantly on the verge of starvation. Reduced to pauperism, they endeavoured to atone for their poverty by systematic highway robbery. The Samawa district subsided once more into anarchy.

A form of live-and-let-live was established between the tribes and the government. The tribes remained more or less independent, and fought out their private quarrels without reference to the government. The majority of the tribal shaikhs never entered into a town, nor placed themselves within reach of the authorities. Similarly, the latter confined their activities to the towns and to their offices, making little attempt to bring the tribes under control.

By the end of 1923, the pacification of the remainder of the Euphrates tribes had proceeded so satisfactorily that the time appeared to be ripe for bringing the notorious Beni Huchaim under government control.

The Iraqi officials on the spot, however, reported that no attempt to establish government authority would be possible, unless severe punitive action were first taken to raise the prestige of government.

It is possible, as this narrative will show, that the opinion thus expressed by the local officials may have been somwhat tinged by their own mentality. The qaimaqam of Samawa felt no desire to embark on the strenuous and even dangerous task of bringing the tribes to heel by gentle but firm administration, when it was possible to terrorize them into submission by an example of the signal punishment of some of the offenders.

Active operations having, therefore, been decided upon in principle, the following questions arose:

(1) Which particular tribe to select for punishment as an example to the remainder?
(2) How to proceed against the tribe selected?

The whole Beni Huchaim group was unanimous in its refusal to recognize the authority of the government, or to pay taxes. In the 1920 Rebellion the whole area had taken up arms. The government had imposed fines on the tribes for their share in the revolt. The Barkat tribe refused to pay. A force of Arab levies was sent by the government to arrest the shaikhs of the Barkat, but the tribe attacked the column and forced it to return to Samawa. So elated were the tribes by this success that they proceeded to raid the caravans on the local tracks and to rob any townspeople of Samawa who were rash enough to leave the town.

In 1922, the local government made a rather half-hearted attempt to collect taxes, but the Sufran tribe, neighbours of the Barkat, drove off the tax-collectors and their police escort.

A tax-collector with a mounted police escort, sent to collect taxes from the Albu Jayyash area, nearly came to an untimely end. As they rode across the rough fields, intersected by irrigation canals, tribesmen could be seen running out of the scattered settlements and lining the canal banks. Soon rifle shots rang out and bullets began to whistle. The tax-collector decided that discretion was the better part of valour and ordered a retreat.

The sight of the column turning back to Samawa, however, only inspired the tribesmen with more excited enthusiasm. The firing rapidly increased. The tax-collector, regardless of the dignity of his high office, departed for Samawa *ventre-à-terre*!

The mounted police endeavoured to effect a more decorous withdrawal until one of them was wounded, while the horse of another was killed beneath him. A somewhat dishevelled column eventually regained the safety of the walls of Samawa.

One of the most remarkable features of this chaotic situation was that the main railway from Baghdad to Basra, on which the life of Iraq very largely depended, ran through the centre of the Beni Huchaim country. Presumably the tribes believed that to tamper with the railway would compel the government to take action, and realized that it would be a mistake to overplay their hand. The trains continued to run peacefully across twenty miles of country which owned no allegiance to the Iraq Government.

In March, 1923, however, Albu Jayyash pulled out three hundred spikes from sleepers on the railway passing through their land and beat them into daggers, presumably more actively to pursue their tribal rivalries, as daggers do not seem very efficient weapons against the government – not even against the mounted police.

If tradition speaks true, Albu Jayyash had a long record of turbulence, especially in the days of Delli, their former chief and a great fighter. It was believed by the tribes, for some reason, that there were seven Great Powers in the world. On the occasion of some former revolt against the Turks, the tribe had performed a defiant war-dance to the slogan: '*Seven Great Powers and the eighth is Delli.*'

In 1923, Hajji Ajja, the son of Delli, was head of the tribe – a nice little man with a sense of humour and a face deeply marked by small-pox. But no one would have suspected him of being a Great Power!

In view of these lively incidents in the Samawa area, the Minister of the Interior could scarcely be blamed when, in the summer of

1923, he informed the Iraqi Prime Minister that the situation in Samawa was intolerable. To decide how the trouble was to be remedied was no easy task. The British Army had left the country and the R.A.F. had assumed responsibility. It had no ground forces except a few armoured cars, which in any case could not operate in Beni Huchaim country, which was criss-crossed by canals and ditches and entirely innocent of roads.

The formation of the Iraqi Army was already in hand, but it was almost untrained and completely incapable of staging an operation on a divisional scale. In other words, the ground troops to bring Beni Huchaim to order did not exist.

The alternative was to use aircraft, a proposal welcomed by the R.A.F. Air Control in Iraq was still a new experiment, which had been received with no little scepticism by the old hands. The R.A.F. felt itself to be on trial and tended to claim that there was nothing the Army could do which aircraft could not do better. The turbulence of Beni Huchaim provided the opportunity to test these rival theses.

The idea of using aircraft was not distasteful to the civil authorities, who were afraid of another regrettable incident should a small column of ground troops be committed in so difficult a tribal area.

The government was also extremely anxious for the safety of the railway. It was feared that, as soon as action was taken against the tribes, the latter would retaliate by destroying the railway line. Not only so, but there was also a vital railway bridge over the Euphrates at Barbuti, a few miles from Samawa. If this were destroyed, the railway would be out of action for many months, if not years.

When, however, planning reached this stage, a major difficulty was encountered. How were the aircraft to identify their targets? Lower Iraq consists of one vast plain, as flat as the proverbial billiard table. To the west it is bounded by the immense tawny-coloured desert, fading away into pearl grey in the far horizon. Across the flat, alluvial plain ran the two mighty rivers, Tigris and Euphrates, dividing into many streams, canals and ditches, interspersed with green fields and gardens of date palms, and dotted with innumerable little tribal communities.

Each such group in the Samawa area consisted of a mudbrick war-tower, surrounded by a group of *sarifas*, or huts made of reed mats, all exactly similar.

A map of the area had been made during the war, but on too small a scale to show the little tribal hut settlements. Moreover most of the dwellings consisted only of a large reed mat bent over to form a 'tunnel' with the ends blocked. This could be rolled up and loaded on a donkey in a few minutes. Thus the sites of the villages were frequently changing.

In these circumstances, I heard with some alarm that Air Headquarters had decided that, as the Intelligence Officer in the area, I would be held personally responsible that every aircraft attacked the correct target. I went to Samawa, ascended to the flat roof of the government offices and stared east and north over the tops of the date palms. Little could be seen but a flat mud-coloured plain, intersected by the banks of irrigation channels in the middle distance, shutting off any further view. In the foreground, three or four miles away, were a few of the usual groups of reed huts, each with its central war-tower. Obviously nothing could be done by direct observation from the ground.

So complete had been the independence of the tribes from the government that it seemed to be almost impossible to collect any data from the civil officials in Samawa. Both tribally and topographically the area was so little known that it was apparent that no aerial or military operations could be undertaken without extensive previous reconnaissance. I was ordered to start work immediately.

To commence this task, I set out one day from Roumaitha on horseback, accompanied by Flight Lieutenant Guy Moore, R.A.F., and in the course of a five day ride through tribal country, visited the Dhuwalim, Iyajeeb, Zayyad, and Barkat. Part of the object of this expedition was to prepare a sufficiently accurate sketch map, to enable aircraft to identify the individual villages of any tribal chiefs, who refused to surrender to the government.

This was by no means an easy task. The lists of the tribes, sections and shaikhs were very imcomplete, while the whole area was covered with a network of canals and dotted with innumerable villages.

The arrival of a force of police in the district would probably have been the signal for a rally of the tribes to attack it. On the other hand, chaotic as the area was, the chiefs were thought to be wise enough to understand that British officers in uniform could not be robbed nor killed with impunity. We therefore decided to carry out the tour unostentatiously without any escort. We accordingly set out with my servant Ali and with a simple tribal guide.

The tribes proved to be exceedingly friendly. Indeed, in every state of society, anarchy tends, after a period to right itself. A number of the chiefs was probably secretly desirous of the establishment of a just administration. Particularly the tribes on the lower reaches of the canals stood to gain by the existence of a central authority, which could prevent the upstream tribes from damming the rivers and depriving them of irrigation water.

Unfortunately, however, affairs kept moving in a vicious circle, for if the tribes made any advances to the government, the reply they usually received was that they must immediately commence paying taxes.

It appeared to us that the area could have been brought under control by administrative means without preliminary punitive operations. Such a result could only be achieved if the civil administration would take two essential steps. Firstly, to replace the qaimaqam of Samawa by a really first class administrative official. Secondly, that the government inaugurate the new policy with some positive measures, such as the gradual establishment of public security and the inauguration of fair distribution of water for irrigation. It was useless to introduce a new era by demanding taxes, before the tribes could see any benefits which were likely to accrue.

Meanwhile the authorities had decided that the Barkat and Sufran tribes should be selected to be made an example to the remainder. Not that they were any more rebellious than the others, but purely because they were the furthest from the railway, and thus the least likely to retaliate by cutting it.

I accordingly asked the R.A.F. to fly me over the area, but I could only see the same fawn-coloured plain, intersected by many canals and by winding irrigation ditches, with here and there the same groups of huts, clustered round their war-towers. There was no means of telling where one tribe ended and another began, much less of identifying the war-tower of any particular insubordinate chief.

I returned to Nasiriya and mounted the Elephant, while Ali al Yunis saddled the Rat. We rode by easy stages up the west bank of the Euphrates to Samawa. The R.A.F. claimed that they could suppress rebellious tribes without using any men on the ground. I mentally decided that their claims were exaggerated.

The qaimaqam of Samawa invited me to dinner that evening. The police officer and the judge were the other guests. I explained that I proposed to ride out the next morning to visit the Barkat and Sufran.

The qaimaqam was horror-struck and reminded me that no government official had visited these tribes for more than three years.

The police officer made gloomy references to the débâcle suffered
by the mounted police who had so rashly escorted the tax-collector
into Albu Jayyash country. But, in reality, my plan to visit the tribes
was carefully considered. I had noted that all previous attempts had
been carried out in company with a force of mounted police,
armed with rifles and thereby threatening the tribes with force. It
seemed to me a mistake to employ a weak force, which merely invited
attack.

If ground troops were to be used, their numbers should have
been so overwhelming as to render any idea of resistance ridiculous.
No such ground force existed in Iraq, and consequently the only course
was to have no force at all and to arrive as a guest.

We accordingly set out the next morning, Ali al Yunis and
myself. We took with us a local government messenger called Gummaz
abu al Kowd (pronounced *code*). The Kowidda – the collective name of
the Abu al Kowd family – were a small independent section, who
camped along the edge of the desert west of Samawa. They still lived in
tents and bred camels, although they only consisted of seven or eight
families. They claimed a somewhat tenuous relationship with
Shammar, but at the same time were Shiite, although all the desert
tribes were Sunnites. Their conversion to Shiism must have meant
that they had already been several centuries in Iraq.

[When ten years later I was recruiting for the Arab Legion in
Trans-Jordan, several young men of the Kowidda followed me
across seven hundred miles of desert to enlist in the Desert Patrol.]

There were several advantages in taking Gummaz with us on our
first visit to the Barkat. Firstly, he was himself a local tribesman.
whose relatives were camped nearby. To kill him would involve a
tiresome blood feud with the Kowidda, an eventuality perhaps more to
be feared than a government punitive expedition. Secondly, he had a
small job as a local government guard, but no uniform and was not
recognizable as a government employee, except by such as knew him
personally.

Ali al Yunis was, of course, also dressed in Arab clothes. I
was wearing a British Army uniform, but a light Arab cloak thrown
over my shoulders made my appearance inconspicuous. At anything
but very short range, therefore, we passed very well for three Arab
horsemen.

Our plan was to ride through the Barkat area, straight to the war-tower of Khushan al Hamadi, the shaikh of the tribe, and there to invite ourselves to lunch. I was satisfied that, in so doing, the risk was small, for I believed that the tribes were as afraid of the government, as the government was of the tribes.

The summoning of tribal leaders to report to the local government headquarters seemed, in the situation as it then was, to be a mistaken policy. The Turks, in pursuance of their policy of tribe-smashing, had acquired so bad a reputation for kidnapping tribal leaders and throwing them into prison – or even banishing them to Aleppo or Istanbul – that many tribal shaikhs were afraid to report to the government. The officials who represented the new Iraqi Government were, of course, the same men who had previously worked for the Turks – there were no others available.

If the local Iraqi officials had been sympathetic in their outlook towards the tribes and been willing to visit them, these mistrusts might have been overcome. But the officials had been brought up in the Turkish belief that 'progress' was the only thing which could save the country, and that the tribes were the enemies of progress and must therefore be crushed. Why do men always wish to crush and to smash by violence? In fact, as soon as a just administration is established, the tribal system begins automatically to break up and the tribesmen to deal direct with the government.

Anyhow, the idea of a senior government official visiting a tribe outside Samawa would have been denounced as destructive of government prestige. In this respect, I was fortunately placed, for I had no official connection with the Iraq Government. An insignificant and irresponsible British Army captain need not, by his antics, inflict any injury on the dignity of the powers-that-be.

11

The Barkat and Sufran

As we walked and cantered along the dusty track into the Barkat country, Gummaz told us tales of Beni Huchaim and their feuds and battles. Four miles out of Samawa, we passed near an isolated war-tower, without the usual group of reed huts clustering round its foot. It belonged, related Gummaz, to an old man who lived there alone with his daughter.

The old man was at feud with many of his neighbours. When he was obliged to leave the tower, his daughter bolted the door from the inside and sat on the upper floor of the tower with a rifle across her knees to await his return.

'The girl is a dead shot,' said Gummaz, 'so they don't get many callers.' 'I hope she won't have a crack at us,' I remarked, as the silent and apparently deserted tower was only some three hundred yards away. 'She won't shoot if we stick to the track,' he answered, 'but if we rode towards the tower we should probably get a warning shot.' We decided not to disturb the lady in her boudoir.

The sun was already high in the sky and riding was becoming unpleasantly hot, when we forded our horses across the fourth successive irrigation canal and saw, a mile away, across a flat sundried plain, a large war-tower. This Gummaz declared was the home of Khushan al Hamadi, the shaikh of the reputedly wicked Barkat.

Although my calculation of the improbability of our being in any danger from the tribesmen seemed to me sound enough, it was not entirely without misgivings that we approached the settlement. One fortunate circumstance, at least, seemed to be that no one was taking any notice of us. A party of women, armed with small hoe-like axes, was chopping firewood from the low camel thorn shrubs and stacking it in old cloaks or bits of sacking which they had laid out on the ground. (The duties of the sexes are carefully divided – fetching firewood is women's work in the tribes.)

The firewood girls never paused to glance at us, though they would have been the first to scream and run for shelter on the approach of government, the arch-enemy. The shaikh's community looked poor enough. A skinny horse was chained by one foot outside the tower. One or two small cows with all their bones sticking out and a few dirty, almost naked children were the only living things to be seen.

We pulled up outside what seemed to be the guest hut and swung off our horses. Two or three men emerged from the dark door of the hut and took our horses by the head to tie them up. One of them recognized Gummaz, I was glad to see, and shook hands with him. We stooped to enter the low doorway of the guest hut. Three or four men, sitting inside it, rose to their feet.

'Peace be upon you,' we said.

'And on you peace,' they responded.

We sat down, but the appearance of my army uniform seemed to impose restraint on conversation. A few minutes later, a tall gaunt man in his middle thirties entered the hut with an air of authority. 'Welcome to the guests,' he said, as he came forward to shake hands. Then turning to the men sitting round, he said sharply: 'Come along! fetch carpets! Spread them for the guests. Oh, Abbas! Light the fire and put on the kettle. Come on, all of you!'

A heap of thorn bushes was thrown on the fire, for a few minutes we were blinded with acrid smoke, then a flame caught alight, the fire crackled and the blackened kettle was pushed into the blaze. Six little glasses in cracked saucers were ranged on a battered tin tray and Khushan vanished into the tower to return with a bag of sugar and a little tea in the hollow of his palm. Passing these supplies to the tea-maker, he came and sat beside us on the floor.

To begin forthwith to ask questions is both bad manners and liable to arouse suspicion. Khushan must doubtless have been deeply exercised in his mind at the unexpected appearance of a British officer in uniform in his village, when no government official had ventured there for nearly four years. But if he was, he gave no outward sign of his feelings. We discussed the most indifferent subjects – we had come from Samawa – yes, it was still hot for the time of year – did we have trouble in fording the canal – the crossing place had a muddy bottom.

Gradually the tension disappeared, cordiality increased, and the tribesmen began to explain their point of view.

'*Al hukuma alla rasi*,' said Khushan, 'the government on my head' – an expression signifying his respect and his devotion to the authorities. 'But . . .' It was that 'but' which caused him to open his heart. 'But we get no water here for our crops. All the canals leave the river up near Roumaitha, in Albu Hassan or Dhuwalim territory. Then the canals pass through Albu Jayyash country. All these people take all the water when they want it and none reaches us when our crops are thirsty. Why does not the government regulate the water? . . . The government on my head – but we are poor and they say that we owe them thousands of rupees of taxes. How can we pay? There is no money.'

'If you had paid every year, you would not now be thousands of rupees in arrears,' said Gummaz, who, having a government job, could see both sides of the question.

'My brother, how could we pay when we are poor,' said Khushan, spreading out his palms deprecatingly. 'The Dhuwalim take all the water and we have no crops.'

Everything we could see of the Barkat certainly confirmed Khushan's statements about their poverty – the ragged threadbare strips of carpet, the battered teapot, the tribesmen clad only in their shirts and cloaks.

The thought came to me that these poor people, so constantly pressed for taxes, derived little benefit from the government to which they were asked to pay them. There were for them no roads, no doctors, no schools – not even safety for life and property. Every man lived with his rifle beside him even at home. To leave his own tribal area was to take his life in his hand.

We rode back to Samawa in the evening. I, at least, felt a wiser man than I had been when I set out in the morning. The statement by the Minister of the Interior, that the situation in Samawa was intolerable, seemed slightly less obviously justified than formerly. The qaimaqam welcomed me with open arms, like one risen from the dead.

But he showed little enthusiasm for my innocent remark that there was something to be said for the tribes also. This he obviously regarded as one of those silly sentiments which at times are produced by immature young persons ignorant of the facts of life. 'Sons of dogs,' he said. 'Did they not shoot at the police?'

The next day I visited the Sufran in the same manner, but as the distance was greater, the expedition took rather longer and we slept the night with the shaikh, Azzara al Majoon. The Sufran appeared to be even poorer than the Barkat, presumably because they were still lower down the canals. If the Dhuwalim took most of the water, Albu Jayyash received a certain amount, the Barkat little enough and the Sufran scarcely any at all.

Only complete government control could ensure a fair distribution of water, and the Barkat and Sufran should be the principal bene-ficiaries. Yet, in the vicious circle of tribe and government mistrust, the two tribes were dying of hunger, but resolutely refusing to come in to the government.

The canals which should have watered the whole Beni Huchaim country must have been dug by the Arabs from the light of nature. They twisted and meandered over the country and were badly in need of clearing and redigging. The Sufran were so poor that many of them seemed to have given up any attempt to cultivate and were semi-nomadic sheep breeders, living in little ragged goat-hair tents.

For me, October 1923 was strenuous indeed. I spent it riding round the Barkat and Sufran country, sketching in the physical features and the reed hut villages. Although it was only intended to attack the Barkat and Sufran, the target map I was making was to cover the whole Beni Huchaim group, in case action against the first two tribes should result in sympathetic risings by the others. As a result, I was told to cover Albu Jayyash as well.

As my map was to be used from the air alone, it was important to include features which would show clearly from the air. One little group of huts, for example, had beside it a small pond in the shape of a U, which stood out prominently from the air, but would never have been noticed from the ground. In order to ensure that all such air landmarks were included, I returned to Nasiriya, and flew several sorties from there over Beni Huchaim.

In those days, 84 Squadron R.A.F. were equipped with the De Havilland 9A – commonly called the Ninak. In the 1920s, the fuselage of aircraft was not closed in. Pilot and observer sat in separate cockpits, the pilot in front. The sides of the cockpit came up to the observer's shoulders when he was sitting down. His head stuck out into the open air, enclosed in a flying helmet and goggles. But if the observer wished to obtain good vision of the ground, he was obliged to stand up in the back seat and to lean over the side of the aircraft, in which case the side of the cockpit came only a little above his waist. Swinging round in the sky, leaning over the side in a howling wind, trying to see through the goggles, grasping a sheet of paper on which I was trying to write or sketch, was by no means an easy task.

In order to remain over the small area which I was sketching, the aircraft kept turning round and round in a tight spiral, so that at one moment I seemed to be almost upside down, with nothing between me and the ground. Then the aircraft would straighten up and the horizon would seem to swing round and up, as though it were about to hit me in the face.

Then, once again, we would bank steeply, and my right arm would become as heavy as lead, so that I could scarcely raise it, much less write with it. Often we would suddenly be jerked sideways with a sharp bump, caused by shafts of hot air rising from the scorching plain below. I would collapse on my seat with a gasp, my goggles and helmet crooked and my harness cutting into my right shoulder. If I had not been strapped in, I should have fallen out of the aircraft.

Between alternate reconnaissances of the tribes by ground and by air, I was obliged frequently to fly to Baghdad and to go to Air Headquarters to help in the plans and in the preparation of the map.

During October 1923, as I became more familiar with Beni Huchaim and their misfortunes, I began to feel increasingly guilty. Riding backwards and forwards constantly through their little groups of huts, I was always eating their food and drinking their tea and coffee. But at the same time I was plotting their settlements on the map with a view to bombing them.

The only honourable course, it seemed to me, was to tell them exactly what I was doing. This, fortunately, involved no betrayal of the government, because the only object of the operation was to compel the tribes to come in to Samawa and submit. If I could persuade them to do this, then the end would have been achieved without bombing and everybody would be happy.

The only hope of convincing them that it would be better to submit now, was to tell them that they were going to be attacked from the air and that they would be destroyed without any chance of shooting back. I candidly told them that I was preparing the map to be used for the bombing, and that I myself would have to be in the leading aircraft.

The government had agreed that, when the plans were ready, a warning would be sent to the Barkat and Sufran, ordering them to report forthwith to Samawa. I explained this intended procedure to Khushan al Hamadi and to Azzara al Majoon, telling them that, when they received this summons, they should immediately ride in to Samawa and report.

Meanwhile work proceeded at full speed. None of the airfields to be used was serviceable in wet weather and the annual winter rains were already overdue. If they came, the whole operation would have to be postponed until the following April and, before then, anything might have happened.

This urgency not only made it necessary to carry out the operation as early as possible, but also to make it as short as possible. To settle the question by an overwhelming attack in twenty-four, or at most forty-eight, hours, would also reduce the risk of any attempts to sabotage the railway.

On 29 November, special trains left Baghdad and Basra respectively with ground parties, bombs and petrol to establish advanced landing grounds at Diwaniya, Samawa and Ur of the Chaldees – the home of the Patriarch Abraham nearly four thousand years ago.

The attack was to be delivered on the morning of 30 November. As I was to lead the bombers, I was called to Baghdad on 28 November, but, before leaving, I was able to send word to the two tribes that the operation was about to commence. I told them that they would receive the ultimatum twenty-four hours before the bombing and that, as soon as they did so, the two shaikhs were immediately to ride in to Samawa.

I waited in vain in Baghdad to hear that the tribes had complied with the summons. To me, the government atmosphere seemed to be entirely erroneous, for they visualized fierce warlike tribes defying the world. I had lived among them for six weeks. The problem seemed to me that of coaxing timid deer, rather than standing up to savage tigers.

It was still nearly dark on the morning of 30 November, when I was woken up by an orderly and told that the aircraft would take off in one hour. Khushan and Azzara had obviously failed to report.

The plan was to employ all available aircraft and to fly as many sorties as possible continuously. All aircraft were to take off from their home bases – Hinaidi outside Baghdad or Shaiba outside Basra – and to fly to their targets and drop their bombs. Thereafter 84 Squadron were to return to Ur, bomb up, and keep attacking continuously for the rest of the day.

From Baghdad, No. 1 Squadron in single-seater fighters and 8 Squadron in ninaks were to fly to their targets and then land at Samawa, fill up and keep continuously attacking for the rest of the day. One flight of 45 Squadron was to operate from Diwaniya, and six aircraft from 30 Squadron were to work from Hinaidi.

I was to open the ball by leading the first attack in a ninak of 8 Squadron. It was with mixed feelings that I heard, as I climbed into the cockpit, that we were carrying a 550 lb bomb, and that so large a bomb had never before been dropped from a ninak. The pilot, however, thought that 'it ought to be all right with luck'.

We took off in formation, and as we rose slowly from the ground with a roar of engines, I looked round to see the other machines just behind us, their propellers flickering, the helmeted heads of the pilots and observers protruding from the fuselages. Gradually the fawn-coloured summer landscape of Iraq opened beneath us. Behind us, the city of Baghdad was veiled in a thin morning haze of bluish smoke, the Tigris twisting through it like a silver ribbon.

Already, ahead of us, the Middle Euphrates with its many streams separating from and rejoining the river, its date palms and its rice fields, lay like a dark green patch on the beige-coloured desert. Soon we were passing over Diwaniya, and I could see where the Euphrates reunited into one stream below Samawa and, further ahead, the dark patch of the palm gardens beyond Nasiriya.

In those days the bomb-sight was a primitive contraption on the outside of the fuselage, just in front of the pilot on the starboard (or right-hand) side. The pilot leant over the right side of his cockpit and manoeuvred the aircraft about until the sights were aligned on the target below. It was the observer, however, who actually released the bomb. A series of wires ran over pulleys on the fuselage from the bomb-rack underneath the wings and up into the observer's cockpit. When the pilot saw the sights were aligned, he raised his hand and the observer pulled the toggle on the end of the wire.

I leant far over the side, watching pass beneath us the little town of Roumaitha, the palm gardens and fields and little hut villages of Albu Hassan and the Dhuwalim. There was Shaalan albu Chon's guest hut, with the tops of the palm trees around it, looking like small cabbages. There were Albu Jayyash and the broad Euphrates passing under the railway bridge at Barbuti.

The wind was from the north, behind us. We, therefore, made a détour west and south of Samawa, so as to come up into our target facing up wind. The aircraft banked steeply – now the Barkat villages were directly ahead of us – and we were running straight in on our target.

My map had been photographed and mounted on a card of a size convenient for pilots to look at in their cockpits. Every pilot had received a copy. All the targets were numbered on the map. Our target was Number 14.

I could see the pilot look at the map, then over the side of his cockpit at the ground. He nodded his head and slipped the map-card into a wallet on the side of his cockpit. He was holding the stick with his left hand, his right arm rested on the right-hand side of the cockpit, ready to give me the signal. Target No.14 was now straight ahead of us. I could see it coming nearer, for a moment it was hidden behind one of the wheels of the undercarriage, then it re-appeared – the war-tower, the group of reed huts, the canal, the solitary palm tree – I knew them now so well.

I gripped the toggle of the bomb-wire, the sights crept forward towards the target, up went the pilot's hand, I gave a tug on the toggle. Suddenly the aircraft shot up into the air, as the weight of the big bomb came off it. I turned quickly and looked over the side towards the rear. I could still see the huge bomb going down and down until I lost sight of it. I glanced up quickly to see the other machines of our formation coming in over their targets. Then I looked down again, just in time to see a great fountain of smoke and dust shoot up into the air on Target 14.

We banked gently in order to circle round and land at Samawa. The Barkat villages were dotted now with geyser-like spurts of smoke. A new formation, like tiny specks, was coming in from the south. Suddenly the Sufran area also was covered with bursts – it must be 84 Squadron coming in from Shaiba. Already we were losing height passing over the Euphrates, up came the ground to meet us, the palm gardens of Samawa were on our right and then, with a quick sideslip to lose height, we touched down on the dusty airfield of Samawa.

My flying duties were now over. All the aircraft had found their targets by the use of my map. In his final report on the operation, addressed to the Air Ministry, the Air Officer Commanding was to report that 'by means of this map, it was possible and even simple to ensure that any bombing which took place was concentrated without error on any particular village or villages which might be selected.'

Bombing continued all the day of 30 November and in the morning of 1 December until, in the afternoon, Khushan and Azzara came into Samawa. I was walking through the bazaar going to the government offices, when I suddenly met them face to face. For an instant I wondered what reception they would give me, now that I and my compatriots had inflicted on them such an overwhelming disaster.

But I was not long in doubt. Both broke into broad smiles as soon as they saw me and, running forward, they shook me by the hands, crying: 'Welcome! Welcome! How are you? Here we are, you see. We have come into the government as you ordered.'

'If you had come in before the bombing, it would have been better,' I said. 'Meanwhile tell me what happened. Were many killed?' 'There were no killed but one old woman,' said Khushan, but I did not know if he were telling the truth. Certainly the casualties were very few. I had told them beforehand exactly when the bombing would take place. Moreover the fact that we, the leading formation, circled round Samawa and came in from the south, had given them an extra four or five minutes grace. During this interval, everyone had raced out of the villages and had lain down in the irrigation ditches all round. 'Where are all your people now?' I asked. 'We do not know,' said Azzara al Majoon. '*Wallahi shettu*, by God, they have scattered.'

It was true that all pilots had reported the area to be empty and lifeless. In the evening of 1 December all the shaikhs of Albu Jayyash came in also without being summoned, to make sure that they were not next on the list. On the morning of 2 December a force of three hundred mounted police rode out from Samawa into the country of the Barkat and the Sufran and, moving from village to village, they razed all the war-towers to the ground.

The police were covered in this operation by No. 1 Fighter Squadron in Snipes, but in actual fact they did not encounter a single living soul. The Barkat and Sufran had vanished from the face of the earth. The police column returned to Samawa on 4 December.

The next morning all the shaikhs of Beni Huchaim arrived in Samawa, uninvited and unannounced. The effect of the operation on this notoriously turbulent area had certainly been well-nigh miraculous, especially if only one person had been killed.

On 10 December, the Minister of the Interior arrived in Samawa, accompanied by his adviser Mr. (later Sir) Kinahan Cornwallis. Seventy shaikhs and village headmen were assembled to hear a speech by the Minister, in which he ordered every chief to return home and to demolish his own war-tower.

It is true that all the settlements of the Barkat and Sufran had been destroyed, but the settlements themselves consisted only of reed huts which the tribesmen themselves could rebuild in a few days at scarcely any cost. The human casualties had probably been fewer than in one of the many tribal fights, which had been unending since 1920.

My sympathy for the tribes was somewhat weakened by an incident which occurred in the Sufran. The tribe was divided against itself, and the feud had, on several occasions, led to fighting. On 30 November, when the bombing continued all day, all the tribesmen sheltered in ditches or crept down the canal beds and over into the areas of neighbouring tribes. But as soon as darkness fell they all returned to their homes to see the effect of the bombing. One such group of the Sufran discovered, amid the chaos of craters where their huts had been, a large unexploded bomb. Carrying it carefully between two men, they travelled a mile across country to the site of a village with which they were at feud.

The men of this other community had also returned to see the damage and were sitting in a circle on the ground, round a small fire which they had lit. The enemy party crawled cautiously up to within a few yards of the circle, laid the unexploded bomb there, packed round it dry grass and straw, and set a match to it. A minute or two later, the bomb exploded, causing perhaps more casualties than the day's bombing by the aircraft.

The incident was to me a revelation. It seemed incredible that, in such a day of universal ruin for the whole tribe, these men should still pursue their feud against their fellow tribesmen with so much bitterness.

Both the R.A.F. and the Iraqi authorities were not a little elated at the triumphant success of the operation. The turbulent Beni Huchaim, to quell whom a British infantry division was believed to be necessary, had all hastened in to Samawa, unsummoned, to make their submission.

At this stage, however, the authorities made a capital mistake – the same mistake as had been made by the Peace Conference at Versailles. Having at length defeated the enemies who had caused them so much trouble and expense, they resolved to inflict upon them so much damage that they would never again be able to offer any opposition.

The civil authorities, therefore, sent for Khushan al Hamadi and Azzara al Majoon, and told them that their tribes must hand in all their rifles within forty-eight hours. The two shaikhs bowed and withdrew – forty-eight hours passed, and nothing happened. It is probable that the government did not have the imagination to visualize what their ultimatum meant.

In all the Middle Euphrates tribes every man owned a rifle. Many ancient feuds divided all these people, and the Barkat and Sufran. If the latter two tribes alone were disarmed, their tribal enemies might overrun them or drive off the few goats or sheep which now constituted their sole earthly possessions. The police would not be able, in such circumstances, to give them protection. At any rate the tribesmen preferred to die rather than give in their rifles. They did not defy the government – they just vanished.

Having over-called their hand, the authorities now found themselves in a dilemma. The operation had been an astonishing success – every tribe in the area had hastened voluntarily to submit. But now government had issued a further order to the Barkat and Sufran, which the latter had not obeyed and which the powers-that-be were unable to enforce. As a result, the end of the operations threatened to be an anti-climax.

I was convinced that a great psychological opportunity had been missed. The government had made an impressive display of power, and everyone had made a grovelling submission. It seemed to me that this was a moment for generosity, for the proclamation of a new era, for the entertainment of all the shaikhs to a banquet and for the discussion with them of an equitable irrigation system. But the civil authorities took a narrower view. 'Now that those hated tribes are defeated,' they thought, 'let us trample them under foot, and make sure that they can never rise again.'

12

Landing in the Blue

The triumphant operation against the hitherto irrepressible Beni Huchaim seemed likely to peter out in an anti-climax.

I was summoned to a conference of senior officials and – as the R.A.F. intelligence officer – I was asked where the Barkat and Sufran had gone, as their tribal lands were now deserted. I did not know. We flew all over the area at a low altitude without seeing any signs of life. A few miles north of the Barkat area, however, in the Jezira Desert, we saw a large encampment of black tents.

Their great size, so different from the wretched little tents of the Sufran, scarcely bigger than a bedspread, convinced me that these must be some of the aristocratic Sadoon, formerly the princes of the neighbouring Muntifiq district.

We landed again at Samawa, and I suggested to the Group Captain that we land a ninak beside this camp to enable me to ask the tribesmen some questions. The suggestion was not at first received with much enthusiasm. Aircraft, it was said, were built to land on aerodromes. To land them in the open country was to take an unnecessary risk. Besides which, the tribe might be hostile and attack the aircraft on the ground.

Others, however, were anxious to try it, saying that they could choose a flat piece of desert to land on. Eventually permission was granted. We decided to take one ninak, with myself as passenger, and three single-seater Snipe fighters.

The plan was that one Snipe would land first to see if the ground were fit, as the Snipes could land and take off in a very small space. If the Snipe pilot fired a green light, the ninak was to land beside the Snipe, while the other two Snipes circled overhead ready to use their front guns to cover us, in case the tribe proved hostile and attacked the aircraft on the ground.

We duly arrived over the large tented camp and, having circled round once or twice, one of the Snipes went down to land. Meanwhile a rather stout little man had emerged from the tents and was standing alone in an open space in front of the camp, waving his cloak, bowing, saluting and obviously making every friendly gesture of which he could think. I felt sorry for the poor little man, whose frantic gestures and portly figure seemed to me pathetic. He little knew that we were as frightened as he was about this somewhat precarious operation.

Meanwhile there was nothing we could do but circle round and round, watching our Snipe pilot, who had climbed out of his machine and was pacing up and down, surveying the ground on which the ninak might land. Eventually he chose a strip which satisfied him and fired his green light signal. My pilot banked steeply and we flew away in a wide circle to come in and make a perfect landing fifty yards from the Snipe.

I slipped out of my harness as quickly as I could, climbed out of the aircraft and walked across the three hundred yards of intervening desert towards where the little man was still bowing and waving.

But no sooner did I do so than half a dozen horsemen emerged from the tents and galloped towards me at full speed. Personally I was satisfied that they were friendly – they did not appear to have any weapons and one was waving his cloak as he rode. But just as I went forward to meet them, a Snip roared over my head at about a hundred feet. For an anguished second I thought that he was going to open up with his front gun on the galloping horsemen, but instead of doing so, he pulled up in a steep climbing turn over the tents.

As I had expected, the people of the camp were Sadoon. They welcomed me with an enthusiasm in which their fears of the circling aircraft doubtless reinforced their traditional hospitality. 'It's time for lunch,' they cried in chorus. 'Do us the honour!'

If I could have accepted their invitation, I would probably have been able to establish mutal confidence and they would have told me all they knew. But with the deafening roar of the Snipes circling just above our heads, the atmosphere was too hectic. My inquiries about the Barkat and Sufran produced only blank faces. By Allah, they said, nobody had heard any news of them.

There was no other means to find out than to ask. Half the two tribes might have been sitting in those great tents for all I could tell, but the roaring of the Snipes overhead scarcely produced the most favourable atmosphere for a confidential chat. I shook hands all round and climbed back into the cockpit.

The ninak opened up and roared off down the desert in a cloud of dust, and then rose into the air. I waved to the little group on the ground, who waved back to me, doubtless with undisguised pleasure at our departure. We were no nearer to finding the Barkat or the Sufran, but it had been an amusing little experiment, which was to bear fruit in the future.

Two days later, I had an idea. We were already well into December, the month in which the shepherds always moved into the desert west of the Euphrates. I had myself seen that many of the Sufran were shepherds. What more natural than that they should have crossed the Euphrates and moved out in their tents into the desert? I obtained leave to fly on a reconnaissance keeping a few miles south of the Euphrates. Sure enough, about sixteen miles south-east of Samawa, just where the Sufran shepherds could be expected to move out, I located a small group of tents, exactly similar to those which I had myself seen in the Sufran country.

There was no intercommunication between pilot and observer in the ninak. I lent over the pilot's cockpit, nudged him in the back and pointed to the ground. He nodded and came down to about fifty feet, at which height we flew round and round choosing a smooth place to land. At length he was satisfied, pulled up in a steep climb to fire a light into the ground to get the wind direction and circled round to land.

By the time we eventually landed, there was not a soul to be seen. The little tents were void of life. It took me a long time to find anyone to whom I could speak. At last, seeing me alone and unarmed and, by this time, a long way from the aircraft on the ground, two men came cautiously back to me. They proved to be the Tobah, a small tribe even poorer than the Sufran and their neighbours on the south. After a non-committal chat to ease the tension, I asked if they had seen any Sufran anywhere. They replied that none had crossed the Euphrates.

It was a joke among Beni Huchaim that the Tobah could run so fast that they could overtake a galloping gazelle. A story used to be told that a Turkish military column was once marching up the Euphrates and captured a man of the Tobah, who was taken before the commanding pasha for cross-questioning. After a time, seeing a space of open desert in front of him, the prisoner suddenly shouted a rude remark about the pasha's wife and made a dash for it. The pasha, with a furious oath, called to his mounted escort to catch the man, but all the Sultan's horses and all the Sultan's men were unable to overtake the fugitive!

At last, we realized that trying to find the Barkat and Sufran fugitives among the tribes of Beni Huchaim was like looking for a needle in a haystack. They could have been located in time by unobtrusive intelligence methods, but roaring formations of aircraft were scarcely a suitable instrument.

Arabs have many honourable traditions concerning the protection of fugitives and distressed persons. It is only necessary for such a person to enter one of their tents or huts, and cry 'I am under the protection of this house,' for all the men to leap to their feet to defend him, even if he be a complete stranger or a tribal enemy. In this manner the Barkat and Sufran had infiltrated into the surrounding tribes who wuld never reveal their whereabouts.

The excitement gradually subsided and the tribes trickled back and re-erected their reed huts. The authorities wisely forgot their demand for a surrender of rifles. I still could not help feeling that a great psychological opportunity had been missed of winning, not the submission, but the loyalty and affection of these tribes. But such an idea was foreign to the mentality of the local officials, to whom tribes were the enemies of progress and thus to be crushed.

The operations, however, had in thirty-six hours put an end to the constant anxiety caused by the turbulence of the Middle Euphrates. This was, indeed, no mean victory, even if we discount my more utopian visions of winning the tribesmen's love. But the effect was not limited to the Samawa district alone.

Up and down the Euphrates and the marshes and across to the Tigris, the turbulent tribesmen realized that a new era had dawned. Tribal rebellions were a thing of the past.

Such had been the effect of air control in the plains of Iraq. The bombing of the Barkat and Sufran had been an operation of great precision, made possible by the slow speed of flight of the aircraft of the 1920s, and by the fact that their fuselages were open and that it was possible to lean over the side and sketch the details of the countryside and the landmarks visible from the air.

But the result had also emphasized the vital importance of intelligence, if individual villages were to be pinpointed from the air, in an area without large-scale maps. And the ability to obtain such detailed information rested upon the peculiar mentality of the tribesmen themselves who, while ready to shoot at the police, deemed it a duty to receive and to welcome a guest, although he was mapping their villages with a view to bombing them and told them so.

Had the tribes been inspired by real hatred, it would have been impossible for me to ride round their country without an escort. But all Arab tribal hostilities in Iraq, though they caused many casualties, were modified by their casual methods and by the codes of honour and tradition which controlled their actions.

It is an accepted belief in Europe that primitive man was fierce, cruel and savage, and dragged his women about by their hair. The intimacy which I formed with many shades and varieties of tribesmen in the Arab countries have often caused me to doubt these easy assumptions of the superiority of our 'civilizations'. The tribes were not, of course, as primitive as the original cavemen of the pre-historic ages, but they appeared to be divided from us by a long interval of time.

The gap, however, whether long or short, had not resulted in a corresponding difference in morality, honour, kindness or affection, for in some of these directions their standards were higher than our own. Indeed the cold-blooded and deliberate cultivation of hate seems, in some cases, to be a characteristic of our modern civilization.

[Another remarkable contrast between them and ourselves is found in our respective treatment of women. The killing of women is regarded with horror by the tribes, whereas we not only indiscriminately bomb great cities, but terrorists leave time-bombs in public places, or even assassinate women for political reasons. It would be more consoling if we could believe that the human race is growing more compassionate, more tolerant and more loving, but my experience has not convinced me that this is true.

There was an irony, it seemed to me, in the horror of Arab tribesmen at the idea of killing women. How often had I been told by Westerners, that they never could feel any sympathy for Arabs owing to the manner in which they treated their women.

The real difference between East and West in this matter, I suggest, is that the modern trend in the West is to claim that women and men are virtually the same. Among the Arabs, the emphasis was placed on the absolute difference of the sexes, which were not the rivals but the complements of one another. Men and women led quite different lives. In some ways women were worse treated than they are in the West, in some ways better. The sexes, however, were never rivals.

In passing, it may be of interest to note that the late Professor Levi-Provençal, probably the greatest modern authority on the Arabs in Spain, wrote in one of his works that it was the Arabs who taught the West Europeans to be courteous to women.

The tactical use of aircraft for internal security, which we developed in the 1920s, is no longer applicable. Modern aircraft fly so high and so fast that detailed observations of the ground is no longer possible. Moreover the pilot and observer can no longer look over the side. Whether helicopters have taken the place of the slow-flying aircraft of the 1920s, I am unable to say, for I have never worked with them.

The technique of landing here and there in the country to talk to the people was an accidental by-product of the Barkat and Sufran operations. It was to prove the key to the next type of operation in which we were to be engaged, as succeeding chapters will show. Merely for the purpose of talking to the people, in a country involving great distances such as Iraq, the helicopter would certainly have been safer than our rash landings, crashing into shrubs and leaping over sand dunes.

But modern military aircraft, which need such a long runway to land or take off, could, of course, scarcely have survived even one landing in the open countryside of Iraq.]

The operations in the Beni Huchaim had been solely concerned with internal security. But Britain's most important commitment to Iraq had been her defence against external enemies. This obligation she had fulfilled during a period of four years, while Turkey had been threatening to seize the Mosul district. She would, indeed, undoubtedly have done so, had not Britain championed the Iraqi cause.

No sooner was the Barkat and Sufran operation concluded, than I was ordered back to Nasiriya, where new storm clouds were gathering on the horizon.

13

Raiding to Kill

In or about 1742, a man called Muhammad ibn Abdul Wahhab began to preach a Muslim religious revival in Nejed. At first he met with little response until one Muhammad ibn Saud, a minor shaikh of the Anaiza tribe, declared himself a convert, and proceeded to support the movement with armed force. By 1770, most of the inhabitants of Central Arabia had joined the revival, whether by persuasion or coercion. Soon the Wahhabis, as they were called, were attacking the towns on the Euphrates and in 1803 they took Mecca. In 1810 they almost reached both Baghdad and Damascus.

Europe was at the time torn by the Napoleonic Wars and the Ottoman Empire was helpless. The Sultan delegated Muhammad Ali, the Albanian dictator of Egypt, to suppress the Wahhabis, which he did in a war lasting from 1812 to 1816. The Egyptian Army subsequently retired, and Nejed remained in confusion, the Saud family gradually regaining their influence.

When the British Army landed at Basra in the First World War, Nejed was divided into two states. The southern half was ruled by Abdul Aziz ibn Saud, while the northern portion was governed by Ibn Rasheed, with his capital at Hail. (Map 1, page 14)

Before the First World war, the Ottoman Empire held a garrison in the Hasa, on the Persian Gulf, but, in 1912, Ibn Saud had overrun this force and annexed the province. Seeking an ally upon whom he could rely if the Ottomans reacted, Ibn Saud established a liaison with Britain through the Resident in Bushire, an official of the government of India.

In 1912, Ibn Saud, at war with his rival, Ibn Rasheed, had promoted a revival of Wahhabi fanaticism, to assist him in his operations against Ibn Rasheed. The latter, who was losing ground, appealed to the Ottoman Empire. But if the revival of Wahhabism was an imitation of the fanaticism of the eighteenth century, a second part of Ibn Saud's plan was original.

Assisted by the religious leaders of the movement, he formed his bedouin tribes into religious communities, which were denoted *Al Ikhwan*, or The Brethren. Tobacco, music, silk and worldly vanities in general were forbidden, and the Brethren swore to devote their lives to the forcible conversion of the world to the Wahhabi sect.

In the winter of 1913-14, Captain W. H. I. Shakespear, then the British Political Agent in Kuwait, visited Ibn Saud and discussed with him an alliance with Britain. When the First World War began, Ibn Rasheed declared for the Ottoman Empire. Thus the rivalries of the Nejed princes conformed to the pattern of the Great War.

Ibn Rasheed's power extended over the desert west of the Euphrates and thus threatened the flank of the British Army moving up that river. In January 1915, Shakespear persuaded Ibn Saud to attack Ibn Rasheed, and an inconclusive battle was fought at Jarab, in which Shakespear was killed. Thereafter Ibn Saud remained in his own territory until the end of the war. Part of the reason for his inactivity may have been due to the support given by Britain to another Arabian prince, the Sherif Husain of Mecca.

In the summer of 1920, Ibn Saud eventually marched on and captured Hail and the Rasheed state ceased to exist. Ibn Saud thereby became the sole ruler of Nejed, or Central Arabia, and the neighbour of the newly established state of Iraq. In the same year, as a result of the various postwar settlements, three new Arab states received rulers of the Sherifian family of Mecca, which Ibn Saud considered to be a rival to his own dynasty. Sherif Husain became King of the Hejaz, the Ameer Abdulla became ruler of Trans-Jordan, and the Ameer Faisal was crowned King of Iraq. Ibn Saud suspected that the appointment of three Sherifian rulers was a British intrigue directed against himself.

Britain was, at this period, unfortunate in enjoying too great a reputation for cleverness. The British Government was regarded as an Olympian power which inspired and controlled every political movement in a Machiavellian pursuit of its own interests. In reality, Britain rather resembled the proverbial old hen, flapping and cackling confusedly in her attempt to restrain the violence of the numerous Arab ducklings which she had hatched. One of her best-intentioned efforts was the attempt to secure a treaty of friendship between Iraq, with its Sherifian king, and Nejed under Ibn Saud.

Delegates from the two states met in the spring of 1922 at Muhammara near Basra, but failed to agree. Eventually a treaty between Iraq and Ibn Saud was drawn up and signed at Uqair in the Hasa, largely as a result of the persuasive personality of Sir Percy Cox, the British High Commissioner for Iraq, who acted as mediator. Attached to the treaty were a series of documents called the Uqair Protocols, drafted by Sir Percy, which laid down the frontier between Nejed and Iraq. Ibn Saud accepted the frontier unwillingly.

In the autumn of 1922, Ibn Saud's situation was somewhat as follows:

(a) Principally as a result of the religious enthusiasm which he himself had deliberately stirred up, he had defeated his rival, Ibn Rasheed, and was the sole ruler of Central Arabia.

(b) His fanatical followers, however, claimed that it was their religious duty to conquer the whole world for Wahhabism and they were totally unprepared to halt at a political frontier which someone had drawn on a map.

(c) Abdul Aziz ibn Saud himself, however, was a man of penetrating intellect and was aware, to some extent at least, of the power and resources of the nations of Europe. He was thus anxious to avoid a collision with Britain, but was unable to convince his followers. For ten years he had been deliberately fanning their fanaticism and now found it difficult to eat his own words.

The Ikhwan, therefore, were clamouring to be led on to the conquest of Iraq for Wahhabism, as they had conquered Ibn Rasheed.

The Iraq Government, newly established in Baghdad, regarded these problems from an entirely different angle. Still dominated by the Ottoman mentality, it was anxious only for progress, westernization and modernity. Tribes were not modern and should be abolished, especially bedouin tribes in the desert. What did it matter if the Ikhwan raided and killed the Iraqi tribes? Bedouins were of no interest or value to a modern government anyhow.

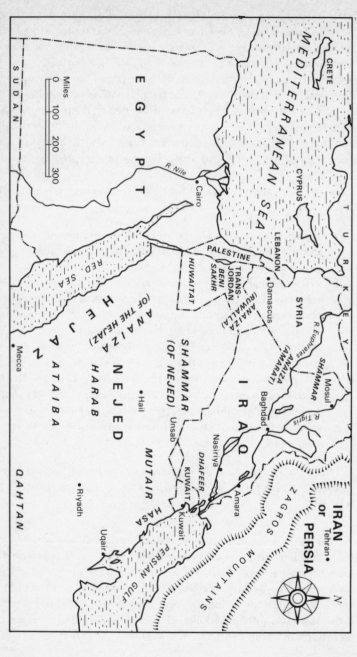

Map 8 The Principal Bedouin Tribes of North Arabia

130

After the signature of the treaty and protocols at Uqair in December 1922, the remainder of the winter 1922-23 passed more or less quietly on the newly designated Iraq–Nejed frontier. I was in the Dulaim district at the time, concerned with the possibility of a war with Turkey over Mosul.

In the autumn of 1923, as already related, I had been brought back again to the Lower Euphrates, where the operations against the Barkat and Sufran had ended, once and for all, the long-dreaded turbulence of the tribes on the Euphrates. In December 1923, I returned from Samawa to Nasiriya.

The desert south and west of the Euphrates extended unbroken for seven hundred miles to the northern end of the Red Sea. The area nearest to the Euphrates was the grazing ground of the bedouin tribe known as the Dhafeer. North-west of them lay the Amarat Anaiza whose chief, Fahad ibn Hadhdhal, I had visited from Al Qaim. South-west of the Dhafeer lay Shammar, the defeated former supporters of Ibn Rasheed and now Saudi subjects. South of the Dhafeer were Mutair, recognized as Saudi subjects and including some of the most fanatical communities of the Wahhabi brethren. These were the great tribes of camel bedouins, who spent nearly all their lives in the desert.

But along the banks of the Euphrates, dwelt a swarm of shepherd tribes, who summered close to the river, their sheep being unable to endure the desert heats in summer. In November and December, however, when rain began to fall, the desert was suddenly clothed with grass, and pools of rainwater formed in the rocky valleys. Loading their tents and baggage on donkeys, the shepherds trekked into the desert, travelling perhaps as far as a hundred or a hundred and fifty miles away from the river bank and the nearest government post. During this period, from November to April, the shepherd tribes were scattered far and wide over an area of some thirty thousand square miles of open desert, lying between the Euphrates and the Iraq–Nejed frontier, as defined in the Uqair Protocols.

During his long years of war with Ibn Rasheed, Abdul Aziz ibn Saud had evolved a system of Ikhwan strategy against which the Iraqi shepherds were helpless. The Wahhabi tribes were able each to concentrate raiding parties composed of some three of four thousand camelmen. These they would hold back in readiness until their spies had located a suitable target. Then, one evening before sunset, they would set out, march all night covering perhaps seventy miles and surprise their victims in a wild charge at dawn.

Our aircraft were not allowed to cross the Iraq–Nejed frontier in looking for raiders. The result was that the Ikhwan could cross the frontier at dusk and reach objectives seventy miles within Iraq by dawn. In other words, it was not possible for aircraft to arrive in time to protect shepherd camps from dawn attack within this seventy-mile belt.

The factor which added such a peculiar poignancy to these raids was massacre. The Ikhwan killed all males in cold blood, even small boys or male babies in arms. Women were not killed and the survivors of one of these raids consisted only of a weeping and wailing crowd of exhausted women and girls, who had probably straggled back on foot in panic flight over a hundred miles of desert.

In December 1923, when I returned to Nasiriya from the Samawa operations, the shepherd tribes were already out in the desert, but as no government official of any kind had ever entered the desert west of the railway line, no one had any idea where they were.

Although the Ikhwan were desirous of extending their raids into Iraq, the Treaty of Muhammara and the Uqair Protocols might have preserved the peace if only the Iraq Government and Ibn Saud had been involved, assisted by the mediation of Sir Percy Cox, representing Britain. But the arrival of the Ameer Faisal as King of Iraq immediately roused the suspicion of Ibn Saud and made his co-operation uncertain.

Unfortunately, due to postwar economy, the subsidy which had in the past been paid by Britain to Ibn Saud was terminated. He could scarcely avoid connecting the cessation of the subsidy with the arrival of King Faisal in Iraq.

The endless rivalries of the princes of Arabia often expressed themselves in terms of the seduction of one another's tribes. None of them could afford to maintain a regular army and thus their military power depended on the number of tribes who owed allegiance to them. During the summer of 1923, certain shaikhs of the Dhafeer, an Iraq tribe, paid allegiance to Ibn Saud. As against this a small number of Ikhwan, who had incurred the anger of Ibn Saud, fled to Iraq where they were not only welcomed by King

Faisal but, from the safety of Iraq territory, were permitted to engage in pilfering raids against the subjects of Ibn Saud.

In December 1923, therefore, tension between King Faisal and Ibn Saud was mounting, owing to these intrigues. Meanwhile, however, the Iraq shepherds, utterly unaware of these political rivalries, were scattered far and wide over the desert.

As hostilities in the desert seemed more than probable, the first step seemed to me to be to obtain some topographical knowledge of the area. I accordingly hired two riding camels from the Dhafeer and, one morning in January 1924, I crossed the railway line, heading south-west towards the distant blue ridges of unexplored desert. The only traveller who had crossed the area before had been Leachman in 1912, travelling in disguise. I was accompanied as usual by Ali al Yunis and by one Shammari and one Dhafeeri, as protectors against those tribes.

We spent some three weeks in the desert, travelling down to Al Amghar, at the northern apex of the Neutral Area. We visited and slept with many tribal camps, both bedouin Dhafeer and shepherds. The latter enquired anxiously regarding relations between the Iraq Government and Ibn Saud. Many asked frankly why the Iraq Government did not protect them from Ikhwan raids, although it taxed them. (Map 9, page 136)

On my return to Nasiriya, I worked hard to produce a new one-over-a-million map of the desert, based on the topographical information which I had collected. Now, at least we had some geographical information on which to base our intelligence reports.

In March and April 1924 I was absent on two months' leave. During my absence, Faisal al Duweesh, chief of the Ikhwan tribe of Mutair, delivered a massive raid on the Iraqi shepherd tribes at Unsab. Many Iraqis were killed and thousands of sheep, donkeys, tents and property were looted.

Returning from leave in April 1924, I found the remnants of the Iraqi shepherds huddled in panic on the west bank of the Euphrates. For the previous ten years Ibn Saud had been universally known as the ally of Britain and in receipt of a British subsidy. Thus when raided by his followers, the Iraqi nomads were convinced that these attacks were being connived at, if not encouraged, by Britain. Considerable bitterness was roused by this delusion.

Meanwhile, however, on the other side, the petty raids carried into Nejed by the Ikhwan refugees and encouraged by King Faisal were assumed by Ibn Saud to be supported by Britain, as mandatory for Iraq. Thus, while Ibn Saud and King Faisal intrigued against one another, both sides blamed Britain!

Throughout the summer of 1924 the Ikhwan refugees in Iraq continued their petty forays into Nejed. There could be little doubt that the Ikhwan were merely biding their time until the shepherds moved out into the desert in the winter and offered the Nejed tribes a lucrative objective, incapable of resistance.

Accordingly, in October 1924, I submitted proposals for the forthcoming grazing season. Firstly, I suggested that Ikhwan raiding provided more than enough work for one Intelligence Officer and proposed the appointment of an S.S.O. solely for Ikhwan defence.

Secondly, it was hopeless to fly endless air reconnaissances over the desert when the pilots had no idea where to look for raiders. It was obvious, however, that the raiders' objective was the Iraqi shepherds. Thus, when looking for Ikhwan raids, the most hopeful method was to visit the most advanced Iraqi shepherds every day and check their safety.

Such a method made it necessary for us to know every day where the leading Iraqi tribes were and to secure their co-operation in camping where we told them and in following our instructions. This was in itself no easy task, because the Iraqi tribes suspected that we were in reality in league with the Ikhwan. Months of patient visiting and talking to the tribes were needed before we could convince them that we wished to help and not to betray them.

No reply was received from Air Headquarters to these proposals until December, when the tribes were already moving out. I was then made responsible for intelligence concerning defence against the Ikhwan, with the title of S.S.O. Ikhwan Defence.

At the same time, in December 1924, a detachment of R.A.F. armoured cars was sent to carry out a reconnaissance in the desert. This operation might have been useful as a training exercise in desert driving, but it was not linked in any way with the general defensive situation. The cars nowhere approached within seventy miles of the frontier. That is to say they did not approach the danger area. In the middle of December they returned to Baghdad in order to be back in their barracks in time for Christmas.

Moreover the use of British armoured cars in the desert was rendered difficult by the high standard of physical comfort to which the men were considered to be entitled. The whole column, for example, had to make a long halt at midday in order to cook a hot meat meal. At the same time, the necessity for the daily issue of fresh meat and bread required the supply of rations by air, involving a prohibitive amount of flying.

The raiding season was about to begin and the Iraqi shepherds were already far out in the desert. Aircraft, even if they could ever overtake raiders, could only inflict light casualties on scattered camel riders. But if armoured cars could overtake them on the ground, they might inflict on them a defeat which would cure them of raiding for ever. Armoured cars were, therefore, the answer to our problem, but to me in my enthusiasm they appeared only half-hearted in their operations.

I was young and arrogant, and insufficiently respectful to my seniors. Moreover I was a junior Army officer addressing the R.A.F. In my report to Air Headquarters, I compared the operation to sending the fire brigade for a drive around the town and then allowing all the men to go on holiday for Christmas, on the grounds that there were no houses on fire at the moment. The tone of my report was resented. Operations against the Ikhwan were to last for six years, but I was never able to secure the co-operation of the armoured cars.

I was too inexperienced to appreciate the value of talking things over. I should have gone to Baghdad, made friends on the staff and discussed the whole problem with them. But I was too devoted to the tribes to be willing to absent myself for a long trip to Baghdad.

The concentration of large forces of raiders south of the frontier could not be concealed and we were able to obtain warning from Kuwait or from desert travellers when a raid was in preparation. But we could never tell when the raid would come, and sometimes the enemy remained concentrated for a long time to allow the first alarm to subside.

This factor was peculiarly difficult in dealing with the R.A.F., who might declare an alert when the first reports were received. Then two or three weeks might elapse without incident, sarcastic remarks were passed about the usual panic, the alert was cancelled – and then the blow fell.

I continued to receive reports of the imminence of a heavy Ikhwan raid by Faisal al Duweesh the chief of the Mutair tribe, but

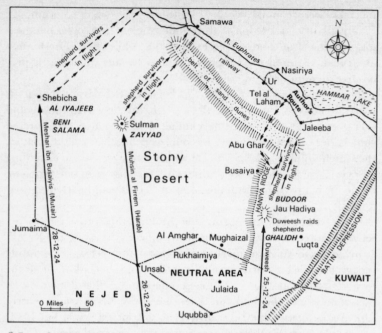

Map 9 The Killing Raids, December 1924

the powers-that-be showed no signs of interest. Unfortunately heavy rain had fallen in the desert in the area within seventy miles of the frontier and the rolling hills were covered with fresh green grass. To my horror I heard that several large groups of shepherds had ventured forward into this tempting grazing. I immediately sent a message by a camelman warning them of an impending raid and ordering them to move back. My messenger returned to report that the grazing was excellent and the shepherds refused to move. I had no means of defending them, and decided in desperation that I would myself ride out to them, and try and persuade them to come back.

I set out from Tel al Lahm station with four camelmen on Christmas Eve 1924, to visit the shepherd camps and bring them back. We slept the night with a small camp of Dhafeer and set out early next morning, intending to sleep the next night with the most advanced shepherd camps, at a place called Jau Hadiya.

It was about noon the next day when we topped a long ridge of the rolling desert hills and suddenly saw, in the valley beyond, an

136

animated scene. The valley was full of sheep, donkeys, horsemen and women and children on foot, all running as fast as they could towards the north, urging their flocks before them with sobs and pathetic cries. Just at that moment, a mile away to the south, we saw, appearing over the top of a low down, a long line of camel riders, some of them carrying large green war-banners, in hot pursuit of the fugitives.

On both flanks other camel riders dashed forward with a view to cutting off the fugitives who, abandoning their sheep, ran for dear life from their death-dealing pursuers. We joined the fugitives, endeavouring to ascertain what had happened. Most of them could only cry wildly 'The Duweesh! The Ikhwan' – but a few who had retained their wits were able to explain that the southernmost camps of shepherds had been overrun at dawn that morning by a wild mass of camelriders and all their men had been killed.

The tribes camped a little further north had fled incontinently with the enemy in close pursuit and this *sauve-qui-peut* had now been going on for six hours, more and more of the panic-stricken shepherds being overtaken and killed. The camel riders were now less than a mile from our position, but we could see that they lost time by stopping to kill their victims and then to round up the sheep and donkeys.

My four bedouin companions were now highly alarmed and kept urging me to trot on and leave the shepherds to their fate, as the five of us could do nothing to defend them. But I could not bring myself to be so abject as just to desert these miserable people and run, especially as it was the government which I served which was responsible for their safety.

[More than fifty years have elapsed since that day of anguish, but I can still in my mind's eye see those terrified women, dragging and carrying their exhausted children, throwing panic-stricken glances behind them at the pursuing camelmen, and crying passionately for help – 'O God! O Muhammad! O Ali! O God protect us!']

We continued for perhaps two hours to ride in the midst of the fugitives. Then, at last, the pursuers seemed to be falling a little further behind. The evening was already drawing in and I decided to ride ahead as fast as we could, hoping to give the alarm and to obtain aircraft to bomb the raiders the next day. Our camels being already exhausted, I and one of my bedouins borrowed two horses and set out at a gallop for Jaleeba railway station, which we reached just after dawn in a state of exhaustion.

Within five minutes, the railway telegraph clerk was despatching a 'clear the line' telegram to Air Headquarters, reporting the raid and asking for the immediate despatch of aircraft. But, in all the emotion and excitement, I had forgotten one point – the day before had been Christmas Day. My signal reached Baghdad at dawn on Boxing Day – all offices were closed and half the personnel were on leave. So I spent the day in the tiny railway station at Jaleeba, only some fifty miles from a large Ikhwan raid.

The next morning three aircraft were made available and we overtook the raiders, just setting off for home with the loot. With so few aircraft, we could do them little harm, but at least the R.A.F. and the government were now convinced that raids of massacre did occur.

It was not till four days later that reports were received that another Ikhwan raid had massacred shepherds of the Zayyad tribe at Sulman. A flight of three aircraft were sent from Baghdad to investigate. Flying over the wells at Sulman, they found rows and rows of tents and thousands and thousands of camel and sheep. The raiders of the Harab tribe had camped for four days to rest on the site of the battle. The aircraft were unarmed and could only fly helplessly round and survey this most perfect of targets.

A few days later, yet another raid was delivered on the Beni Salama shepherds at Shebicha, but news of it did not reach the government until a week later, when exhausted survivors reached the Euphrates on foot.

This outburst of raiding and massacre galvanized the Iraq Government and the R.A.F. into sudden activity. As recommended by me the previous October, an advanced post and landing ground was established at Abu Ghar, thirty miles out in the desert beyond the railway. Here the Iraq Army erected a wireless set, beside which I camped, being thus directly connected with Air Headquarters.

A strong British diplomatic protest was sent to Ibn Saud which, coupled with the simultaneous reports of air action against the raiders, persuaded him to prohibit further Ikhwan raiding. Another favourable factor, from the Iraqi viewpoint, was that Ibn Saud had declared war on King Husain of the Hejaz and that the full strength of the Ikhwan were committed in that area.

From the grazing point of view, the spring of 1925 was disastrous for the Iraqi tribes. The belt of desert seventy miles north of the Iraq-Nejed frontier was clothed with long grass and wild flowers.

But the remains of the shepherd tribes stayed crowded into the area round Abu Ghar, which had missed the early rains. Every morning the little ragged tents were surrounded by dead sheep, camels and donkeys, which had died of starvation – a truly heartbreaking sight.

14

The Nomad Life

The spring of 1925 passed with only minor alarms in the Southern Desert. Ibn Saud with all his forces, including the Ikhwan, was waging war against King Husain in the Hejaz, and was desirous of peace on the Iraq frontier till the Hejaz war was over.

The shepherds had returned to the banks of the Euphrates and only the Dhafeer bedouins were still grazing their camels in fancied security in the desert. Then suddenly, on 22 June, 1925, a raiding party of Mutair arrived without warning, swept up one thousand seven hundred Dhafeer camels and recrossed the Nejed frontier before reports of the incident reached either the tribes or the government.

The Iraq Government was indignant at this outrage, after the peaceful promises given by Ibn Saud three months before. The Dhafeer were assured that their camels would be returned and were forbidden to raid back. But as summer passed into autumn and there was no sign of restitution, the Dhafeer followed the course natural to them. Faced with starvation, they set out in small groups to raid some camels back from Nejed.

It was the British Government which rose to the occasion, by sending a diplomatic mission, under Sir Gilbert Clayton, to discuss the Iraq frontier with Ibn Saud. The war was still continuing in the Hejaz, but the British party passed unmolested through the Sherifian lines and met Ibn Saud at Bahra, on the road between Mecca and Jidda.

As a result of their conference, the Bahra Agreement was signed on 1 November, 1925. Ibn Saud and Iraq both agreed to inflict severe punishment on raiders and to abstain from seducing the loyalty of one another's tribes. Both governments had made these promises before, but the fact that a new agreement had been signed did result in a relaxation of tension. Moreover it was obvious that, at least while the Hejaz war lasted, Ibn Saud genuinely wanted peace with Iraq.

Unfortunately, however, the Dhafeer camels were not returned, with the result that the victims continued to recoup themselves by stealing camels from Nejed, thereby, it was to be feared, giving the Ikhwan an excuse to raid again. In December the shepherds, too confident the year before, were afraid to move out beyond the fort at Abu Ghar.

Our intelligence sources from Nejed, however, confirmed that Ibn Saud had issued strict orders against raiding Iraq and, moreover, all the Ikhwan were away in the Hejaz. As a result of the Bahra Agreement, the British and Iraq Governments announced peace and few if any aircraft patrols and no armoured cars were made available for the frontier.

In the Southern Desert, I found myself left to my own devices. The rôles of the shepherds and myself were reversed. The year before they had moved out and I had tried to hold them back. Now I saw that if they did not move out, what flocks had survived the previous winter would die.

In one important respect the situation had changed since the year before. In 1924 the shepherds had believed that Britain was the ally of Ibn Saud to destroy them. Now they were satisfied that we were trying to help them, but they concluded that Ibn Saud was too strong for us, and would conquer the world.

After a discussion with Ajaimi ibn Suwait, the shaikh of the Dhafeer, we evolved a plan. He was positive that the shepherds would die on the gravel plain outside Abu Ghar fort sooner than face further massacres unless I myself lead them out. He volunteered himself to move with his immediate followers towards the Neutral Area if I would go with him.

Arab nomads, shepherds and bedouins alike, have black goat-hair tents. Only governments use white canvas tents. The sum total of equipment which I possessed for desert operations was a Ford van and a one-hundred-and-twenty-pound white canvas tent. Loading the one on the other, and accompanied by a driver and two bedouins, we opened the campaign. (Map 9, page 136)

Ajaimi ibn Suwait and his Dhafeer struck camp from Abu Ghar and pitched their tents fifty miles to the south at Luqta, with my little white tent beside them. The shepherds sent scouts to see where he had gone. They found him camped in luscious grazing at Luqta, with a little white tent. 'What is that white tent?' they asked. 'O that's the government,' said Ajaimi casually.

The shepherds went back to their tents. 'Ajaimi is all right!' they said, 'he has the government with him!' Slowly they moved forward, filling the area from Luqta to Abu Ghar, but always keeping the little white tent and Ajaimi's big black tent in front of them.

Sometimes it was nervous work. Rumours came that Faisal al Duweesh had returned from the Hejaz. Now and again the shepherds panicked and fled. To show our defiance, we moved southwards and camped at Rukhaimiya in the Neutral Area, where the grazing was splendid.

When the weather grew warmer, we slowly moved back to the north. The great camels walked ponderously beneath their huge humps. The sheep, goats and lambs were in fine condition, the tents were full of milk and butter. The Ikhwan had not come.

These months living alone with the bedouins, eighty miles south of the nearest government post and wireless set at Abu Ghar, I gradually obtained new insights into the nomad way of life.

For many thousands of years, certainly from before Old Testament times, the great majority of the human race was divided into two groups – the stock-breeders and the cultivators. In some continents, doubtless, there were men who lived by hunting alone, but no trace of these has survived in any of the countries where I have lived. In Britain, and indeed in Europe as a whole, the two vocations could be combined, owing to the fact that the damp climate produced everywhere sufficient grass for grazing. Thus the agriculturalist could, in addition to ploughing and harvesting, keep sheep or cattle, and there was sufficient grass near the settlement to enable these animals to live without going far afield.

In large areas of other continents, particularly Asia and Africa, this was not the case. Here rainfall is so light that grazing is scanty, or so variable that, in most years, some area or other will be completely missed by the winter rains and will remain parched and dusty for a whole year. Thus the cultivator, who could not leave his ploughed fields, was unable to find grazing near by to allow him to keep flocks of animals. The occupations of stockbreeder and agriculturalist could consequently not be combined.

As a result, the inhabitants of these countries remained, for thousands of years, divided into two distinct halves, the graziers and the farmers, the nomadic and the settled. These two differing ways of life produced entirely different cultures, resulting in rival communities which often regarded one another with hatred and contempt.

In studying the characteristics of nomadic and agricultural societies, we may begin with their attitude to war. The settled farmer has all his wealth bound up in his dwelling, his land, his trees and other immovable objects. Should he abandon these to an enemy, he at once becomes a starving fugitive. These factors compel the cultivator to put up a stubborn defence should he be attacked.

At the same time, agriculture is a laborious task, leaving little physical energy or time for other violent exercise. Moreover farming occupies most of the year with seasonal tasks, making it difficult for the agricultural worker to absent himself for long periods. Thus we find the farmer to be peculiarly stubborn in defence, but to show no relish for military adventures.

These two characteristics lead to two more. First he regards war with horror and, if attacked, his sole desire is to win as quickly as possible, by fair means or foul. Secondly, his sole object being defence, he tends to live in villages and he realizes that, in order to attain security, every member of the community must be obliged to share in the defence.

The characteristics of agricultural communities in war may, therefore, be summarised as follows:

(a) Stubborn defence.
(b) Dislike of military adventures.
(c) The determination to win by fair means or foul.
(d) The idea that all members of the community must share in the defence.

The small town largely shares in the mentality of the agricultural community, for it possesses fixed assets. Being richer than the village, it sometimes surrounds itself with walls, a further indication of its purely defensive attitude.

The nomad outlook on war is exactly the reverse. His wealth does not consist of immovable property, houses, land or orchards, but in highly mobile horses, camels, sheep or goats. It is unnecessary for him to die in the last ditch to defend such property against a superior enemy when, more often than not, he can save his wealth completely by a rapid retirement. Not only so, but flocks of animals are such unwieldy things that, in a pitched battle, they probably stampede, disperse or are slaughtered in large numbers, even if their owner be eventually victorious.

All these considerations point to the fact that, in the defensive, the nomad will normally evade attack by a superior enemy by a skilful retirement. Only in the very last resort will he dig in and fight to the death as the villager must.

These factors are further emphasized if we consider the political results of the war. The villager will fight desperately to save his home and his land but, once conquered, he can only surrender. Tied to a piece of land on which alone he can make a living, he is obliged to submit to whatever oppression or humiliation is imposed by the conqueror. If he be allowed to remain on his land, he will perforce bow his head to oppression, over-taxation, blows, insults, or even the violation of his women.

The nomad, on the other hand, if he finds himself surprised by overwhelming numbers, will probably not fight at all. His unwieldy flocks make a desperate resistance impossible. He will ride out to meet the enemy commander and offer his submission. But this he will do with his tongue in his cheek. No sooner have the hostile forces withdrawn than, rather than submit to humiliation, he will pack up and migrate as fast as possible to some far country where he can once more be a free man. Thus we find that the nomad, although so weak and unstable in defence, possesses a much more independent mind than the villager and is more tricky, more haughty and more resentful of insult.

These factors explain Ibn Saud's unwillingness to accept a geographical frontier with Iraq which left an area of desert inside Iraq territory. Such an arrangement limited his autocracy over his own tribes. As long as there were deserts beyond his control, any nomads with whom he was angry could slip away into Iraq territory beyond his reach.

We have hitherto considered nomads and settled communities in defence. When we consider the offensive, the contrast between the nomad and the villager is equally great. The cultivator is tied to his fields by an endless round of labours. The nomad has very little work to occupy his spare time and is, of course, always mounted on a horse or camel and inured to long journeys. He is thus admirably fitted for offensive military expeditions, both because he has not enough work to occupy his energies and because he is naturally hardy and mobile.

As a result, military adventures become the pride, the glory and the pastime of the nomad. Moreover, these adventures being largely offensive, the life of the community does not depend on their success in the same way that the survival of the village depends on a successful defence. Thus the nomad tends in war to seek personal glory for himself, rather than the service of the community. This peculiarity, as we shall see later, was likewise a characteristic of the chivalry of Western Europe in the Middle Ages.

This competition in performing glorious deeds was the life passion of the nomads – the feats of arms performed were more important than victory. There is no glory to be derived from killing a man in his sleep or from shooting him in the back.

As a result, there arose a system of individual challenges and of jousting with the lance in pursuit of personal fame (also a naive readiness to surrender and to admit defeat when outnumbered, because victory was not really the main object of the war). In such a war between bedouin gentlemen, there was a lack of hatred or resentment between the combatants and a ready generosity to acknowledge the noble acts performed by the heroes of the other side. The corollary was, however, a haughty scorn for settled communities, who fought to win and not according to the rules.

A less attractive side to this nomadic outlook on war was jealousy and boasting. The object of the bedouin raider not being to serve a cause but to attain personal distinction, a man is often torn by jealousy of others of his own tribe who perform more spectacular deeds than himself. This jealousy of one another is distasteful to Europeans, though it can probably be matched by the jealousies and struggles for precedence of the European nobles of the feudal age. It is an essential, though unattractive, peculiarity of a 'chivalrous' culture.

Before 1914 the chief weapon among Arab bedouins was the lance. When pitched battles occurred between tribes, the two sides would first line up against one another. Then champions would canter out into the space between the two armies, calling out the names of their ladies, their sisters or of their camel herds. A challenger would then ride out from the other side, and the two would ride against one another with their lances while both armies looked on. This custom is certainly more than two thousand years old – witness Goliath and David.

On 5 August, 1192, on the Third Crusade, the Muslim and Crusader armies faced one another on the plain outside Jaffa, commanded respectively by Saladin and Richard Coeur-de-Lion. 'The King of England,' laments Baha-al-Deen, the biographer of

Saladin, 'lance in hand, rode along the whole length of our army, and not one of our soldiers left the ranks to attack him.'

The last occasion on which this procedure was followed in bedouin battles was at Jumaima in 1910, in a battle between Shammar under Ibn Rasheed, and Anaiza, under Ibn Hadhdhal. The First World War followed, and immense numbers of rifles fell into the hands of the tribes. This resulted in the disappearance of lances and of the old customs of personal challenges between champions.

The Prophet Muhammad preached in Arabia from 613 to 632 A.D., when he died. In the ensuing year, the Arabs burst out of their desert peninsula and swept across Egypt and North Africa. In 712 they conquered Spain and continued to rule a great part of the peninsula until 1492, a period of seven hundred and eighty years. For some of this time they also ruled part of the south of France.

To appreciate for how long the Arabs dominated Spain, we may note that seven hundred and eighty years ago today takes us back to Richard Coeur-de-Lion. During the greater part of this period, 712-1492, the Arab culture of Spain was considerably higher than that of France or England. Inevitably the French and then the English imitated Arab culture, just as the Africans imitate European culture in the twentieth century.

The spearhead of the Arab conquests consisted of the bedouin tribes, who brought with them to western Europe the chivalrous customs of the wars of the desert. Thus, when Richard I landed in Palestine on the Third Crusade, he found opposed to him Muslim knights brought up in the same traditions as he had learned as a boy in Aquitaine.

The bedouin idea that war was glorious dominated Europe for seven or eight hundred years, until the Renaissance. The ancient Greeks and Romans had fought to win, by fair means or foul, for they were based on city communities. The renaissance of classical culture in the West put an end to war for personal glory – war in which to fight honourably was more important than to win the battle.

Nevertheless, the spirit of *beaux gestes* in war survived here and there in Europe long after the Renaissance. A typical example is the possibly apocryphal story of Lord Charles Hay at the Battle of Fontenoy in 1745. When the English guards found themselves face to face with the French guards, he stepped out of the ranks, swept off his hat in a courtly bow, drank to the health of the French guards, and invited them to fire first.

Perhaps also, especially in Britain, we may claim that the spirit of Arab chivalry survived in our own feeling of sport. To play up and play the game was more important than to win the match. To have a good game, closely contested but in a clean and sportsmanlike manner, was the test of a successful match.

But, in recent years, this spirit has also rapidly lost ground. Utilitarianism has completely ousted romance. The West has discarded the old bedouin ideals that to fight nobly is more important than to win the battle. Sport has largely become an 'industry', with money as the incentive, and to win the aim, by whatever means are available.

When speaking of nomads in this chapter, I am, of course, referring to the camel nomads of the Arabian deserts with whom I lived. Few people in the Western nations today realize the immense rôle which nomads have played in world history. For all nomads have always shared the qualities of extreme hardihood, mobility and a lack of hard work to absorb their energies. They possessed the additional advantage that they could go to war accompanied by their women and children, and by their livestock which constituted all their worldly possessions. Townsmen and villagers, on the contrary, were obliged to leave their families and their property behind them when they went to war, with a large percentage of their men to guard them.

A nomad tribe or nation could thus advance in a solid mass like an army. Against such an invasion villagers were helpless, for they could not concentrate a sufficient force in the field. Only great cities could hope to resist, for they could surround themselves with walls which could not be overwhelmed by a mounted charge.

The Roman Empire was overrun by nomads although, unlike the Mongols, the barbarians were not inspired by hate but, in a sense, by admiration. They conquered the Roman Empire because they wished themselves to become Romans.

The Mongols destroyed the splendid civilizations of the Arabs and the Persians out of hate. Pouring into some peaceful and civilized countryside, they easily overran the rural villages, whence they herded the young men together in gangs of slaves. They then massacred the remainder of the citizens, regardless of age or sex.

When they besieged a walled city, the gangs of prisoners which they had collected were driven in front of them up the breaches in the walls, thereby reducing the casualties among the Mongols to a minimum. When the city was taken, it was completely destroyed and every single inhabitant was killed.

The extremely arduous life led by nomads inspired them with contempt for people who slept in beds and who shut the doors of their houses. The Mongols claimed it to be a duty to exterminate all such decadent peoples from the earth. The steppes of Russia, Siberia and Mongolia were the homes of the nomads who repeatedly destroyed the civilizations of Europe, southern Asia and China.

The Arab bedouins shared with the northern nomads the warlike qualities produced by hardihood and mobility. But they developed one quality, which seems to have been peculiar to them alone – they invented romantic, sporting war between themselves – the original and most remarkable system they bequeathed, as we have seen, to Europe, where it developed into our medieval chivalry.

To the bedouins, then, war was not a desperate matter of life and death, but rather a romantic excitement to break the monotony of the pastoral life. An occupation in which many men are killed must inevitably give rise also to tragedies, bereavements, widows and orphans. But the bedouins did not, of course, view their raiding from outside as we did. In 1925 it was still their normal way of life, which seemed to them both natural and inevitable.

The reader, however, may well be puzzled by the contrast between the massacring raids of the Ikhwan, and the 'sporting' raids of other bedouins. The sporting variety is undoubtedly several thousand years old, but, during that period, Arabia has periodically been swept by waves of religious enthusiasm. The original wars of conquest in the seventh century may be classed as one of these, though less bloody than subsequent outbreaks.

The Carmathians, in the tenth century, constituted a fanatical religious outbreak in central Arabia, which not only swept the desert, but reached the gates of Cairo, Damascus and Baghdad.

The Wahhabis did the same at the end of the eighteenth century, using the same methods of massacre as their predecessors the Carmathians. As already stated, Ibn Saud in 1912 revived the fanaticism of the Wahhabis, when he raised the Ikhwan.

To the religious fanatic, all the human race except his own sect are enemies of God, deserving extermination. With such persons, there can be no question of sport, honour or fair play. Yet, curiously enough, the romantic aspect of war survived even during periods of fanaticism, in so far as only men were massacred and women were not molested, which is more than can be said of wars in many self-styled civilized countries. Then, at last, when the fanatical phase died down, the old honourable and sporting customs returned.

Nomads remained a scourge and a menace to civilization as long as the wild mounted charge was a formidable method of tactics. The nomads were always able to obtain swords, lances and bows and arrows. It was the appearance of complicated manufactured weapons which gradually put an end to their domination.

For firearms, and later vehicles, could only be manufactured in cities, and cities were the traditional enemies of the nomad. Thus we, on the Iraq-Nejed frontier in the 1920s, were perhaps the last exponents of the terrible age-old struggle between the massacring nomads and the defenceless agricultural population of the Euphrates valley.

Today the wheel has turned full circle and nomads are perhaps the most defenceless of all types of communities. Most of them live on vast open plains which, owing to lack of water, were impassable to the cavalry and infantry of the armies of only seventy-five years ago. Today, these immense plains form ideal terrain for armoured vehicles. The great distances involved, formerly an impassable obstacle to pedestrian armies, are crossed in a few minutes by modern aircraft and there, in the open plains, the great nomadic herds offer an utterly indefensible target to bombs and machine-guns.

Never was there a greater or more complete reversal of fortune. Our efforts to defend the Iraqis from the Ikhwan passed unnoticed in the great world, and even in Iraq. Yet we may perhaps claim that we were the last to engage in a type of warfare which had occupied – and terrified – mankind for many thousands of years.

15

Arabian Knights

In this chapter, I have collected some of the notes on bedouin life which I wrote down during my three months' residence with the Dhafeer in the winter of 1925-26.

One direction in which the way of life of Arab nomads differed from that of villagers was in their treatment of women. The farm worker is doomed to a life of hard, physical labour. It would perhaps be unreasonable to expect him to encourage his wife to sit at home, while he spent twelve hours a day ploughing or reaping. Thus we find that the women in agricultural communities share with the men, to some extent at least, the drudgery of working in the fields.

In this respect, again, we find the nomad practice directly opposed to the agricultural. Compared with the farmer, the nomad had little heavy manual labour to perform. On the other hand, his passion was personal distinction. Perhaps it is natural, when men seek fame, that they should desire to secure recognition of their prowess by women. Again, the virtual exemption of the women from heavy labour enabled them to retain their beauty, thereby rendering them more attractive than the horny-handed females of the village.

To the villager, the woman is a worker and the producer of children: to the nomad, she is the arbiter of man's glory, courted, sung and praised. It should be noted, however, that the nomad woman, though better treated than her village sister was not the 'equal' or companion of men. The respect and admiration which she commanded was due essentially to the fact that she was absolutely different from man. Man was the warrior and the statesman, woman the beauty and the mother. 'Equality' of the sexes means nothing in chivalry. The two sexes are entirely different creations of which neither is superior or inferior.

This essential contrast was emphasized by the careful division of duties between the sexes. Fetching water by hand was a woman's duty, as was collecting firewood which, consisting of small desert thorny bushes, was a light load. Men, however, drew water from the wells, which was a heavier task and, of course, above all, men looked after and guarded the horses and camels.

Women were everywhere the arbiters of man's prowess. Champions, riding against one another with the lance, would call out the names of women, either their loves or, curiously to our ideas, their sisters. Sometimes, in pitched battles, women in gaily decorated camel litters were carried into battle in the midst of their tribal contingents, for whom they formed rallying points. In the heat of battle the girls would stand up in their litters, let their long hair fall over their shoulders, bare their breasts, sing the ballads of past heroes, or urge on the wavering warriors by name. Needless to say the girls were never interfered with by either side. Here are a few stories illustrating the bedouin attitude to women.

Sultan ibn Suwait was a famous shaikh of the Dhafeer, three or four generations ago. It is related that somewhere on the Hejaz border, many hundred miles from the Dhafeer camp, a girl was once robbed by a raiding party who took her camel. The name of Sultan ibn Suwait was known throughout Arabia and, in her resentment at such treatment, the girl cried out, 'Oh that Sultan were here to defend a woman.' The gossip of the desert repeated the story till it crossed Arabia to the Dhafeer camp. Sultan swore that no maiden should appeal to him in vain and crossed four hundred miles of desert with a raiding party to obtain redress for an unknown girl.

Two of the most powerful tribes in Arabia were Ataiba and Qahtan, whose shaikhs, Ibn Humaid and Ibn Hadi, were in the old days always at war. Once upon a time Ibn Hadi had a most beautiful daughter who resolutely refused to marry any of the many suitors who presented themselves. The then Ibn Humaid was a famous raider and had carried plunder and war through the camps and herds of Qahtan. His prowess was the talk of every camp and fireside in Arabia.

In Ibn Hadi's tent many long and anxious debates were held as to how to resist the daring assaults of Ibn Humaid and Ataiba, and the Qahtan shaikhs swore to sacrifice their camels as a thank-offering if their ever-victorious enemy should fall into their hands. One day yet another suitor presented himself at the tent of Ibn Hadi to solicit the hand of his daughter and her father came in to consult her. But she answered that she would never marry at all, unless she could find a bedouin chief, the most gallant in war, the most generous, the most handsome and the most witty of the Arabs. The suitor retired discomforted.

But a Sulubbi, one of the tinkers of Arabia, a menial who goes from tribe to tribe mending pots and pans, had overheard the conversation. 'There is only one man, my little mistress, who answers the description you gave,' whined the tinker, 'and that is Ibn Humaid.' 'Oh, if only I could see him once,' said the maiden, 'but he is an enemy and Qahtan have sworn to sacrifice their camels if they could kill him.'

The tinker wandered off and one day told the story in the camp of Ataiba, where it came to the ears of Ibn Humaid. That night he slipped away from the camp unnoticed and, riding alone for several days across the desert, reached the camp of Ibn Hadi. At night, with only his drawn sword in his hand, he slipped into the camp and crawled into the tent of Ibn Hadi, where his daughter was sleeping alone in a curtained apartment. Waking her quietly, he told her who he was and they remained talking in whispers until dawn appeared. The girl implored him to go, saying that he was courting death, but he refused, and soon the appearance of broad daylight made escape impossible.

In bedouin camps, the chief makes coffee early in the morning and the men of the tribe collect in his tent to drink it and discuss the affairs of the day. Soon the tribesmen began to collect in Ibn Hadi's tent, until all the leaders were present, talking and drinking coffee and divided only by a curtain from their bitterest enemy, Ibn Humaid of Ataiba.

Then the girl stood up and, looking over the curtain which divided the guest part of the tent from that of the family, said to her father, 'O father, I ask you to grant me a request.' 'It is granted before you ask it,' replied her father, with whom she was his favourite child. Turning to the assembled chiefs of the tribe, she said, 'You are all witnesses of my father's promise.' 'We are witnesses,' they answered.

Looking to her father again, she asked him to spare the life of Ibn Humaid. The old man merely told her not to be silly. Ibn Humaid had done great damage to Qahtan and anyhow he was hundreds of miles away in the tents of Ataiba. When she answered that he was in the tent, Ibn Hadi leapt to his feet, but the girl cried out, 'O Qahtan! you were witnesses of my father's oath!' The old men intervened, saying that it was true, the girl's request had been granted. Ibn Humaid emerged as an honoured guest, and Qahtan, to fulfil their vows, sacrificed their camels to celebrate the wedding feast.

Such stories could be endlessly multiplied, for romantic courtship played an essential part in the emotional make-up of the bedouin and his pursuit of glory.

We have seen that personal distinction, rather than service to the community, was the principal objective of the bedouin warrior. This avidity for personal fame likewise characterized other customs for which Arab nomads were peculiar. The most striking of these was perhaps generosity.

The maintenance of life in a bedouin community, depending on herds of animals, was liable to extreme vicissitudes. Firstly, the clumsy size of the great flocks, in a community constantly at war, rendered them always liable to be looted by an enemy. This situation introduced an element of instability into life, which might well result in a man being one day the richest of the tribe and the next day entirely destitute. But this destitution in itself was by no means hopeless, because the victim might in time be able, by raiding other people, to restore his own fortunes. The bedouins had a saying that the wealth of this world was like dirt on the hands, always coming and going.

At the same time, the necessity of being able to load up all one's possessions every day on camels made the accumulation of reserves of wealth almost impossible. This way of life induced a detached manner of looking on worldly wealth and a completely improvident outlook on the future. At the same time, the thirst for personal distinction encouraged men to perform the most extravagant acts of generosity to appeal to the imagination and gave rise to fantastic standards of munificence.

Thus we find bedouins, after undergoing almost incredible hardships for a quite trivial gain, prepared to give away all they possess merely in order to perform a theatrical gesture. The attitude of the villager was entirely different and his plodding and laborious life, combined with the possibility of accumulating wealth in a fixed dwelling place, made him essentially thrifty and provident.

Hospitality was the most obvious form assumed by this desire to shine in generosity. Needless to say, every nomad keeps open house, or at least open tent, at all hours of the day and night. Indeed the tent is normally divided in half by a curtain, one half for guests and the other for the family. Moreover custom prescribed that guests, who may be complete strangers, must be fed and waited on for three days before the host can enquire where they came from or what is their business.

The same generosity is extended by nomads to all poor persons. In a bedouin tribe no human being, however poor, old, deserted, weak or diseased is ever neglected. Amongst bedouins it is impossible to die of hunger, and a bedouin shaikh may often be seen after a feast himself distributing meat, bread and rice to a crowd of poor children or sending selected morsels over to the tents of old women or widows camped nearby.

The meanest and the poorest of nomads will literally kill the last animal he owns to provide a feast for a guest, who may be a complete stranger and who is quite probably a rich man who customarily overeats. On the northern Hejaz border there were nomads so poor that they had no tents and lived in caves or beneath the shrubs of the desert. But these people, if they saw a traveller passing by, would run out and waylay him, and compel him, almost by force, to turn aside in order that they might kill the last goat they owned in the world to make him a meal.

A typical nomadic scene is that given in Genesis XVIII. Abraham 'sat in his tent door in the heat of the day. And he lifted up his eyes and looked, and lo! Three men stood by him; and when he saw them he ran to meet them from the tent door, and bowed himself to the ground, and said, "My Lord, if now I have found favour in thy sight, pass not away, I pray thee, from thy servant. Let a little water, I pray you, be fetched and wash your feet and rest yourselves under the tree. And I will fetch a morsel of bread and comfort ye your hearts; after that ye shall pass on; for therefore are ye come to your servant" – And they said, "Do as thou hast said." and Abraham hastened into the tent unto Sarah and said, "Make ready quickly three measures of fine meal, knead it and make cakes upon the hearth." And Abraham ran unto the herd and fetched a calf tender and good, and gave it to a young man and he hasted to dress it, and he took butter and milk and the calf which he had dressed and set it before them; and he stood by them under the tree and they did eat.'

Abraham is believed to have lived about 1800 B.C. This little scene, therefore, took some three thousand eight hundred years ago and yet every small detail coincides with what I so often saw. Notice that Abraham *ran* to meet the men and invite them, although they were complete strangers, and persuaded them to stop by saying that he would only just fetch a little bread and water. How often has the same been said to me – 'just a bit of bread quickly'. But no sooner had he induced them to sit down than he runs off and kills his best calf. And finally, having prepared a banquet, he himself stands to serve them while they eat. For the nomads to this day carry hospitality so far that the host, having ruined himself to provide a feast for a complete stranger, will not eat with him, but insists on remaining standing to wait upon him.

In the tents of the shaikhs, it was common for slaves at dinner time to stand outside and call, 'Let anyone who wants to eat come to dinner. Anybody who does not come has only himself to blame.' Incidentally, slavery is, of course, no longer legal but in many cases the descendants of former slaves consider themselves part of the family and have remained with it voluntarily, generation after generation.

Ibn Muhaid, a great shaikh of Anaiza, made himself famous through one winter of drought and famine because his slaves called every night before his tent for all who were hungry to come and dine, and it is still a saying in northern Arabia, 'Ibn Muhaid is calling to dinner.' Our Lord's parable of the man who sent his servants into the highways and hedges to compel men to come to his feast was no exaggeration.

To provide only enough food for the guests would have been considered extremely mean by Arab tribes. Even in the month of Ramadhan, when the whole tribe was fasting, bedouins would kill two or three sheep to make lunch for an honourable guest, although most of the food would be wasted or spoilt.

But they will not even limit their fantastic hospitality to human beings. The semi-mythical hero, Antar ibn Sheddad, on the occasion of his wedding, is said to have slaughtered hundreds of camels on the hills in order that the wolves might also join in the festivities. I myself knew a man with the Dhafeer called Ma'ashi al Dhib, or the Diner of Wolves, who, if a wolf howled behind his tent at night, would take out a kid and tie it up in the desert. 'No guest,' he would say, 'shall call on me in the evening without dining.'

In addition to the three main characteristics of this bedouin culture – glory in war, a romantic attitude toward women and lavish generosity – they possess other customs of a similar nature, with the same imaginative appeal. One of these is the obligation to defend the weak, or any person appealing for their protection. A bedouin would often risk his life to protect a stranger, a cripple, a sick person, a widow or an orphan who had appealed to him. The reader will recognize the resemblance between such customs and the knights errant of mediaeval Europe who derived similar ideas from the Arabs of Spain.

An incident which occurred not many years ago in the Ruwalla may serve to illustrate this custom. The Mashhur family were connections of the Shaalan, the shaikhs of the Ruwalla. One of the chiefs demanded something from an old woman of the Sherarat, a low-caste tribe whom the bedouins affected to regard with contempt. The woman appealed for help to Ibn Mashhur, who championed her cause and rescued her from his own shaikh, and from the oppression of which she complained.

I have already mentioned that bedouin champions sometimes called the names of their sisters as battle cries. Ibn Mashhur, to commemorate his knightly act, thereafter used as a war cry 'I am the brother of Rabda,' the name of the old tinker woman whom he had protected.

Another nomad custom is the protection of any person who appeals to the tent. In 1924 I rode across the Syrian desert on a camel from Iraq to Trans-Jordan. When among the Beni Sakhr tribe in the latter country, I noticed a boy who obviously came from some tribe six hundred miles away on the Persian Gulf. He told me the following story. He had accompanied a large raid of Ikhwan from Central Arabia, who had attacked the Beni Sakhr the year before, killing many of the tribe and plundering great numbers of their camels.

Our youth, who came from the Mutair tribe, the followers of Faisal al Duweesh, was wounded in the battle and fell unconscious from his camel. He did not recover consciousness until the cold early dawn next morning. The Beni Sakhr had stripped him naked and left him for dead on the ground in front of their tents. Scrambling dizzily to his feet, he walked shakily towards the tents. A man was sitting in the nearest tent who, when he saw him, seized his rifle and ran out to kill him, crying for revenge for his brother who had been killed in the battle the day before.

But in his excitement the man worked the bolt of his rifle feverishly and two rounds jammed in the breech. The wounded boy staggered past him and fell into the tent. The tent-owner immediately put down his rifle, spread a carpet and began quietly to make coffee for the guest. Once he had entered the tent he was safe, and in fact he remained with the Beni Sakhr for several years. Here we see the two codes overlapping. The Ikhwan were religious fanatics who had massacred many of the Beni Sakhr, including the tent-owner's brother. Yet the protection of his tent outweighed, in the opinion of its owner, the desire for revenge for his brother.

An attractive custom among Arab nomads was the establishment of perpetual friendly relations as the result of a kind act. Early in the last century, an internal struggle for precedence took place in the Shammar tribe in Nejed, between two rival chiefs, Ibn Ali and Ibn Rasheed. The Ali family were successful, and Abdulla ibn Rasheed and his brother were driven penniless from the tribe which they had aspired to lead. They reached what is now Jordan, their worldly goods consisting of one camel between them, and dismounted at the tent of Al Khuraisha, the chief of Beni Sakhr. The shaikh was away but the family and servants entertained the guests hospitably. Unfortunately, during the night, their one camel died, exhausted by their flight from Central Arabia, and in the morning they were obliged to continue their journey on foot.

A short way from the camp, they met a bedouin riding towards the tents. He stopped them and asked the news, and they told him that they were travellers, that they had spent the night in Al Khuraisha's tent and that their camel had died. The rider asked whether their host had not supplied them with another, but Ibn Rasheed answered that the host was away. Thereupon the rider dismounted and, couching his camel, compelled them to mount; then, admitting that he himself was the chief, he swore that no guest of his should arrive riding and leave his tent on foot.

Many years later, Abdulla ibn Rasheed returned to Shammar, drove out his rival, Ibn Ali, and became Ameer of Northern Nejed, where he maintained the state of a prince in Hail. As long as he or his descendants ruled, a period of over fifty years until they were driven out by Ibn Saud in 1920, the Khuraisha family were treated by them as friends and allies, the recipients

of honours and gifts, in memory of the camel given by the old
Khuraisha chief to Abdulla ibn Rasheed in his destitution.

A pleasant incident occurred a few years ago between the tribes
of Anaiza and the Huwaitat. Auda abu Taya, shaikh of the
Huwaitat – the ally of Lawrence – led a raid against Anaiza. As
the Huwaitat charged down upon the enemy, one of the latter
threw himself on the mercy of Auda. The latter accepted his
surrender and assured him no harm would come to him, but the
man asked for a sign from Auda, which he could show to other
members of the raid as proof that the chief had granted him his
life. Auda hastily took the kerchief from his head and threw it to the
man, riding on bareheaded into the battle.

Several years later, Auda received a message from a man of
Anaiza that he was looking after a flock of goats for him. Left
with Auda's kerchief after the battle, the man was unwilling to
make away with his protector's property, so he sold the kerchief and
bought a nanny goat. After many years of breeding, the goat had
produced a flock, when a desert traveller was entrusted with the
message for Auda. The latter had long ago forgotten the incident,
had never known the man's name and their two tribes were still
at war. But the Anaizi had refused to forget the kindness.

King Abdulla of Jordan once told me a pleasing story. His
father, the late King Husain of the Hejaz, was, before 1914, Sherif
of Mecca. Although the Turks were the nominal rulers of the Hejaz,
control of the tribes was left very much in the hands of the
Sherif. One day Sherif Husain and his son, Abdulla, were travelling
in the desert with a caravan which was carrying their tents and
supplies.

The sherif decided to ride on ahead to choose a spot for the
midday halt and cantered on with Abdulla till they came to some
trees by a well, where they dismounted to await their followers. Some
camels were grazing near by, in charge of a small boy and his
smaller sister. With the freedom of bedouin children, they came
over to ask the news of the travellers, whom they obviously failed
to recognize.

The sherif enquired their tribe and was told the Begoom. 'Are
you not afraid,' asked Sherif Husain, 'to graze so near the boundaries
of the Ataiba tribe, who might loot your camels?' The small boy
was lying on his back, waving his feet in the air. 'Silly old man,'
he said, 'you don't understand anything.' Husain replied, 'I don't

understand what?' The little boy was laughing in a most vulgar and disrespectful manner. 'Don't you know,' he asked, 'that as long as old Husain is in control, we have nothing to fear from raiders?'

At this stage the caravan and escort came in sight and the little boy, to his terror, discovered that he had been talking to the sherif himself. But Husain was so pleased at this artless testimonial that every year thereafter until his exile, he summoned the boy and his sister (now both grown up) to Mecca and sent them home with gifts of food, clothing and money.

I have already said that one of the characteristics of the bedouin is love of a dramatic gesture. In this connection, an interesting custom is that of the *jaha* or deputation. For some offences, particularly those involving honour or personal dignity, the damages awarded under tribal law are so heavy as to be almost impossible for a poor man to pay. The injured party, moreover, will often refuse absolutely to accept any settlement of such a case. In these circumstances there may be nothing for it but to collect a deputation of the shaikhs and notables of the tribe, who arrive at the tent of the offended party. He prepares a feast for them but, when it is laid out, they refuse to eat until he promises in advance to grant their request.

The notables mediate, point out the advantages of a reconciliation and assure the offended party of the contrition of the offender. Only when the former, with a noble gesture, agrees to pardon the injury he has suffered, will the deputation partake of his food. Those who accuse the bedouin of being greedy for money must appreciate that often a poor man, who stands to receive large damages, will with a dramatic gesture forgo it all at the request of an honourable deputation.

The same spirit will often be shown even in minor matters. A man may complain against another for an unpaid debt, but if the debtor can humble himself in public to say 'I ask you to excuse me, O brother of Wadhha,' (naming his sister), the creditor will probably with a dramatic gesture cancel the whole debt.

Among pure nomads, the chiefs exercised virtually no authority, except such as depended on their own personality. This was due to the mobility of their followers. Any tribesman who resented the attitude of his shaikh could move away and join another tribe or section.

In any case, the simplicities of the nomad life made social distinctions impossible. The fact that everything had to be loaded on camels made the use of furniture impossible. The greatest shaikh and the humblest herdsman were obliged equally to sit on the ground.

These notes have been included in this narrative because the bedouin way of life has already almost ceased to exist. With oil wells and pipe-lines covering large areas of Arabia, industry, and with it materialism, will soon spread over the desert. The next generation of the knights of Arabia will be more familiar with the spanner than the lance. Indeed the whole trend of the Middle East today is imitation of the West in the search for industrialization and money – the very developments which seem to have caused so much discontent and unhappiness in the West.

Under the influence of this tendency, the educated citizens of the Middle East regard the bedouins and their way of life with dislike and contempt, as holding back the industrialization and the modernization of their countries. Indeed, when speaking to foreigners, they will often deny that such people as bedouins even exist.

Such is the frequent course of social change. The old system is regarded with shame and aversion and all traces of it are deliberately obliterated. Only centuries later are antiquarian societies formed painfully to rescue from deliberate and intentional oblivion the noble customs of their ancestors, once again held in honour.

But however despised the romantic and uneconomic past culture of the Arab nomads may be, there can be no doubt that a thousand to twelve hundred years ago it constituted the much admired model on which arose the structure of mediaeval European chivalry.

16

Dyarchy

The system set up for the government of Iraq in 1921 involved the double-manning of a number of appointments. During Turkish times the great majority of the senior appointments in the administration had been held by Turks, who had now disappeared. In addition, the Ottoman Government itself had been corrupt, out-of-date and inefficient.

As a result, the British Government considered that the establishment of an administration on modern lines necessitated the assistance of a number of British officials to help their Iraqi colleagues. The ministries included British advisers, although the executive authority rested with the Iraqi Minister. The same system applied to the police, the post office, the public works and other departments.

For general administration, the country was divided into provinces, known as divisions, each under a mutasarrif or governor, who held authority over all civil departments in his area. At the mutasarrif's elbow was a British official, known as the Administrative Inspector, who possessed no executive authority. This double-manning of senior appointments was known as dyarchy.

The ideal form of government, it has been said, would be despotism and an angel from heaven, a solution impossible of practical application. But dyarchy was an even more impracticable solution (if there can be degrees of impossibility) for it necessitated the presence of two angels from heaven.

I cannot avoid the opinion that British administrative advice and help was of great benefit to Iraq, enabling her to build up competent services in every department within five or six years. Yet efficiency often clashes with politics. The imposition of advisers conveyed to the Iraqi officials a suggestion of inferiority. If no British advisers had been imposed on them, it would have taken much longer to set up the administration, but no political resentments would have been incurred.

The French seizure of Syria, moreover, contrary to British promises, created the suspicion that Britain intended to establish colonial rule in Iraq – a suspicion which was entirely unjustified. It must be remembered that the Woodrow Wilson plan for mandates was originally purely idealistic. It was thought to be the positive duty of the leading nations to assist new countries to form modern administrations and much of this idealism persisted in Britain, though the Iraqi nationalists did not realize the fact.

Yet another, and insuperable, complication was that the country was out of control and Iraq had no forces of her own with which to establish order. The use of British forces to establish public security was, therefore, inevitable, a necessity which rendered unavoidable a British share in the government which was to direct the operations.

[Looking back, fifty years later, on the stresses and strains in Iraq in the 1920s, the frictions seem to me to have been due to the same factors as have since caused such untold confusion and misery in the world. There were no divergent interests between Britain and Iraq which could not have been solved by quiet negotiation. But the possibility of a smooth and amicable hand-over was destroyed by suspicion, resentment, impatience and, above all, by political agitation, leading to violence. The use of violence itself led to an exacerbation of hatreds, when in reality no violence had ever been necessary.]

In 1926 I received a letter from the War Office in London notifying me that I had been long enough absent from the regular Army and that I would shortly be recalled. I was utterly dedicated to Iraq and to love of its people and was unable to contemplate the possibility of leaving the country and returning to the barrack square in England. I accordingly resigned my commission in the British Army.

Meanwhile, the adviser to the Ministry of the Interior, Mr. (later Sir Kinahan) Cornwallis, hearing of my predicament, offered me a ten-year contract with the Iraq Government in the appointment of an Administrative Inspector. I was overjoyed at the opportunity of remaining in Iraq and signed the contract in November 1926. From the point of view of a worldly career, the decision was rash.

The Anglo-Iraqi Treaty was to last for only four years from the date of ratification of the Allied peace with Turkey (which took place on 6 August, 1924), that is to say until 6 August, 1928. Thereafter the Iraq mandate would end, the country would become completely independent, and it was extremely doubtful whether British Administrative Inspectors would remain. I had, therefore, exchanged a regular commission for a nominal ten-year contract which would, in practice, probably be terminated in two years. But my decision was emotional rather than wise. I loved Iraq and could not contemplate leaving her.

I had been an Army officer since I left school in August 1914. Now I found myself a civilian, with an almost valueless contract which would probably be terminated in two years' time.

I was posted as Administrative Inspector to the Diwaniya Division on the Middle Euphrates. The mutasarrif was an experienced administrator, who had served under the Ottoman régime and we co-operated very loyally and happily together.

The task of setting up a just and reasonable administration seemed to be almost insuperable. The whole division or province, was entirely agricultural and many of the most inextricable problems concerned land.

In the earliest times, some three or four thousand years ago, the land was thought to belong to the local tribal god. As the centuries passed, these ideas gradually developed into the belief that the land, like the rain and the sunshine, belonged to the one true God and could not be monopolized by men. In Ottoman times the conception that God was the landholder changed into the principle that all land belonged to the state. Then an exception came to be made for houses and gardens. The builder of a house or the planter of an orchard acquired the right of ownership, but the wheat and rice lands remained the property of the government.

While, however, such theories might be accepted in principle, the cultivated lands were in practice occupied by communities and by individuals. These people dug irrigation canals, erected water lifts, sowed and reaped. Each man, in fact, owned his plot of land from the produce of which he lived. As the custom was that a man's inheritance was divided up equally between his heirs, not inherited by the eldest, many of the plots were extremely small.

Since everybody in the community knew everyone else's plots of land, they sold freely to one another for cash, the community witnessing the deal, without any records on paper. It was, indeed, impossible to preserve records of land sales as the country had never been surveyed. But tribal land ownership did not always so smoothly pursue the even tenor of its way. The tribes were all armed and out of control. There were fights and land was seized by force, then re-conquered. As nobody had any legal tenure, it was difficult to decide to whom the land 'belonged' at any given moment. The example of the Fatlah tribe will serve as an illustration.

The Euphrates, which from Ana to Ramadi had run in a single channel between rocky desert hills, split up at the Hindiya Barrage into many different streams. One of these flowed southwards through the little market town of Shamiya.

The river below the town was occupied by the Fatlah tribe, cultivators of rice lands and date palms. In 1870, the shaikh of the Fatlah was a certain Faraun – the Arabic for Pharaoh, a monarch whose despotism his namesake aspired to imitate. Faraun was a great baron who distributed the irrigated lands on the Euphrates to his tribesmen with a lordly hand. No government authority existed in the area. It never occured to Fàraun that one day the tribesmen to whom he apportioned the land would claim before the law to be the equals of his own descendants.

Faraun died in 1903 and his sons succeeded to his authority. All the tribal lands were open rice fields with no trees. The Ottoman Government did not attempt to extend its control to Shamiya until 1909. In 1911 many of the tribesmen began to plant date palms on their plots of land.

In 1912, however, the sons of Faraun rebelled. A Turkish military force arrived in the area, the rising was suppressed, the sons of Faraun were imprisoned and their lands declared confiscated. The tribesmen made direct contact with the government as independent citizens, and divided up the shaikhs' land between them.

In 1915, when the British landed in Basra, the Ottoman Government proclaimed a Holy War and called on the tribes to raise levies to fight the British. This could only be organized through the shaikhs. The sons of Faraun were accordingly released from prison and given full official support. Naturally the first thing they did was to wreak vengeance on their own tribesmen who had occupied their lands. From this date, a bitter feud commenced between the descendants of Faraun and their own tribesmen.

During the war years, first the Ottoman and then the British O.E.T.A. supported the authority of the shaikhs as the easiest way of maintaining law and order, thereby enabling them to continue the oppression of their own tribesmen. During the 1911 to 1914 period, while the shaikhs were in prison, the tribesmen had planted date palms on their lands. When I arrived in Diwaniya in 1926, the shaikhs were demanding a share of the date crop from these trees, although they had had no share in planting them.

None of the parties to these bitter disputes possessed any documents or legal tenure and thus their quarrels could not be referred to the law courts. The only solution was an investigation by an administrative official and a common-sense compromise settlement.

When I was in Diwaniya in the summer of 1927, the Ministry of the Interior deputed me personally to investigate the whole problem and to make recommendations for a final settlement between the shaikhs and the tribesmen. As an Intelligence Officer, I had developed a technique of going and living with people about whom I wished to obtain information, a method rendered possible by Arab standards of hospitality.

I spent many long days in the flaming heat of an Iraqi summer, walking over the swampy rice fields and talking to shaikhs, tribesmen and local officials. If witnesses had been called to an enquiry in a government office, they would all have recited carefully prepared but mendacious statements. By means of informal chats in their own homes, I discovered far more about their problems than could ever have been elicited in a court of law. Finally I submitted proposals for a settlement to the Ministry of the Interior. The sequel will be told later.

Unfortunately for me, the mutasarrif, my colleague, was transferred when I had been about two months in Diwaniya. Lateef Beg, the new mutasarrif, arrived in Diwaniya and took over. He was a former Turkish Army officer who had fought with Faisal and Lawrence and had returned to Iraq when the French drove Faisal from Damascus. In the 1920 Rebellion he had ambushed a British column and killed several men. By this means he had become something of a hero to the Nationalists.

The tribes of the Diwaniya division had done most of the fighting in the 1920 rebellion and were still looked upon as potential trouble makers. No sooner was Lateef Beg made mutasarrif than the Nationalists urged him to win the shaikhs over to the Nationalist Party by administrative favouritism. This meant bringing pressure on tax assessors to reduce their taxes and ensuring that, whenever they were involved in a dispute, they should win the case.

Shortly after his arrival Lateef Beg and I drove over together to Shamiya. My report on the Fatlah had been submitted to the Ministry of the Interior, but no reply had been received from them. Lateef and I sat talking to the qaimaqam in his office. When I had occasion to leave the room for a few minutes, Lateef hastily ordered the qaimaqam to give a third of the date crop from the tribal date gardens to Abdul Wahid, the leader of the descendants of Shaikh Faraun, who was a member of the Nationalist Party. A few days later an order was received from the Ministry of the Interior accepting my proposed settlement for the Fatlah disputes and ordering the mutasarrif to enforce it. He was thus obliged to cancel his order to the qaimaqam to allow Abdul Wahid to collect a share of the tribesmen's date crop.

Under the Ottoman régime, the produce of the land was directly taxed. Each year, the harvest was estimated or measured and the cultivator was taxed on the amount of grain he harvested. It was a bad system for it did not encourage the farmer to increase the productivity of his land. On the contrary, if he left all his land fallow, he paid no taxes at all.

The rice crop, which was the most valuable, was measured by parties of men with ropes before it was harvested. But other grain crops, wheat, barley, maize or millet, were 'estimated'. A party of officials rode round the fields and estimated – or guessed – the amount of grain. Sometimes this was done while the crop was still standing, sometimes on the threshing floor. To estimate accurately was a highly skilled occupation, but the system also facilitated favouritism and even bribery.

It so happened that the winter crops had been estimated in the Afek sub-division and the result had been sent to the Ministry of Finance. The latter, however, suspected that the larger landowners had been underestimated, while the poor had been overcharged. It accordingly adopted the unusual procedure of ordering that the wheat and barley crops of Afek be measured by rope, a procedure which was carried out before the arrival of Lateef Beg, when I was acting mutasarrif.

The resulting figures showed that the rich shaikhs had indeed been let off too lightly, while the poorer cultivators had been overtaxed. The shaikhs hastened to Baghdad to complain and, by political manoeuvring in the capital, succeeded in having their taxes reduced. Meanwhile, Lateef Beg had arrived. The shaikhs returned to Diwaniya in high fettle with letters of recommendation to Lateef from the Nationalist Party, urging him to help them.

A short time afterwards, the leader of the rich shaikhs, a certain Hajji Mehedi, with an armed following, prevented the government irrigation engineer from examining the Afek irrigation canals, which were reported to be silting up. The silting of the canals would, of course, have ruined Hajji Mehedi and his followers, but he was not looking so far ahead. Elated by the support of the politicians in Baghdad, he was anxious to show his power by defying the local government.

I urged Lateef Beg to order the police to investigate this armed obstruction of a government official. I recorded the result in my diary:

I had it out with Lateef Beg today. I told him that it was a capital mistake to support people like Hajji Mehedi for political reasons. They only interpreted such action as weakness, and defied government authority as a result. I expressed the view that, unless he put his foot down, the Afek area would get out of hand.

He assured me that he had no desire to favour anybody for political reasons, but that he wanted to avoid having a row with the ministers, who were all his friends, and who kept writing him private letters urging him to 'help' certain people. He went on to say that he had never wanted to come to Diwaniya, that he had protested all along, and that he only wanted to get away from it now.

He was, of course, partly right. Certain politicians in high places do not care about administration, but they want their political supporters favoured and they tell Lateef to do it.

Another common form of intrigue was the organization of petitions, bearing hundreds of illegible signatures, seals and thumb impressions, or of telegrams to the Ministry, which were subsequently published in the press. The Nationalists were alleged to be instigating a petition among the Diwaniya tribes urging the abolition of British Administrative Inspectors. Other shaikhs came to me, offering to get up a petition in my favour, but I told them on no account to do anything of the kind.

At one time there was a strong rumour, which even reached Baghdad, that Lateef was organizing a petition against me. I asked him if it was true but he replied, 'I have heard those stories too, but they are lies.'

In our personal relations we were always polite and even cordial, in spite of the intense atmosphere of intrigue with which we were surrounded. I find this entry in my diary. 'I am always hearing tales of what Lateef has said against me and I have several times said to him, "People tell me that you find it difficult to work with me. If you really do so, do please tell me what the trouble is." He several times replied with genuine cordiality (it seemed to me) that he had never said anything of the kind, and that he and I were dear old friends.'

Indeed I noticed that, if I stayed five or six days in the office, talking to him every day, we became quite warm and affectionate. But I always felt an urge to get out and see the people in the out districts – after all I was called an inspector of the administration. As a result, I would go away on tour for three or four days – to see the measurement of the rice crop or to study some tribal dispute. When I returned, I would find Lateef cold and formal. Obviously letters had arrived from Baghdad, or some intriguers had told him stories against me.

'I cannot help liking him,' I wrote on another occasion, 'but I always feel he is susceptible to influence. He has never had a chance here in Diwaniya. The politicians in Baghdad keep writing to him to work administrative ramps to help their political supporters. If he does so, I protest. If he does not, he is abused by his political friends in Baghdad. If his ramps are made public, he is obliged to cancel them and feels that he has lost prestige. Yet I still like him. If it were not for the politics, we should be happy together.'

On 24 July, 1927, I received a letter from the Adviser to the Ministry of the Interior, informing me that the British Government had suggested the opening of negotiations for a new treaty, and had invited King Faisal to London. The existing Anglo-Iraqi Treaty had only one year left to run. The negotiations, however, did little to reduce the atmosphere of intrigue. The Nationalists seem to have felt that a disturbance on the Middle Euphrates, ostensibly directed against the British, might be a means of bringing pressure to bear on the negotiators.

One of the complications in this tangle of intrigues was that the only force in Iraq available to suppress rebellion was still the R.A.F. Thus if the Nationalists raised a tribal rising, the British would have to suppress it, a development which the Nationalists could claim as proof that Britain was the oppressor. Anticipating events, it may here be noted that the negotiations encountered no great difficulty and that, a year later, Iraq achieved complete independence and became a member of the League of Nations. It is probable that this would have happened in any case, even if there had been no Nationalist Party and no political agitation. There was much opposition in Britain herself to the continued British presence in Iraq. Nevertheless the political animosity which had been engendered most tragically and unnecessarily remained.

Is it possible now to deduce any lessons from the tragedy of Anglo-Iraqi relations? Britain had occupied Iraq in the First World War in the course of operations against Turkey, without thought of the ultimate settlement. In the course of the operations, however, it did emerge that the route from Egypt to Iraq and down the Persian Gulf would constitute an alternative way to India and Australia other than the Suez Canal. A friendly Iraq would form a staging post on such a route.

That Britain had no intention to use force against Iraq seems to be proved by the fact that, soon after the Armistice, almost all the British forces were withdrawn, with the result that there were virtually no troops in the country to suppress the 1920 Rebellion.

We must also allow for the fact that Britain felt a responsibility to help Iraq to stability and prosperity. It is too cynical to represent Britain as solely motivated by greed or by her own interests.

On the other hand, the Iraqis had been profoundly affected by the confused promises made by Britain to the Sherif of Mecca, to the French and to the Zionists, some of which were incompatible. The Arabs had inherited a cynical political outlook from the Ottomans, and were impressed by the apparently vast power of the British Empire. Such an immense power, they thought, could not possibly make a mistake, and hence its conflicting promises were attributed, without a second's hesitation, to deliberate treachery.

They failed to appreciate, indeed they rejected the idea with contempt, that democracy and bureaucracy are often extremely inefficient and, at the same time, that British policy was frequently deeply affected by moral or political idealism. As a result of their completely different assumptions and mental backgrounds, mutual confidence between Britain and the Iraqi Nationalists was virtually unobtainable.

Should Britain then have refused the mandate for Iraq? Had she done so, Turkey would almost certainly have invaded and annexed Mosul and northern Iraq. At a later date, Ibn Saud might well have destroyed the young nation or at least thrown it into confusion.

Where such passionate political emotions are evoked, mere administration passes unnoticed. Yet it is true that the Ottomans did indeed leave Iraq in an extremely primitive and chaotic condition. Moreover, all the senior officials having been Turks, no experienced administrative or technical officials remained. I cannot help feeling that Britain rendered great services to Iraq in organizing such humdrum services as the police, the post office, the public works, irrigation and finance.

Such administrative assistance was, admittedly, only required for a short time until Iraqis could be trained, and the seven years' duration of the Iraq mandate was probably sufficient. Nevertheless these services were indeed rendered and were extremely valuable, though they were scarcely noticed by the world at large, in the passionate political atmosphere of nationalism.

[The moral, it seems to me, writing fifty years later, points to the terrible dangers which lie in the impatience, suspicion, intolerance and violence, which are latent in human nature. In fact, there was from the commencement no cause for conflict between Britain and the Iraqi Nationalists.

But once violence has been used, the after effects may remain for generations or even for centuries. The result was the 1920 Rebellion, leaving its inevitable legacy of violence, hatred, resentment and the desire for revenge, which continued through the Second World War, although there was in reality no cause for conflict.

The tragedy has since been endlessly repeated all over the world. Politicians in many different countries have acquired the technique of stirring up to violence the people of their nations and urging them on to murder, terrorism and civil war.

The world has not yet grasped the lesson that violence only makes every problem worse, and that violence, once used, continues to produce violence, for generations and for centuries.]

For myself, the year 1927, when Lateef Beg was with me in Diwaniya, was perhaps the most unhappy of my life. I was devoted to the Iraqis of all classes – government officials, cultivators, shepherds, bedouins – excepting perhaps the politicians. I was realizing increasingly what immense scope existed for the improvement of the administration, how co-operative everybody was in introducing such reforms and how appreciative they were of services rendered to them, if inspired by genuine love. I was ready to throw myself into the work with all the enthusiasm in my nature.

My experience in the First World War had shown me both the value and the joy of comradeship in such a labour of love. And then I found myself thwarted at every turn by those who wished to use administrative favouritism to gain political supporters, regardless of the good of the country.

Even worse, I found myself betrayed by my closest colleagues, not because we were enemies or because they disagreed with my views but, often unwillingly, because they felt themselves obliged to assist the intrigues of the politicians to whom they owed their positions. Being of a somewhat emotional nature, the lack of frankness of some of my colleagues caused me acute unhappiness.

For the rest, 1927 left me ever afterwards with an intense aversion to party politics which so often tempt those who indulge in them to place the interests of their party before those of their country.

17

Back to the Desert

While I was engrossed in land disputes or in measuring the rice crop in the Diwaniya and Hilla Divisions, events had been taking their course on the Iraq-Nejed frontier. I have already mentioned the signature of the Bahra Agreement between Iraq and Ibn Saud on 1 November, 1925, in which both sides agreed to prevent their tribes from raiding. The two governments also agreed not to seduce the tribes of the other party from their allegiance.

The signature of the agreement had led to an immediate détente and the winter 1925-26 had passed without raids, though I had been obliged to live with the tribes in a white tent, to give them the courage to move out. In reality, the absence of raids during that winter had not been due to the Bahra Agreement but to the fact that Ibn Saud and the Ikhwan had been absent, fighting King Husain in the Hejaz.

Meanwhile the British and Iraq governments and the R.A.F. had declared themselves satisfied that permanent peace had been established between Nejed and Iraq. All defensive organization was dismantled and even defensive planning was abandoned.

In October 1926, however, shortly before I left Nasiriya, a large raiding party of Shammar from the Jezira in northern Iraq passed down through the desert west of the Euphrates and looted considerable numbers of camels from the friendly neighbouring state of Kuwait. I had long been arguing with Baghdad that the Iraq government *must* assume control of its own deserts and that, to do so, it was essential to establish police posts equipped with wireless on the important wells.

The raid on Kuwait had nothing to do with Ibn Saud, but it reinforced my arguments for desert police posts. I had recommended the establishment of a police post at the wells of Busaiya. It so happened that the Shammar raid had watered there. This clinched the

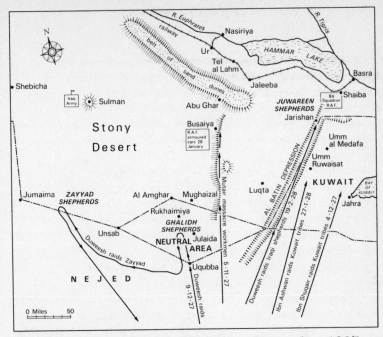

Map 10 The Renewal of Raiding, December 1927

NOTES: (1) On 5 November, 1927, a Mutair raid massacred the workmen building the fort at Busaiya.

(2) On 9 December, 1927, Duweesh massacred Iraqi shepherds in the Neutral Area. Aircraft flew over during the massacre, but did not realize what was happening.

(3) Duweesh did not return home, but proceeded west and raided Zayyad shepherds on 19 December near Jumaima.

(4) On 4 December, 1927, Ibn Shuqair raided Kuwait tribes.

(5) On 27 January, 1928, Ibn Ashwan raided Kuwait tribes at Umm Ruwaisat in Kuwait.

(6) On 19 February, 1928, Duweesh raided Juwareen shepherds at Jarishan, only fifty miles from the R.A.F base at Shaiba. Retiring raiders were bombed on 19, 20 and 21 February. One aircraft was shot down in flames.

(7) In January 1928 R.A.F. armoured cars were sent to Busaiya, as static guard for workmen building the post.

(8) During these operations, I was in Diwaniya. I returned to the desert on 2 March, 1928.

argument. The erection of a police post at Busaiya (Map 9, page 136) was sanctioned in February 1927, four months after I had left the Southern Desert.

In September 1927, a party of twelve workmen were sent to Busaiya to build the post, with an escort of seven policemen. On the night of 5-6 November, 1927, a raiding party of Ikhwan Mutair rushed the camp and massacred workmen and police alike. The government, however, decided to continue the work, and more workmen were sent out under an escort of R.A.F. armoured cars.

Meanwhile the situation in Nejed had undergone a complete reversal. In 1924-25, Ibn Saud had been in complete and absolute control. He had allowed the Ikhwan to raid Iraq out of hostility to King Faisal, who was secretly encouraging pilfering raids into Nejed. During 1925 and 1926, both Ibn Saud and the Ikhwan had been away fighting in the Hejaz.

Early in 1927, however, the Hejaz war was over and all the Ikhwan were back in Nejed. Ibn Saud had now achieved as much as he considered possible. Both Iraq and Trans-Jordan were under British mandates and he did not wish to fight Britain.

Their victorious and immensely lucrative war in the Hejaz had, however, only whetted the appetite of the Ikhwan for more conquests. Worse still, the tribes of Ataiba and Mutair claimed that they had conquered the Hejaz, not Ibn Saud, who had no regular army and who relied upon his tribes to do his fighting. The chiefs of these two tribes were now so arrogant that they would no longer take Ibn Saud's orders. There is little doubt that they had decided to overthrow him and to divide Arabia between them.

Had they rebelled directly, however, the remainder of Nejed would have rallied to the King. But when they announced their intention to raid the 'infidel' Iraqis, the rest of Nejed could not but sympathize. Thus the real object of their attacks on Iraq was the overthrow of Ibn Saud himself.

The bomb did not take long to burst. On 4 December, 1927, Mutair raided the Kuwait tribes at Jahra, at the head of the Bay of Kuwait. On 9 December, Faisal al Duweesh massacred the Ghalidh tribe of Iraqi shepherds in the Neutral Area. An R.A.F. air reconnaissance flew over while the battle was in progress, but failed to realize what was happening. The Duweesh did not return home but continued to the west and, on 19 December, raided and slaughtered Beni Huchaim shepherds near Jumaima. Ibn Saud was at his capital, Riyadh, but took no action.

A lull followed the December raids, the Ikhwan waiting to see if Ibn Saud would march against them. As, however, nothing happened, they interpreted his inaction as weakness. On 27 January, 1928, Ali ibn Ashwan of Mutair raided the Kuwait tribes at Umm Ruwaisat in Kuwait territory, only seventy-five miles from Basra.

On 19 February, the Duweesh raided the Juwareen tribe of Iraqi shepherds at Jarishan, only fifty miles from the R.A.F. camp at Shaiba. Had he gone straight on, he might have reached Shaiba itself. The R.A.F. was flying all over the desert, but was unable to see the raiders. On this occasion they overtook the retiring raiders with their loot on the 19, 20 and 21 February, one aircraft being shot down in flames.

The R.A.F. and the Government were taken completely unawares by this sudden tornado of killing raids. All the previous defensive arrangements had been disbanded and the personnel dispersed. The R.A.F. now hastily established an operational headquarters at Ur.

The Government at last was thoroughly roused. Detachments of the Iraq Army were sent to Busaiya, Sulman and Shebicha, and permission was given for aircraft to cross the Iraq-Nejed frontier.

I was still employed as Administrative Inspector of the Hilla and Diwaniya Divisions, far from these stirring events. Suddenly I received a telegram transferring me to the Southern Desert. I left Diwaniya on 2 March, 1928. I was told that I had been posted as Administrative Inspector, Southern Desert, but my duties were not defined. As there was no administration, there did not seem to be anything to inspect. The area was full of R.A.F. and Iraq Army and I was a solitary civilian.

The Duweesh had been so successful that other tribes were stirred to follow his example. The chief of these was Ataiba, under Sultan ibn Humaid. On 24 March, he set out with a force allegedly twelve thousand strong to raid Iraq. In reality, however, it was probably too late for so large a force, as the water pools in the desert were drying up. Anxiety remained acute until the middle of April when it was reported that Ibn Humaid had turned back.

Meanwhile, the British Government had despatched Sir Gilbert Clayton to meet Ibn Saud in Jidda. It was he who had negotiated the Bahra Agreement in 1925. On 21 April, 1928, I left Baghdad by air with the Adviser to the Ministry of the Interior, Mr. Cornwallis, and joined Sir Gilbert Clayton in Jidda.

From the commencement, agreement was impossible. The real dispute was not between Ibn Saud and Iraq, but between Ibn Saud and the Ikhwan rebels. The latter, whom the conquest of the Hejaz had made insufferably arrogant, were determined to overthrow the King. The latter had trained the Ikhwan as the spearhead of his army and had encouraged their fanaticism in order to defeat his Arab rivals, Ibn Rasheed and King Husain. But now his frontiers marched with Iraq and Trans-Jordan, both British mandates. He realized that he could not fight Britain, but he could not avoid a clash with her unless he could bring the Ikhwan to heel. However he was passionately desirous to avoid a civil war.

In this dilemma, he wished to persuade the British and Iraq Governments to demolish their police post at Busaiya. He hoped then to return to the Ikhwan and say, 'Look, by diplomacy I have achieved what you failed to do by force. Leave it to me to deal with Iraq.' It is unlikely that this would have brought back the Ikhwan to obedience, for they were already determined to dethrone him. But he clutched at the hope, like a drowning man.

The Iraqi case was that, in former times, their government had no control in the desert. Their bedouins, in those days, used to steal camels from Nejed, which caused Ibn Saud to protest vociferously. At last the Iraq Government was establishing police posts in the desert, and had, indeed, put an end to all raids into Nejed. But now Ibn Saud was demanding the removal of the police posts, which would lead to a resumption of raiding. He could not have it both ways.

Ostensibly the negotiations were between Britain, Iraq and Ibn Saud. In fact, we were all on the same side, facing the rebel Ikhwan. There could be no peace until they were brought to heel, but Ibn Saud was unwilling to admit that he could not control them. After weeks of futile talking, we returned to Iraq.

We were back in Baghdad at the end of May 1928. It was evident that the winter 1928-29 would witness a hurricane of killing raids, if not open war with Nejed. We had six months to prepare.

Meanwhile I had already drawn up a plan and had submitted it to Baghdad before we went to Jidda. The key factors on which my plan was based were the following:

(a) Air reconnaissance over so vast an area (about two-thirds the size of England) had completely failed. The Duweesh had come within fifty miles of the R.A.F. base at Shaiba. It was obvious that some ground scouting force was necessary.

(b) Even when aircraft overtook raiders returning home with their loot, the casualties they could inflict were negligible. A ground fighting force was essential.

(c) The Iraq tribes were numerous and armed with rifles, but had no discipline or organization.

(d) The 45,000 square miles of the Southern Desert produced excellent grazing in winter and spring, supporting hundreds of thousands of sheep and many thousands of camels. These animals died if they could not move out into the desert and the shepherds and their families were faced with starvation.

(e) I was a solitary civilian. All I could do immediately was to organize an efficient intelligence service in Nejed which I had begun to do as soon as I arrived in the desert in March 1928.

(f) The police posts at Busaiya, Sulman and Shebicha were valuable as bases for the storing of petrol and ammunition and as wireless stations which could transmit reports to the government and to the R.A.F. But they were immobile. The grazing round the posts was insufficient for the hundreds of thousands of animals in the desert. What was necessary was the formation of mobile armed detachments which could camp with the tribes in their grazing area.

The tribes themselves, in my plan, were to be trained to concentrate round these mobile camps and help to defend themselves. I accordingly requested sanction to form a Southern Desert Camel Corps, partly on camels and partly in vehicles, armed with machine-guns. These vehicles could provide ground patrols in front of our tribes to watch for raiders. In the event of an Ikhwan raid, the machine-gun trucks would concentrate our tribes and fight back. A copy of my proposals was submitted to the Air Officer Commanding, who noted on them in pencil, 'I do not agree. I do not want the police to fight.' This comment was sufficient to delay the issue of machine-guns from March to September 1928, the precious summer months during which the crews could have been under training.

The A.O.C.'s note revealed the fundamental difference of outlook between the R.A.F. and myself. The Air Officer Commanding looked upon the Iraqi tribes as civilians. In the event of an alarm, he wished them and their flocks to evacuate the desert and collect behind the police posts, leaving some seventeen thousand square miles of desert grazing unusable. He was then prepared to cover this vacant area with great numbers of air patrols which, however, had never been able to locate raiders. Even if they did identify a raid, the number of casualties they could inflict from the air was no deterrent.

After endless correspondence, the Iraq Government, in September 1928, sanctioned the following force, to be known as the Southern Desert Camel Corps:

70 camelmen
30 machine-gunners in trucks
8 miscellaneous trucks and vans, bought in Baghdad
4 new Ford trucks each mounting a Vickers gun
2 Wireless vans.

Although there were hundreds of wireless sets in Iraq, no other other department would lend us two. As a result, two sets were ordered from Britain, and arrived a year later.

During this summer of 1928, I made a close study of ancient desert methods of warfare and discovered that there was indeed a technique for defence. Although bedouin wars seem to consist mostly of raid and counter-raid, defensive battles had formerly taken place in the days when Arab princes controlled large numbers of tribes.

The tactics of the desert defensive battle consisted in pitching all the tents near one another, with the tent ropes overlapping and all the animals packed in together behind the tents. This formation presented a solid obstacle to the wild mounted charge. The objection to this method was that the flocks could not graze. As a result, the defensive formation could only be maintained for about two days. This limitation laid a heavy responsibility on the commander not to concentrate all the tribes until the day before the expected attack, and on the tribes to come immediately when summoned. No such operations had been carried out for many years and no one alive among our tribes had ever actually taken part in them.

Such accurate timing required extremely reliable intelligence. It was necessary to keep sufficient agents with the enemy tribes to ensure that one agent would accompany every enemy raid, would desert his comrades at night on their approach march and would come over to us with accurate information.

I planned to use my hundred men of the new Desert Force to form the nucelus of this tribal defensive formation. If the R.A.F. had agreed to allow their armoured cars to support us, this plan would have been infallible. But Air Headquarters would not hear of such proposals as co-operation with tribes. They continued to demand that all 'civilians' be swept out of the desert and that aircraft be left to deal with the raiders.

In November 1928, the rebel Ikhwan tribes of Mutair, Ataiba and the Ajman unfurled their war banners and declared their intention of raiding Iraq, whether Ibn Saud liked it or not.

I hastened to Baghdad to make final arrangements with the Iraq Government and the R.A.F. The Iraq Army came nobly to our assistance. They were already holding Busaiya, Sulman and Shebicha. They now agreed that a detachment of a motor machine-gun company should accompany the Southern Desert Camel Corps and myself, forming a mobile force to move with the largest possible concentration of Iraq tribes. This assistance was doubly welcome because the Iraq Army had wireless sets.

Returning from Baghdad I called a meeting of all the Iraq nomad tribes of the Southern Desert, bedouin and shepherds alike. We met at Samawa and all the tribes pledged themselves to move with us and camp and fight under our orders. The R.A.F. agreed to begin air patrols forthwith, instead of waiting until the first raid had taken place. Early in December we moved out with the Desert Force and camped at Mughaizal. The tribes camped all around us, some even going forward into the Neutral Area.

At this critical moment, the British Government suddenly issued an order that aircraft were not to approach within twenty miles of the frontier. As our camp at Mughaizal was almost on the frontier, this meant that the R.A.F. would in future reconnoitre for the enemy *behind us*.

The British Government had failed to grasp the situation. They intended this order to be a concession to Ibn Saud. In fact, it might have sealed his fate. The Ikhwan rebels were about to attack Iraq against Ibn Saud's orders. If they won a great victory and returned with immense loot, the other tribes would join them and Ibn Saud would be overthrown. If, on the other hand, the rebels were

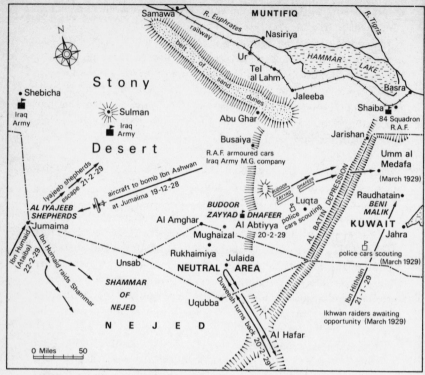

Map 11 Our Stand at Abtiyya

NOTES: (1) R.A.F. armoured cars and Iraq Army at Busaiya, forbidden to move further forward.

(2) Grazing necessity obliged our tribes to move to the Neutral Area.

(3) On 19 December, 1928, we bombed Menahi Ibn Ashwan's raid at Jumaima.

(4) On 21 January, 1929, Ibn Hithlain (Ajman) raided Iraqi Beni Malik shepherds in Kuwait territory. We could have intercepted him, but were forbidden for diplomatic reasons to enter Kuwait.

(5) On 17 February, 1929, we drew up our tribes for battle at Al Abtiyya.

(6) On 20 February, 1929, Duweesh arrived at Julaida at midnight, but turned back.

(7) On 22 February, 1929, Ibn Humaid arrived at Jumaima, but shepherds had gone. He raided Nejed Shammar, subjects of Ibn Saud.

(8) On 23 February, 1929, we left Abtiyya, and marched in formation with our tribes to Umm al Medafa, in Kuwait territory.

defeated, the other tribes would remain loyal to him and would enable him to defeat the rebels.

On 16 December, 1928, an exhausted bedouin agent reached my tent at Mughaizal. He reported that a small Mutair raid under Menahi ibn Ashwan had watered at Al Hafar on the 15 December and was going to seek for isolated shepherd camps near Jumaima. I collected my old bedouin experts and we calculated that he would reach Jumaima on 19 December. The R.A.F. fortunately agreed to let me fly to Jumaima that morning, when, lo and behold!, there were the raiders, whom we duly attacked. This incident was most encouraging, as showing what could be done with our new intelligence system.

The Ikhwan, who maintained a highly efficient spy organization among our tribes, soon discovered that air patrols were no longer flying along the frontier. As a result, many camps of nomadic Ikhwan moved north of Al Hafar, only a few miles from our own tribes in the Neutral Area. This close proximity greatly increased our anxieties, but it also made it easier for us to insinuate spies into their camps. Soon ample information was received that the rebel Ikhwan were coming. Ibn Humaid with Ataiba was to advance on Sulman, the Duweesh with Mutair on the Neutral Area and Ibn Hithlain with the Ajman was coming up from the Hasa.

Our force was too small to divide up. We accordingly cleared the area in front of Sulman, inviting all the tribes to join us in the Mughaizal area, where the grazing was sufficient for everybody.

At dawn on 21 January, 1929, Ibn Hithlain with the Ajman raided the Iraqi Beni Malik shepherds in Kuwait territory. We, at Mughaizal, were ideally placed to cut off the raiders with our armed trucks, but we were forbidden to enter Kuwait territory. Thus a priceless opportunity to teach the Ikhwan a lesson was missed.

Meanwhile I had decided that, if the Duweesh came, my little force would unship their machine-guns and dig in, forming a central redoubt. The tribes would then be marshalled on either side of us in a long line, the tents pitched so close to one another that the tent ropes crossed. The camels would be couched and hobbled so that they could not move, the sheep and donkeys packed between the tents. All this was explained in detail to all the tribes.

At this critical juncture, I received an order that only four Iraq army machine-guns were to remain with us, the rest of their machine-gun company retiring to Busaiya. I implored the R.A.F. to send us their armoured cars, which were at Busaiya, but they refused. Article 3 of the Uqair Protocol had stated that neither side should 'concentrate troops' in the vicinity of the border. As a result, the British Government had ruled that no 'military' should go in front of Busaiya.

I pointed out that perhaps fifteen or twenty thousand fanatical Ikhwan were marching on Iraq and could reasonably be considered as Nejdi 'troops'. Air Headquarters replied that, if attacked, I could retire on Busaiya fighting a rearguard action. This remarkable order seemed to reveal the complete inability of the authorities to understand our situation. The tribes might form a solid line with their tents close-packed and pegged down and their animals in between. But how could such an agglomeration of women, children, tents and animals fight a rearguard action against continuous mounted charges? While we were daily anticipating a desperate battle, the British Government was preoccupied with the nice interpretation of diplomatic agreements.

At dusk on 15 February, 1929, one of my best spies arrived at my tent at Mughaizal. He reported that the Duweesh with ten warbanners had set out two days before to attack us at Mughaizal. I called in my most trusted bedouins of the Camel Corps and we reckoned that the Duweesh would attack us at dawn on 19 February. We had three days to concentrate our tribes and take up our battle position. Two hours after our spy's arrival, we dispersed our desert police cars to bring in all our tribes.

I had already chosen our defensive position at Al Abtiyya, a few miles north of Mughaizal. The principal reason for the choice was that there were there large pools of rainwater. Ample water close at hand was essential for so large a concentration of tribes.

The last of our tribes arrived on the evening of the 17 February, completely exhausted after, in many cases, covering forty-five miles in thirty-six hours. Most of the shepherds, including the women and children, had covered the distance on foot. On 18 February another of my spies arrived. He had marched for two days with the Duweesh's advancing force and then had slipped away and come on ahead. He stated categorically that the Duweesh would attack us at dawn on 20 February.

I signalled the date to Baghdad and asked if a section of R.A.F. armoured cars might join us but received no reply. A tremendous concentration of mobile fire power was located at Busaiya, consisting of the R.A.F. armoured cars and the Iraq Army machine-gun company. If these had encountered the Duweesh's raid, they could have inflicted casualties which would have put an end to Ikhwan raiding for ever. If this had occurred, the rebellion would have collapsed and Ibn Saud would have regained his power. Yet, in fact, I was doubtful whether this force would support us even if we were attacked.

I could only imagine that this extraordinary uncooperative attitude was due to the British Government, who regarded us as some kind of Sherifian supporters, fighting Ibn Saud, whereas, in actual fact, our defeat of the rebel Ikhwan would save Ibn Saud's throne. I accordingly remained at Al Abtiyya with four Iraq army machine-guns and the Southern Desert Camel Corps, seventy strong. On my right were the Zayyad shepherds, on my left the Dhafeer bedouins, and the Budoor shepherds in second line. On the 18th and 19th all roused their ardour with war-dances.

These four days which we spent lined up at Al Abtiyya, awaiting the Duweesh's attack, were a period of intense anxiety. Even in an attack in France in the First World War, it was possible to be killed, wounded or taken prisoner. But the Ikhwan took no prisoners. If you were not killed outright in their charge, you were seized by two or three men and thrown on your back, while one of them cut your throat with a knife. In a defeat, there would be no survivors.

But I personally found the strain of the situation much worse than I had experienced in the First World War. In France, I had been supported by the company of all my comrades. Even if one were to be killed, there seemed to be comfort in the thought that he and so many of the boys would be together.

But at Al Abtiyya, I was not only alone – I was responsible for the whole operation. The British Government and the R.A.F. disapproved of the fantastic idea of helping our tribes to defend themselves. Although they had a powerful ground force only fifty miles away, they would not help us. If I and all the tribes were massacred, their blood would be on my head alone.

At the first pale light of dawn on 20 February, we sent out two cars on patrol to the south. If they sighted the enemy, they were to fire red very lights to give us a few minutes to prepare and to send off a wireless message. I hoped that aircraft would come to our assistance, even if the armoured cars would not. But it was doubtful what action aircraft could take if the battle were already in progress.

Now that the crisis had come, I did not feel afraid. We laughed and joked, drank tea and coffee. Gradually daylight came. The men began to cook a meal. The Duweesh had not come.

For another three days we remained in a state of acute tension. Then we were able to piece together the story. The Duweesh had fully intended to raid us at dawn on 20 February, as our spy had reported. Meanwhile he had placed a spy in our camp, with orders to slip away on the night of the 18-19 February and, to meet him at Julaida, thirty miles south of Al Abtiyya, at midnight on the night of 19-20. After receiving the spy's report, he could cover the remaining thirty miles before dawn.

This spy had been in our camp on 18 February, had seen our tribes lined up to fight and had observed their war-dances. What is more, he had seen three aircraft land beside our camp. He met the Duweesh at Julaida, told him of the concentration of tribes, of the war-dances and, above all, of the aircraft. A frenzied council of war was held at midnight on the well of Julaida. At length the great Duweesh gave the order to retreat. For nine years the Iraq tribes had lived in constant terror: that night the tide turned.

On 17 February, an agent of mine from Hail had told us that Sultan ibn Humaid of Ataiba was advancing with a large force, intending to raid Iraq shepherds at Jumaima, the same day that the Duweesh raided us at Al Abtiyya. At the same time, I heard to my horror that the Iyajeeb shepherds, contrary to my orders, had actually moved to Jumaima. I spent a frenzied three days sending cars and camel police to order them back. Finally on 21 February, they complied. The next morning Ibn Humaid attacked their camp site to find it empty. Unwilling to return home empty handed, he raided neighbouring camps of Shammar in Nejed territory and some caravans of Nejdi merchants.

This action was to save Ibn Saud. While the rebel Ikhwan were declaring their intention to destroy the 'infidel' Iraqis, they enjoyed considerable sympathy from the other tribes of Nejed. But when they failed to defeat any Iraqis, but attacked other Nejdi tribes, and even caravans of Nejdi merchants, it became obvious that their motivation was not religious. The townspeople and the remaining tribes of Arabia immediately rallied to Ibn Saud. Indirectly, we could claim to have made a major contribution to this result by foiling the rebel Ikhwan's grand offensive.

[Writing nearly fifty years later, it is interesting to examine the long-term results of the events of February 1929. If the Ikhwan rebels had defeated Ibn Saud, Arabia would have relapsed into tribal anarchy. There would have been no stable government from which the oil companies could have obtained concessions, with all the world-wide results in the Second World War and on the development of Western industry. Today Saudi Arabia is a wealthy and important nation, exercising a wise and moderating influence on international affairs.

It seems fantastic to claim that all these results stemmed from the failure of the Nejed Ikhwan rebels to raid Iraq in February 1929. It is even more difficult to believe that Iraq was not primarily defended by the British and Iraq Governments, but by the courage of the nomadic tribes of Iraq whom everyone affected to despise. Yet such was indeed the actual fact.]

18

Nemesis

When the Duweesh had turned back from attacking our position at Al Abtiyya, he had not disbanded his force. He had bivouacked south of the frontier, some sixty miles from us – a single night's march. He knew as well as we did that we could not keep our tribes concentrated indefinitely – indeed the water at Al Abtiyya was already exhausted. There were only two areas where there was sufficient grazing for so large a concentration of tribes as we had – the Neutral Area and northern Kuwait. (Map 11, page 180)

The Neutral Area was too risky with the Duweesh's war-banners only fifty miles away. Besides which, the R.A.F. would not fly over it.

The position in Kuwait was different. The R.A.F. – both aircraft and armoured cars – could operate in Kuwait, but the Iraq Army and the Desert Police could not. By a remarkable piece of diplomatic nicety, I personally was allowed to enter Kuwait territory by day, but not to sleep there. At length a compromise was reached. Permission was given for all the Iraq tribes, the Desert Police and myself, to camp in Kuwait territory, but not the Iraq Army. But what was even better, we were given a section of R.A.F. armoured cars to accompany us.

We moved the seventy miles from Al Abtiyya to Umm al Medafa, almost in military style. I laid down the destination for each tribe every day, all keeping close together, while our police car patrols covered them from the south. At Umm al Medafa, we camped on a rainpool as large as a lake. The grass all around was knee-deep.

The Desert Camel Corps Ford vans, mounting their machine-guns, daily patrolled the southern frontier of Kuwait. The Ikhwan were immediately south of the border and many skirmishes occurred between them and our patrols. But for our cars, the rebels would have raided often into Kuwait. The Desert Police, whom the A.O.C. did not want to fight, proved to be the only people who did any fighting. Not that they were more warlike than the R.A.F., but they were operating in their own country and knew exactly where to find the enemy. The R.A.F. on the other hand, was strange to the desert and, moreover, directly commanded from an office chair in Baghdad.

I had served for five years with the R.A.F. and was extremely attached to them, especially to the pilots with whom I had flown endless weary hours. My mistake was not to spend more time in Baghdad to establish personal relationships with members of the staff. Or perhaps, alternatively, to ask for an R.A.F. staff officer to visit me in the desert.

March 1929 was a happy month indeed, camped as we were in luscious green grass, surrounded by our triumphant tribes. Soon the camels were almost too fat to walk, and the sheep and lambs frisked and played. All too soon came the hot April sun, the grass began to shrivel and the shepherds moved off to return to the Euphrates, afraid of being caught in waterless desert with their flocks of sheep.

Ibn Humaid's attack on Shammar and the Nejdi merchants, and the failure of himself and the Duweesh to raid any 'infidel' Iraqis, saved Ibn Saud's throne. The King moved immediately to the town of Buraida, called on the loyal tribes to join him, together with a double levy of the townsmen of Nejed. Meanwhile the loyal tribes began to raid the rebels. Civil war had begun.

On 29 March, the rebels fought a pitched battle with Ibn Saud's levies at Sibilla, ninety miles north of Riyadh. After a desperate swaying hand-to-hand struggle, the rebels were eventually defeated. Faisal al Duweesh was shot through the stomach during the action and subsequently surrendered to Ibn Saud. As he appeared to be dying, the King allowed him to return to his tribe. Ibn Humaid refused to surrender and retired to his home the other side of Arabia. The rebel cause seemed to be lost.

But the third rebel tribe, the Ajman, had not been present at Sibilla. When Ibn Saud seemed completely victorious, the Ajman suddenly defeated a column sent against them, killing its commander, a cousin of the King. Suddenly the hopes of the rebels revived. Meanwhile, the fiery summer heats had put an end to large-scale battles, but in Nejed the loyal and the rebel tribes continued to raid one another.

Our Desert Police cars continued to patrol north of the Nejed

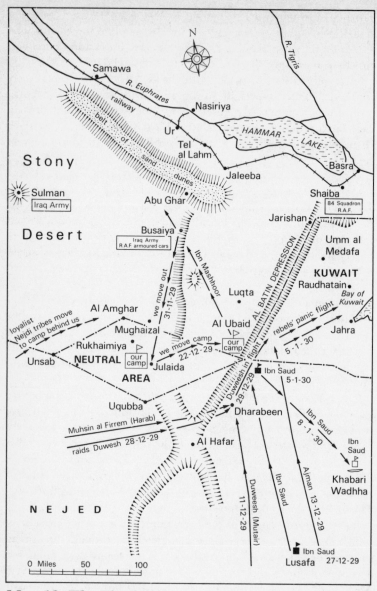

Map 12 The Final Act

frontier. On 29 July, a Mutair raiding party looted two hundred camels from the Dhafeer from a point in Kuwait territory some fifty miles south of the R.A.F. camp at Shaiba. Two police vans, each armed with a Lewis gun pursued the raiders, put them to flight and recovered the looted camels.

In August 1929, a much larger raiding party of Mutair raided some Nejed Shammar, camped in Iraq territory north of Jumaima. Again two Desert Police trucks armed with machine-guns overtook the raiders, scattered them in flight and recovered all the loot. These victories were due to the issue of these machine-guns, which the Air Officer Commanding had attempted to veto a year before on the grounds that he did not want the police to fight. Yet, on the whole, the success of the operations was due to the moral effect of the presence of the R.A.F. behind us.

The Southern Desert Camel Corps had become famous all over Arabia. In the process, they had acquired a nickname, the origin of which was unknown, but which they adopted as a battle cry. The name was *Al Aujan*, or The Crooks. In every battle and skirmish in which they took part, they tore off their headgear, loaded their guns, and drove at the enemy, crying '*Al Aujan! Wain al Aujan!* – The Crooks – where are the Crooks – where are the gallants!'

Towards the end of the summer Ibn Humaid surrendered to Ibn Saud. He was imprisoned in a dungeon from which he never emerged. The tribe of Ataiba returned to their allegiance. There remained only Mutair and the Ajman.

In November 1929, we moved out with the Iraq tribes and the Southern Desert police and camped in the Neutral Area. The Iraq Army was not with us. Meanwhile Mutair and the Ajman had decided to seek asylum in Iraq and were crowding up towards the frontier a few miles south of us. On 13 December a deputation of shaikhs of Mutair arrived at my tent, begging leave to move to Iraq. Simultaneously a number of loyalist Nejed tribes, afraid of the rebels, crossed the frontier and camped behind us, begging our protection from the rebels.

After eight years of terror, it was deeply moving to see both the rebel Ikhwan and Ibn Saud's loyalist tribes imploring our protection. Nevertheless our situation was precarious. Ibn Saud could not move out until sufficient rain had fallen to form pools of water in the desert. If I now curtly refused permission to the rebels to enter Iraq might they not attempt to overrun our camp and scatter into Iraq to escape Ibn Saud? I had with me only forty camel police and four trucks mounting machine-guns. I accordingly once again ordered our tribes to take up a battle position around us.

At this stage, half my troubles were ended by the arrival, on 21 December, of the Chief Air Staff Officer, Air Commodore Burnett, at our camp. This was the first occasion, in five years of hostilities against the Ikhwan, that a senior R.A.F. officer had visited me in the desert. Of course, as soon as he arrived on the site and saw the situation, he fully appreciated our problems. Thereafter, co-operation with the R.A.F. was smooth and easy.

On 27 December, 1929, Ibn Saud with his main army arrived at Lusafa, some one hundred and twenty miles south of our camp, which we had meanwhile moved to Al Ubaid, overlooking the Kuwait frontier. The fugitive Mutair and the Ajman, in a state verging upon panic, were streaming into Kuwait territory immediately opposite to us, beyond the border.

On 28 December, a large raiding party of Harab, a tribe loyal to Ibn Saud, attacked Mutair at Dharabeen. The latter fled incontinent without resistance, as the Iraq shepherds used to do. How, indeed, were the mighty fallen! A further deputation of Mutair, under Hazza al Duweesh, had meanwhile arrived at my tent, imploring to be allowed sanctuary in Iraq. The British and Iraq Governments, however, had pledged themselves to Ibn Saud not to give sanctuary to the rebels and we sternly refused their entreaties. As a result, they surged northwards into Kuwait territory.

Air Commodore Burnett was not a little perplexed. It was easy to promise Ibn Saud not to admit the fugitives, but when crowds of them, men, women, and children (not to mention camels) poured across the border, it was not possible to shoot them down. Only one group, Ferhan ibn Mashhoor and sixty followers, were allowed sanctuary. They were Syrian subjects, of the Ruwalla tribe, who had gone over to Ibn Saud and joined the Ikhwan. They were disarmed, conducted to Busaiya and subsequently repatriated to Syria.

The Air Commodore and I drafted terms to be offered to the rebels. The chiefs were to give themselves up, and the tribes to be collected and disarmed, and allowed to remain in Kuwait territory until negotiations could be completed with Ibn Saud. Air Commodore Burnett flew to Baghdad with these terms, which were approved. On

1 January, Faisal al Duweesh and Naif ibn Hithlain, shaikh of the Ajman, reported to our camp and the terms were explained to them. They asked for twelve hours' grace to return to their tribes and think over the terms. They did not come back.

On 5 January, 1930, however, all the rebels beyond the frontier suddenly panicked and fled in utter disorder towards Jahra. At his request, I accompanied the Air Commodore with a column of armoured cars in pursuit of them. They were utterly demoralized, fleeing pell-mell to the north, the desert behind them strewn with their possessions and with abandoned camels and sheep.

How often had I seen the unhappy Iraq shepherds fleeing in just such anguished terror from these same pitiless Ikhwan. Yet I did not feel elated. There was something painful and humiliating in seeing other human beings reduced to a state of such insane and abject terror. While I was with the Air Commodore, attempting to round up the fugitives, I was handed a signal from our camp, reporting laconically that Ibn Saud and his whole army had arrived at the frontier, immediately opposite my tent.

On returning to our camp, I found a deputation waiting for me with a letter from Ibn Saud asking what steps the British Government proposed to take to evict the rebels from Kuwait. The leader of the deputation embarked on a violent verbal tirade against the British Government. I replied that I was a servant of the Iraq Government, and could not speak officially for the British Government or the Shaikh of Kuwait. As a private person, I was sure that both Britain and Kuwait would fulfil their obligations.

For the next three days the deputation came and went between Ibn Saud and my tent. The leader spent a good deal of time in violent denunciations of the British, Iraq and Kuwait Governments. Meanwhile the royal army had been accompanied by a number of Chevrolet trucks, which reached the frontier on their last can of petrol. I consequently received a message from His Majesty asking if I could supply his army with petrol. Alternatively he enquired whether the mechanized portion of his army could remain in our camp 'as our guests'. Our administrative arrangements, however, proved adequate and the Saudi battle fleet left the frontier under its own power.

Fortunately the water available on the frontier proved inadequate for Ibn Saud's army, and on 8 January, 1930, he moved away to the south-east to Khabari Wadhha in his own territory. 'God save us from our friends,' I wrote in my diary.

I could not help feeling indignant that the British and Iraq Governments, at this crucial moment, were solely and completely preoccupied with high international politics and with conciliating Ibn Saud. For six years the Iraq tribes had been the victims of massacre and plunder at the hands of the Ikhwan, from which neither government had defended them. Only when the tribes themselves formed up to defend themselves at Al Abtiyya did the Ikhwan respect the Iraq frontier.

Now, at last, the tables were turned and the Ikhwan themselves with immense flocks of looted animals were in panic flight. I accordingly bombarded the Iraq Government with requests to be allowed to seize some flocks from the Ikhwan to offer at least nominal compensation to our own victims of their raids. Or alternatively, to make the eviction of the rebels from Kuwait conditional on the payment of compensation by Ibn Saud for six years of killing raids.

Eventually I received a half-hearted agreement to distribute to Iraqi raid victims any Ikhwan camels I could collect in Iraq territory. By this time the rebels were beyond our reach in Kuwait. We, however, succeeded in collecting a few camels, notably from Ibn Mashhoor, and these I distributed to the best of my ability to former victims of Ikhwan raids. It was no more than a symbolic gesture. In any case, nothing could compensate for the great numbers of Iraqis killed.

A few sections of the rebels attempted to make a dash back to Nejed and surrender to Ibn Saud. They were intercepted by the King's army and every single man was killed, in the same manner as they formerly massacred Iraqis.

On 20 January, the British resident in the Persian Gulf flew to Ibn Saud's camp. On 25 January, an agreement was signed to hand over the rebel leaders to Ibn Saud and to evict the tribes from Kuwait territory. In return, Ibn Saud promised to settle the claims of Iraq tribes for losses in past Ikhwan raids. Once all the rebels had been driven back into Nejed territory, nothing more was ever heard of this clause, nor did the British or Iraq Governments trouble to pursue the matter of compensation for their subjects and protégés.

The British Government, to give it its due, was always anxious to make peace. On 21 February, 1930, a meeting took place on board the British sloop H.M.S. *Lupin*, in the Persian Gulf, between King Faisal I of Iraq and King Abdul Aziz ibn Saud. It would be an exaggeration to say that the two monarchs made friends, but at least they met and conversed.

I had accompanied the Iraq delegation, which consisted of the Prime Minister, Naji Beg al Suwaidi, and the Adviser to the Ministry of the Interior, Mr. (later Sir) Kinahan Cornwallis. The officials of the two governments negotiated a *Bon Voisinage* agreement, which led to permanent peace. Never again did the tribes raid one another across the Iraq-Nejed frontier. It must be admitted that the establishment of this peace was due to the diplomatic efforts of the British Government.

[Nearly fifty years have elapsed since the meeting on H.M.S. *Lupin*. Saudi Arabia has become one of the richest nations in the world. The descendants of the fierce Ikhwan are industrial workers in the oilfields. The desert, once virgin and inviolate, is now surveyed and mapped and crossed by pipelines and vehicles. Times have changed and men, perforce, have changed with them.]

My ideas about the desert had developed greatly since I first became involved in the defence of the Iraq tribes against the Ikhwan. The deserts of Iraq, it seemed to me, were not the useless sandy wastes of popular Western imagination. On the contrary, they were rolling steppes a great part of which were on limestone, not on sandstone. These undulating downs provided the best grazing in the country, capable of producing hundreds of thousands of camels and millions of sheep. Now that the killing raids were over, could not some use be made of such an asset?

For thousands of years, however, the tribes living in these vast plains had been the terror of the settled inhabitants who lived on the banks of the Tigris and Euphrates or on the cultivated hills of Trans-Jordan and Syria. In ancient inscriptions and in the Old Testament we find hostile references to bedouins even before Moses and before the Empires of Assyria or Nebuchadnezzar, and the same dislike was as active in the days of the Ottoman Empire as in those of the Pharaohs.

This intense hatred of the nomads, so deeply engrained in the minds and in the emotions of those who lived in the settled areas, had, it seemed to me, obscured the economic and political potentialities of the desert and its people. The ruling classes and the city dwellers had for centuries suffered so much loss and anxiety as a result of the actions of nomads that they would gladly have seen the whole nomadic community exterminated and the desert left empty and without in-habitants.

While these governments were anxious to be progressive and modern, to develop irrigation, agriculture, education and industry, towards the desert they had no constructive ideas. No positive proposals for converting the desert into a national asset had ever entered into their wildest dreams. The most they hoped was that it would not be a nuisance. Throughout my ten years in Iraq this negative attitude persisted.

For thousands of years the bedouins had remained independent of government control because they alone possessed camels, the only desert means of transport. The increasing employment of aircraft and motor vehicles in the desert had now begun to destroy the inaccessible isolation of the nomads. Gradually the age-old fear of the bedouins had begun to fade, but it did not produce any feeling of sympathy for them as fellow citizens. Roads, lines of telegraph wires, and pipelines were constructed across the desert and more and more Iraqis began to come and go across it in the course of their normal avocations.

In none of them whom I ever met, however, did it inspire any pleasure or interest, still less the desire to know or understand its inhabitants. The existence of bedouins, to the ordinary Iraqi, was just one of those things which made life more difficult, like sandstorms, malaria, mosquitoes or locusts. Presumably it was God's will that such things should exist and the only thing to do was to bear them as patiently as possible.

Now it is true that the bedouin, when he felt himself to be the master, could be extremely brutal and overbearing. It is true, also, that he had for centuries regarded all non-bedouins as a legitimate prey and had done his best to rob them or hold them up to ransom. But it is not possible for so large a community to live entirely by robbery. There was an economic demand for his produce, and if that economic demand were to cease the bedouin would cease to exist also. But as long as this economic demand existed, the bedouins would survive. Even if the existing nomad tribes were exterminated by political or military action, others would spring up in their place to supply society with its requirements.

The true bedouin tribes lived principally by breeding camels. In earlier times, and even to a great extent in the 1920s, the camel was the beast of burden of the Arab countries. Convoys of camels moved from town to town engaged in the transportation of goods. In addition to transport work, however, camels were also used for butcher's meat. It was the cheapest form of meat available for the poorer classes in the cities. Thousands of camels every year were, in those days, exported from Arabia to Egypt for food. [This commerce, however, was cut off in 1948, when Israel was established and severed all land access from Arabia to North Africa.]

If and when the demand for camels ceased, men would necessarily stop breeding them and would perforce earn their living by some other method. Indeed such a change was already taking place in the northern tribes, both Anaiza and Shammar. The former were taking increasingly to sheep, the latter to agriculture. Whether they bred sheep or camels was in any case an irrelevant detail. The point was that the desert was a vast grazing area, producing the livestock needed by the community, including millions of sheep.

In most areas, there was not enough water in the desert in summer for large numbers of sheep. But Providence had arranged that the Tigris and Euphrates came down in flood in April, often overflowing their banks. When the rivers subsided in May, they left wide areas of grass on their banks providing summer grazing. Moreover harvest occurred in the early summer in Iraq, after which time the sheep could be turned into the stubble. Thus, to a great extent, the seasonal migrations of the sheep, the rising of the rivers and the harvesting of the grain crops seemed to have produced a natural annual cycle.

Motor trucks might supersede camels as means of transport, but it seemed unlikely that men would give up eating mutton. Sheep, moreover, produced *semn*, the cooking oil generally used in Iraq, and wool was a major item of export.

But while the people of the desert were thus an economic asset to the community, they were often themselves miserably poor. One of the most distressing aspects of their life was its uncertainty, due to the vagaries of the rainfall. In general, three or four good, or at least average years, would succeed one another. Rainfall would be adequate, the grazing sufficient and the numbers of sheep and camels would increase. But perhaps every fifth or sixth year the rains would fail, the grazing would be scanty and tens of thousands of camels and sheep would die. In most cases enough animals would be left to breed from and the numbers would build up again in successive good years. But every now and again a man would lose all his stock and be left with no capital assets to rebuild his fortune. With the friendly sympathy of the tribal community, the neighbours would endeavour to set him up again by giving him – one a sheep and one a camel. But in a really bad year too many nomads would be destitute and they and their families would be faced with starvation.

It so happened, however, that bad years for grazing were not always bad years for cultivation, nor for date palms. The precarious nature of the nomadic life arose from the fact that they had all their eggs in one basket – grazing. It seemed to me, therefore, that every breeder of camels or sheep should also have a piece of land on which to grow grain crops and, if possible, a garden of date palms.

I was convinced, also, that the positive resources of the desert could be greatly increased. Additional wells or cisterns, and dams across the valleys where water flowed after rain, would increase the number of camping sites. Now grazing was often wasted because there was no water within reach. Again, more nourishing types of grasses could be introduced, possibly imported from Australia, and could be broadcast from aircraft over suitable areas.

Another idea was to import foreign rams from abroad to improve either the meat or the wool of Iraqi sheep. Thus, it seemed to me, much could be done both to alleviate the poverty of the nomads and to build up a valuable asset in the economy of the nation.

These considerations and other similar constructive ideas had occupied my mind during those long nights in the desert watching for Ikhwan raiders, or when driving hour after hour over the dusty undulating hills. The first prerequisite, however, was obviously stability, public security and the end of tribal raiding, for which purpose the government must go out into the desert, which hitherto it had never done.

In the course of the operations against the Ikhwan we had established police posts on the major wells in the Southern Desert. It seemed to me now, that if such posts were also established in the Syrian desert, they would become centres of trade, shops would be opened and merchants would come out there to buy and sell from and to the tribes. A school and a dispensary could be built beside each post – perhaps a few trees could be planted or vegetables grown, constituting thereby a tiny oasis.

[Writing fifty years later, I am bound to admit that few, if any, of my dreams have come true. The first obstacle, I think, was social prejudice. To the vast majority of Iraqis, the world would be a better place if no nomads existed at all. This view is shared by other governments in different parts of the world, for nomads are difficult to control, to classify, to conscript or to regiment. Yet some form of change of pastures for grazing animals is practised all over the world. Even in Austria and Switzerland the cows move up to the mountain pastures in summer and down to the valleys in winter. In Iraq and Syria, however, the ancient social prejudices of the government and of most of the people militated against any schemes for constructive development of desert grazing.

Perhaps, however, an even more decisive element was soon to prove to be the discovery of large amounts of oil. The immense wealth to be derived from these sources made a marginal profit to be derived from the improvement of sheep-raising appear negligible.

Another factor, which acted against government interest in the grazing areas, was the passion to imitate the West, an attitude which the Arabs had inherited from the Ottoman Turks. This resulted in the concentration of their attention on industry and agriculture. Grazing, which did not constitute a major contribution to the economy of Europe, tended, therefore, to be neglected. It must be admitted, however, that the Iraq Government, when the oil revenues began to come in, did invest a large part of them in agriculture and in irrigation. But nobody, as far as I know, ever thought of investing money in grazing.]

19

Ibn Shaalan

Meanwhile, in 1930, a few minor tasks still remained to be done before I could try and persuade the authorities to adopt my plans for the peaceful and profitable development of the desert. The first and most pressing task was to put an end to raiding in the Syrian Desert.

The deserts of Arabia terminate in the north in a triangle of which the apex lies at Aleppo. Almost the whole of this northern triangle is occupied by Anaiza, one of the largest tribal groups in Arabia. There are still many Anaiza in the Hejaz, but these who have migrated to the north have fallen into roughly three groups.

Of these, the western group consists of the Ruwalla and Dhana Muslim and are reckoned to be Syrian subjects. The next group to the east is composed of the Sba and the Amarat who summer on the Euphrates, the Sba normally in Syria, the Amarat in Iraq. Further east still, beyond the Euphrates in the Jezira, live the Fedaan, who are also reckoned to be Syrians.

Three paramount chiefs controlled the great mass of these tribes – Ibn Shaalan the western group, the Ruwalla and Dhana Muslim; Ibn Hadhdhal, the Amarat, and Ibn Muhaid the Fedaan in the Jezira. The Sba had formerly been closely connected with the Amarat, but when the frontier was drawn between Syria and Iraq after the First World War it had left the Sba in Syria and the Amarat in Iraq.

When I had arrived in Iraq the three great Anaiza divisions in the north had been under the leadership of three old men, all of them quite outstanding personalities. Of these, Al Nouri ibn Shaalan held authority over the western group, Fahad ibn Hadhdhal over the Amarat, and Mujhim ibn Muhaid over the Fedaan.

In 1930 Fahad ibn Hadhdhal was dead. Al Nouri, though still alive, lived permanently in his house in Damascus and had

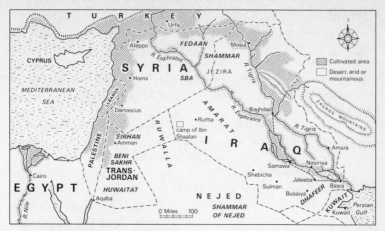

Map 13 The Syrian Desert

abandoned the leadership of his tribe in the desert to his dashing young grandson, Fawwaz. Fahad had been succeeded by his son Mahroot. Mujhim ibn Muhaid in his old age had virtually abandoned nomadism and had taken to cultivating his estates in the Jezira.

These three old men had been calm and wise old sages, with the profound wisdom and knowledge of human life which is sometimes achieved by illiterate old men who have not cluttered up their minds with quantities of irrelevant information derived from books. Gifted by nature with penetrating intellects, their knowledge of life had been acquired by direct observation, uninfluenced by clever theories derived from books or the press.

Whether they loved one another or not I cannot say, but they all three worked together to keep the peace. Each possessed a personality powerful enough to enable him to control his own tribes and an intelligence acute enough to enable him to work with their respective governments.

But the death of Fahad and the retirement of Al Nouri to Damascus left the Ruwalla and the Amarat under the leadership of two young, dashing and perhaps slightly jealous young men. The Ruwalla normally summered near Damascus, the Amarat on the Euphrates, but in winter and spring both moved out to the centre of the Syrian Desert and were liable to meet and intermingle near or south of Rutba.

During the winter of 1928-29, the two young men, Fawwaz and Mahroot, had created a good deal of confusion and alarm by threatening to engage in a pitched battle near Rutba, an embarrassing nuisance to the Iraq Government, which had a police post at Rutba. The overland mail car service from Baghdad to Damascus was plying regularly through Rutba, with convoys of passenger cars.

During the winter of 1929–30, the disturbances in the Syrian Desert assumed a new form. Fawwaz ibn Shaalan was a very young man, dashing, rather nice-looking and vivacious. He was the darling of his grandfather, Al Nouri, who was extremely wealthy and had a handsome town house in Damascus. During the summer, when the Syrian Desert was almost empty, Fawwaz lived the life of a rich young man about town. Money was plentiful and there were many pleasures to be pursued in Damascus and Lebanon. Fawwaz had been educated in Damascus, and spent his evenings in the cabarets of the city, immaculately dressed in a dinner jacket and black tie – a new type of bedouin chief indeed.

When the tribes moved out again in the autumn of 1929 Fawwaz discovered a new form of sport. Accompanied by several Buicks packed with negro slaves armed to the teeth, he amused himself driving out in the desert and rounding up flocks of camels from the scattered camps of the Amarat. Flocks scatter widely in winter to secure the best grazing and two or three flocks of fifteen or twenty camels, each with a herdsman, could be rounded up in a few minutes by four Buicks and driven rapidly away. The owners, mounted on camels or horses, were unable to pursue. The old bedouin raiding, as we have seen, was not without its sporting element, but driving off unguarded camels in Buicks was mere bullying.

The French Mandatory Government had given almost unreserved support to Al Nouri ibn Shaalan, as the easiest method of controlling the Ruwalla, just as the British supported the tribal chiefs in Iraq in 1918 and 1919. As a result, Fawwaz had been born in the purple, with a great deal of money and everything he wanted. With a fleet of Buicks and Cadillacs, he could round up great numbers of camels and be back at his desert camp for tea.

The Syrian Desert was becoming a public highway frequently crossed by convoys of car and buses, while civil air services flew back and forth overhead. If Fawwaz had bullied the bedouins in some remote desert, the Iraq Government might well have regarded his activities with indifference, but these disturbances so near the overland desert route could not be disregarded.

We, in the Southern Desert, possessed the only mechanized force capable of operating in the desert, but in January 1930 we were still engaged in the surrender of the Ikhwan rebels. In February 1930, I was called to attend King Faisal I at his meeting with King Abdul Aziz ibn Saud on the sloop *Lupin* in the Persian Gulf. It was not until the middle of March 1930 that I was free to tackle the Ruwalla problem, and I set out for Rutba with a detachment of Southern Desert armed trucks.

The police at Rutba had collected all the details of the raids which had occurred. Mahroot ibn Hadhdhal, the young shaikh of the Amarat, had inherited the wise moderation of his old father, Fahad, and had forbidden the Amarat to retaliate, with the result that Fawwaz and the Ruwalla had it all their own way. Many hundreds of camels had been looted by Fawwaz and his mechanized negro slaves.

The Ruwalla moved out to the area south and west of Rutba in winter, but returned towards Damascus in spring. The season was now already far advanced and the Shaalan were already moving back towards the Syrian border. If they once recrossed it, no settlement would be possible, at least until the following year. Conferences with the French Mandatory Government to settle tribal disputes had never been successful. They only resulted in unending arguments, in committees, sub-committees, witnesses and evidence, with no tangible result. It was, therefore, essential to act quickly before Ibn Shaalan and his loot could recross into Syria.

I accordingly sent a police car with a letter to Fawwaz, informing him that I had come to settle the trouble between him and the Amarat and asking if we could meet the next day. He was camped some twenty-five miles south-west of Rutba.

The messenger returned with an evasive answer, but informed me verbally that he had received the impression that the Shaalan would move camp at dawn the next day and would march at full speed for the Syrian frontier, which they hoped to cross in the afternoon.

Next morning I accordingly set out for the Shaalan camp at dawn with six armed cars and arrived before they had the time to strike their tents and move off. I had with me a list of claims amounting to several hundred camels taken in different raids. Fawwaz was evasive, but it was obvious that he had no intention of settling anything.

He seemed to be extremely confident and I assumed that he believed that he could keep me in play with talk and argument until the opportunity presented itself to slip away across the frontier into Syria.

I rose from the tent as if to stretch my legs and walked over to where the police armed cars were parked a hundred yards away. There were no camels visible anywhere near Ibn Shaalan's great tent, though there were a great many bedouin tents pitched all around.

One of the men, standing up in the back of one of the trucks, remarked to me that he could see a great many herds of camels in a depression about two miles away. I climbed up beside him and saw them too, though they were invisible from the ground.

I called Fawwaz and told him that I was going to bring in those camels and choose two hundred from them and retain them as security until the claims were settled, then he could cross into Syria. I then sent the armed cars to bring in the camels. We rounded them up in the open desert immediately in front of the Ruwalla camp.

It seemed to me unfair to take the first two hundred camels to hand, as they might include all the possessions of a small number of men. It appeared to me more just to distribute the seizure evenly, taking a few camels from each flock. This perhaps quixotic attempt not to injure anyone unfairly nearly proved our undoing. We seemed to have rounded up about two thousand camels, although I was only asking for two hundred, as surety of the subsequent settlement of our claims.

As all the herdsmen had come with their camels, I asked them to separate into herds, in order that we might take a few camels from each herd. All this took time and it was already past midday when we succeeded in dividing the vast mass of camels each in its own separate herd. I then instructed the herdsmen to bring each herd up one behind the other. As each herd passed us, we would take two or three camels from it and collect them behind us, while the herd passed on. When we had two hundred camels, we would take them in to Rutba and allow the remainder of the two thousand to go.

By this time a large crowd of armed tribesmen had collected all around us. The shaikh's negro slaves were particularly in evidence, gorgeously clad in silk robes, heavily armed and making no attempt to conceal their hostility. I had only twenty-four men, of whom twelve were sitting in our armed trucks, which were full of arms and ammunition. As a result, I had only twelve Desert Police at my disposal to round up and guard the camels I had confiscated.

For an hour or more, we struggled as best we could, in spite of the hostility of the crowd of tribesmen and the mocking jeers of the negroes. We seemed to have collected only some thirty camels, and the sun was already low above the horizon.

A new herd came up and I chose a few camels from it. Then, looking round suddenly, I saw the shaikh's negro slaves driving away the thirty camels which I had previously confiscated. The onlookers, who presumably had been watching for some time while the negroes drove away the camels as fast as I confiscated them, could not conceal their amusement when they saw that I had discovered the game.

As a child I used to have violent fits of temper. I remember well, as a small boy, my mother and I were staying in the country in Norfolk with an almost angelic and sweet-tempered old widow, an old friend of my father and grandfather. In our bedroom my mother spoke sharply to me and I lost my temper. Picking up one of my shoes, I threw it with all my force at a large engraving which was hanging over the bed, shattering the glass to pieces. My mother was horrified and deeply ashamed. How could she tell our kind old hostess that I had smashed up the best spare room? A second after my tantrum, my anger had gone and I was as penitent and as ashamed as was my mother.

Now – worlds apart – on the dusty plains of the Syrian Desert, I again lost my temper. Suddenly I saw red. Jumping into my car, I drove over to where the armed cars were parked, calling to our men, who were dismounted along the edge of the crowd, to follow me. When they had climbed on to the trucks, I raised the signal flag for 'ready for action'. I then drove back towards the crowd of tribesmen, the armed cars following me in line ahead.

I drove in between the mass of camels standing in the open plain on the one hand and the crowd of tribesmen massed in front of the tents on the other. When all six cars behind me had interposed between the crowd and the herds, I gave the flag signal for 'turn to the right into line abreast', thereby bringing the camels in front of us and the great crowd of tribesmen behind us. I then blew my horn and drove into the herds of camels. The drivers of the armed cars realized what was intended and blew the horns of their trucks likewise. In a few minutes, we had the whole mass of some two thousand camels packed in front of us stampeding away as fast as they could travel.

When we cut through between the camels and the crowd of assembled tribesmen, we almost elbowed the latter out of the way. Some indeed had to jump back so as not to be run over. If they had had the presence of mind, they could have jumped on to our trucks and overwhelmed my twenty-four men. But the whole action had taken only a matter of seconds. They were momentarily taken aback and did not know what we were going to do. In the same manner, my hot anger made me drive into the crowd of tribesmen in my private car in a risky manoeuvre, which I should never have dared to undertake in cold blood.

But when we turned to the right into line abreast, sounded our horns and drove the camels away in front of us, the bedouins suddenly realized what was afoot. There were shouts of rage, war-cries and a burst of firing. The negro slaves, as if by magic, seemed suddenly to be all on horseback and galloping after us loading their rifles.

For a time, everything was in wild confusion. The immense crowd of stampeding camels, with the trucks behind them, had raised a pall of dust which completely enveloped us. Shadowy figures of galloping horsemen appeared all around us. Then our machine-guns opened – *rat-tat-tat*! *rat-tat-tat*! They were firing into the cloud of dust, which enveloped both ourselves and our galloping pursuers. From the armed cars, I could hear the war cries of our own men – '*Al Aujan*! *Al Aujan*! *Wain al Aujan*.'

Everything was moving so fast. I was looking to right and left, before and behind – the noise was deafening and the dust made it impossible to see what was happening. A few herdsmen had been riding camels in the midst of their herds when we had driven them off. Now I could see them here and there above the solid mass of camels' backs and humps in front of us, clinging precariously to their saddles, their cloaks flying, while they cast frightened looks at us over their shoulders.

A few seconds later as it seemed to me (but in reality it

must have been ten minutes or more), we began to emerge from the dense dust and from the galloping horses around us. Gradually we reduced our speed and ceased sounding our horns. The camels, exhausted by this mad gallop, dropped back to a trot. Behind us in the distance, we could see the camp of black tents, Ibn Shaalan's great tent and the crowd of tribesmen still in front of it.

We looked round at each other and felt ourselves to see if it had all been a wild nightmare. The camels had settled into a steady jog-trot. We drove our cars slowly side-by-side and shouted to one another to ask each other how we were. Some of the men had thrown off their headcloths and their long plaits of black hair were flying in the wind. They were still wildly excited by the lust of battle shouting 'The Aujan! The Aujan! *Wain al nishama*? Where are the gallants? Where are they?

Four or five miles from Ibn Shaalan's camp, we crossed a ridge and lost sight of the tents. We slowed down to a walking pace, then stopped and rounded up the camels. We then allowed the herdsmen to dismount and told them to walk back to the camp. Half a dozen of our desert soldiers slipped from the cars and mounted camels. '*Doo - ay, Doo - ay, Doo - ay,*' they called, in the melodious language of herdsmen leading the mass of camels on at a quiet walk.

We extended the six armed cars behind us in a half-moon, to act as rearguard. The car crews dismounted and climbed up the hills to prominent viewpoints to see if any of the tribesmen were still following us, while the camels led on slowly towards Rutba. Gradually it grew dark and the cars closed in once again, following the great herd at four miles an hour.

It was nine o'clock at night when we reached Rutba, still driving our vast accumulation of camels before us. '*Subhan Allah! Subhan Allah!* May God be exalted!' exclaimed the Rutba police in amazement, never having seen desert disturbances dealt with by such high-handed methods. Indeed I was half ashamed of it myself, having always believed that no man should ever lose his temper, for I was fully aware that my action was neither calculated nor courageous, but merely the result of a moment's fury.

Next day we sent trucks out to collect the Amarat victims of the Ruwalla raids. The owners of the camels which we had seized also arrived.

Fawwaz ibn Shaalan was too angry to come in person, but his

cousin, Trad ibn Shaalan, joined us in Rutba to represent the Ruwalla. Six years earlier I had crossed the Syrian Desert by camel, accompanied by two bedouins, and Trad had received us in his hospitable tent, had supplied us with food and water, and had repaired our gear for us.

We copied out lists of all the raids which had occurred and called out the plaintiffs in turn. Every man who claimed to have lost any camels took a public oath in support of his statement before a large gathering of Ruwalla and Amarat, the Desert Police and myself. Bedouins, in those days at least, were usually remarkably truthful on oath. It was not, of course, possible to guarantee that none of them would swear to a false number, but I do not think that we were far wrong, and the Ruwalla themselves were present all the time that the swearing went on and while the compilation of the lists was in progress.

In the end, seven hundred and fifty Ruwalla camels were distributed to Iraqi victims of Ruwalla raids. One hundred and fifty camels were directly returned to their original owners, where the Ruwalla themselves witnessed to their poverty. Any camel owners whom the Ruwalla swore to be poor, widows, cripples, or large families were allowed to take back their animals. When all the swearing was over and the lists of incidents and of compensation were complete, the balance of the camels were returned to Ibn Shaalan, together with copies of all the lists.

The seizure of camels from men of the Ruwalla to compensate for animals looted by their shaikhs or by different sections of the tribe may be thought to have been unjust. For though Fawwaz with his Buicks had set the example, other men of the Ruwalla had followed his example to loot what they could. Such methods, however, were justified by tribal custom.

In the case of so immense a tribe, wandering in scattered groups over an area of fifty thousand square miles of desert, it was impossible for an outsider to trace an individual or a sub-section, which had taken part in a certain incident. We had, however, given Ibn Shaalan a list of the Ruwalla raids and of the compensation exacted for each and from whom. Within a tribe, however, and especially one living in tents, nothing could be kept secret from fellow tribesmen.

It would, therefore, now be easy for Ibn Shaalan to send the men whose camels we had seized, accompanied by his negro slaves, to collect the Amarat loot from the Ruwalla raiders and to give it to the persons whose camels we had seized.

The clearest justification for our action, however, was that, from that day onwards, the Ruwalla never again raided the Amarat in all the vast spaces of the Syrian Desert. This was the only occasion in my life when the loss of my temper seemed to produce a beneficial result. Unless I had flown into a rage, I should never have ventured to engage the Ruwalla with only twenty-four men.

Only one other type of raiding had occurred in the Syrian Desert in the winter of 1929–30. In the middle of that winter, when the tribes from Trans-Jordan and Syria mingled in mid-desert with those from Iraq, several small raiding parties from Trans-Jordan had looted flocks of sheep from Iraqi tribes.

It was two hundred and eighty miles from Rutba to Amman, and this sheer distance had hitherto always made it impossible to settle such claims. Indeed, in those days, Trans-Jordan and Iraq lived in different worlds. The Syrian Desert seemed as formidable a barrier as the Atlantic Ocean. Raiders from Trans-Jordan who raided the flocks of Iraqi tribes were, therefore, confident of being able to retain their plunder. Moreover, at that time, the Trans-Jordan Government had not as yet attempted to control its nomads and there were no police forts in their desert.

Being already at Rutba with the armed desert cars, it occurred to me that we might seize the opportunity to settle accounts with the Trans-Jordan tribes also. If these tribes could once be made to give up loot, taken by them hundreds of miles away from Iraq tribes, they would realize that, henceforward, the game would not be worth the candle. I accordingly signalled to Baghdad from the Rutba post, asking permission to drive to Amman to recover the Iraq flocks raided by Trans-Jordan tribes.

We left Rutba on 26 March, 1930, arriving at Amman at noon on the 28th. Six years before, I had ridden across this desert on a camel with two companions. Now I had six armed cars.

The Ameer Abdulla was the ruler of Trans-Jordan. His cousin, the Ameer Shakir ibn Zaid, had been delegated by His Highness to deal with the affairs of the nomadic tribes. He received me in an upstairs office in a house in the little town of Amman. I had brought with me detailed lists of the raids carried out by the Trans-Jordan tribes, together with the date and place of each incident and the numbers of animals claimed by the victims. I laid copies of all the lists before the Ameer.

Rarely in my life have I met with more courtesy, humour and sympathy than I received from the Ameer Shakir. His rather broad face had been badly pitted by smallpox, so much so indeed that he had virtually no beard or moustache. But his facial peculiarities concealed one of the most delightful personalities whom I have ever met. He possessed the impalpable but magnetic quality of being a gentleman, so rare in the world today. He was always at ease himself and never failed to put his guest at ease. His humour was vivacious but quiet and dignified.

It is characteristic of all Arabs that, although they possess a ready sense of humour, they never laugh noisily. This peculiarity seems to be part of that general and particular quality of all real Arabs, a sense of personal dignity, a quality by no means evident in Europeans. The noisy crowds of holidaymakers to be seen in Western countries are foreign to the original culture of the Arabs. Unfortunately the latter have inherited from the Turks the passion for imitating the West and new generations of Arabs are learning to be both undignified and ill-mannered.

But if all Arabs seemed to be naturally dignified, the Ameer Shakir was remarkable, even amongst Arabs, for his quiet dignity, combined with cordiality. Such manners charm all comers and yet their essence is impossible to define in words.

The Sirhan seemed to have been the tribe principally involved in the looting of our sheep. As the end of the spring was approaching, the tribes had moved in from the desert to the edge of the cultivation and were accessible to government authority. The responsible leaders were accordingly sent for and ordered to produce the sheep.

It was already too hot to drive the flocks back across the desert and the Euphrates was nearly five hundred miles away. I accordingly asked for the sheep to be sold and for the money to be given to me to compensate the owners – a proposal to which the Ameer Shakir readily agreed.

It so happened that the price of sheep in Trans-Jordan was much higher than in Iraq. Consequently, when the money which I had obtained from the raiders was distributed to the owners in Iraq, they were able with their compensation to buy more sheep than had originally been raided from them. Above all, however, the action thus taken was a deterrent. Never again did raiders from Trans-Jordan molest the Iraq tribes in mid-desert.

The Trans-Jordan Government was interested in our Desert Police armed cars, as they had no desert forces of their own. I was asked to parade my party in the open space in front of the ruined Roman amphitheatre in Amman, where it was inspected by a number of officials, including the British Representative, Colonel Cox.

Our visit to Amman was to change my life, in a manner entirely unforeseen by me.

Meanwhile the political situation in Baghdad was not an entirely happy one. The tragic rebellion of 1920 had left behind it many resentments and, in spite of the wise and moderating influence of King Faisal I, friction frequently arose between the British and the Iraqis. In the summer of 1929, Abdul Muhsin al Sadoon, a scion of the great Muntifiq family, became Prime Minister. He was a man universally respected and beloved. But the stress of politics and intrigue was too much for him and, on 13 November, 1929, he committed suicide – a martyr to the service of the new Iraq.

At length, on 30 June, 1930, the new Anglo-Iraqi Treaty was signed in Baghdad. The British mandate had already terminated. Iraq was completely independent and was shortly to be admitted as a member to the League of Nations.

Under these circumstances, the Iraq Government let it be known that they proposed to reduce their British administrative staff by sixty per cent. Only four years ago I had resigned my commission in the regular British Army with the intention of devoting the remainder of my life to the service of Iraq. Four years later, when I was thirty-three years of age, owing to a change of policy for which I was not responsible, I was faced with the possibility of dismissal.

Precisely at this moment, I received a notification that the Trans-Jordan Government had finally decided to put an end to desert raiding as had been done in Iraq and to establish government control in its deserts. I was invited to come to Trans-Jordan and undertake the task – a result, doubtless, of that little parade of the Aujan outside the Roman amphitheatre in Amman. This totally unexpected offer was to me literally providential.

Before I left Iraq, I was summoned to the royal palace one evening and there, at a simple private ceremony, King Faisal I presented me with the Iraqi Order of the Rafidain, or of the Two Rivers.

Speaking of the tribes of Trans-Jordan, with whom he had fought and worked (with T. E. Lawrence) in the First World War, the King advised me not to give them money. 'Bedouins can be roused to do anything for honour,' he said. 'But once you give them money, the whole moral tone of your relations with them is lowered.' My own experience has always confirmed His Majesty's views. Arab nomads, in those days at least, must have been one of the most sensitive communities in the world on what they considered to be a point of honour. They were also capable of becoming profoundly committed to personal relationships and to personal loyalties. But money completely undermined their finer qualities.

I left Iraq in December 1930, to my deep regret, for I had learned to love the people of the country. I little knew that I was to spend twenty-six years in Trans-Jordan, and to become even more dedicated to it than I had been to Iraq.

Many of the Aujan resigned when I left Iraq, and followed me across five hundred miles of desert to Amman, where they re-enlisted and became the foundation of the Arab Legion Desert Patrol.

My years in the Southern Desert of Iraq had established a very intimate bond between the desert tribes and myself – a bond forged in the stress of battles and fear, by common dangers faced together. Throughout my twenty-six years in Jordan, men never ceased to come from the Dhafeer, the Zayyad, Shammar and the Amarat to enlist and serve in the Arab Legion.

As the years went by, the recruits who came to Jordan from these Iraqi tribes were boys who had not even been born in those stormy years of the Duweesh, when I was in the Southern Desert. But the tradition was passed on from father to son. As late as 1955 and 1956, boys were arriving to join the Arab Legion, who had been born ten years after I had left their tribes. It is to me impossible not to remember with deep affection these poor people, who for so many years remembered me.

I spent ten most happy years in Iraq. When Iraqis used to visit me later in Amman, I used to amuse them by saying that I was born an Englishman, grew up an Iraqi and had become a naturalized Jordanian. In the end, I was dismissed by the Jordan

Government, and became once more an Englishman. Life is full of vicissitudes.

[Looking back on my ten years in Iraq, it is gratifying to think that the raids of 1929–30 have never been repeated. The desert posts which we founded are still in use today. Not all the reforms of which I dreamed have been implemented – the education of bedouins, the improvement of livestock, the import of better strains of sheep, the sowing of more nutritive grasses. But at least nothing we did was subsequently undone. And still, I believe, round the camp fires, there are old men, white-headed like me, who tell the stories of how we stood our ground at Al Abtiyya and how the Duweesh sent his deputation to beg for mercy at Julaida. I do not know how many are still alive who actually remember me, but I often think of them, and repeat to myself the phrase they themselves use, when speaking of absent friends – 'May God remember them for good.']

20

Noblesse Oblige

Of the forty-two years of my active life, I spent twelve with the British Army and the R.A.F. The remaining thirty were passed serving Arab Governments. During this period, I unconsciously developed certain principles and techniques, to which I added, or which I modified, in the course of my experiences day by day. It is only in the last few years in Britain that I have attempted to marshal the lessons which I have learnt and to commit them to paper.

It may, of course, be objected that experience gained in the Middle East is irrelevant to life in the industrialized nations of the West. This objection contains an element of truth. Nevertheless, basic human nature is everywhere similar and, if we deal mainly in principles, I suggest that we may discover a number of points of general interest.

The first principle which I should like to establish is that which I call *noblesse oblige*. I am convinced that no man should ask his subordinates to do anything which he does not do himself. I do not, of course, refer to technical skills, many of which are highly specialized. But I do believe that if the men start work at eight o'clock in the morning, the senior man should do the same.

The second principle which I discovered by experience is the value of personal relations. Laws, discipline, procedure and regulations are an essential basis of all organization, but they should exist as a reserve, only to be used in emergency. The happiness of our daily work depends on our comradeship and sympathy with one another.

Work should be happy and it is the duty of the senior man, of whatever grade, to make his men happy in their daily routine. There will, of course, be many occasions when the work is mono-

212

tonous or even actually hard and unpleasant. The happiness, therefore, must be derived from pride in our work, and from the spirit of comradeship which binds us together.

Our satisfaction in our work also depends on our knowledge of its value and utility. When commanding the Arab Legion in Jordan, I tried, as often as possible, to address all ranks and to explain to them the general situation and what we were trying to do. In military service, of course, there may be certain subjects which must be kept secret. But we found a wide area of information, which was not secret, but which the private soldier would not discover unless it were brought to his notice. This sharing of information with subordinates creates a sense of partnership which consolidates the whole organization into a single team.

The happiest times of my life were passed in junior positions, as a company commander in the British Army, or with the hundred-man Desert Patrol in Trans-Jordan in the 1930s. In such junior posts it is possible to know every man intimately, his family and his background. Often, in those days, I was able to help these men in their private affairs, to arrange for the admission of their wives and children to hospital, to obtain legal advice in their troubles or to help them in other ways.

Unfortunately promotion to higher posts makes it impossible to know everybody and severs many familiar relationships. Yet even managers or senior commanders can frequently visit their men at work, address them on subjects of interest to them and encourage the junior officers to take a personal interest in them.

One of the beneficial results of constantly visiting subordinates is the ability to know as many people as possible, to recognize them, remember their names and their personal circumstances.

In the course of these addresses or conversations, it is possible to tell them of the objects of the work, to inform them of the successes achieved, of tributes paid to us in the press or by outside individuals and of our superiority over other similar units or groups. By this means, it is possible to rouse in them a pride in the organization to which they belong and in their own contribution to its success.

Another essential aspect of leadership is to remember to thank and to praise those who do well. So many senior men are ready instantly to pounce on a fault, but remain silent when all is going well. Every senior man should always remember to praise, where praise is due.

It is, perhaps, one of the principal errors of our time to think that everything depends on the human brain alone. I do not believe, within limits of course, that this is true. The secret of the success of any organization is the spirit which inspires it.

In 1940, when Britain in arms faced the world alone, Winston Churchill did not rally the nation by promising it more money or a higher standard of living. In his great 1940 speech, he said, 'I have nothing to offer but blood, toil, tears and sweat' – and the people rose like one man and followed him.

In these intellectual times, a serious danger to human comradeship and happiness lies in the theories which we may perhaps call the -*isms*. A group of clever people work out a theory of society which they believe will produce a paradise on earth. We need not hesitate to call such people idealists.

Human beings, however, differ endlessly in outlook and character – there are probably no two identical persons in the world. An intellectual system produced by men is certain to be violently attacked by other groups and only conflict, hatred and violence can result.

The very fact that they see themselves as idealists can make such dream-planners inhumanly cruel. Convinced that they have the solution to all human problems, they see those who differ from them as the enemies of mankind, against whom any act of repression is justified from loss of employment or social boycott to concentration camps beyond the Arctic Circle. The very idealism of the advocates of these intellectual Utopias enables them to act with inhuman cruelty with a clear conscience.

Sometimes they resort to violent action to secure the establishment of their favourite -*ism* in a country on the other side of the world, of which they are completely ignorant. This also perhaps may be a conscience-easer. A man may abandon his wife and children or forge a cheque, but he will carry a banner from Marble Arch to Trafalgar Square demanding the establishment of his particular -*ism* in Timbuktu or the Kuria Muria Islands.

In this respect Christianity has its feet on the ground. Its principles are summed up in the words – love God and your neighbour as yourself. There were problems enough when Christ was on earth – foreign domination, a crushing burden of taxation, poverty, bribery, corruption and violence. But He did not produce intellectual dreams of an earthly Utopia. He told us to love everybody we meet, whether they were attractive to us or not, because the Heavenly Father sends His rain alike on the just and the unjust.

Our theoretical intellectual paradises can often result in cruelty, tyranny and oppression. If we try to love and serve all the people we meet, we are more likely to add to the sum total of human happiness.

Considering the blessings which can result from human comradeship, we come to a subject on which I feel strongly – the ever increasing bureaucracy and the endless hours spent at a desk. The office tends to overshadow the whole of life, making leadership and human relationships increasingly difficult. This unfortunate tendency is felt in every department of life, whether it be administration, the armed services, industry, the church or any other activity.

Paper work makes human relations weaker. Instead of leading his subordinates, the senior man spends all his day at his desk. Moreover the office becomes a routine to which a man becomes so accustomed that he finds it more and more difficult to get out and about.

Personally I found this office life so insidious that I often felt myself obliged to establish my own rules and to compel myself to adhere to them. For example, I would decide to spend three days a week in the office and three days visiting the men at their work, or in the field. On days when I was out, a summary of the office work could be sent round to my house after office hours.

Another insidious danger in increasing office work is that it tends to result in the promotion of clever people, not of natural leaders. All these trends go with the idea that the arbiter of our destiny is the human brain and that our problems can be solved by better laws or better planning, rather than by a better spirit. In reality, if the nation – or any smaller unit – is inspired by the spirit of service, men will of their own accord seek to do what is right. But if they are not inspired by the spirit, but by selfish personal aims, neither laws nor plans can compel them to render whole-hearted service.

On the humble level on which I have served, I have formed the opinion that people do appreciate a man whose life is genuinely dedicated to selfless service in complete sincerity. Such men have seemed to me more effective leaders than the politicians, who seek popular support by promising the voters more money.

Such a life does not only render direct service by conscientiously carrying out its duties. Everyone of us unconsciously influences the people around him, and a life transparently and sincerely devoted to selfless service can change the atmosphere of a whole community.

The press and the general public seem normally to believe that strength is the quality required of a ruler or a commander. I have never held a very senior position, in which strength of character would probably be essential. Personally, however, I have always been a weak man. Any success I may have achieved has been due rather to comradeship than to compulsion.

I cannot avoid the impression that this is the only basis on which the universe can function smoothly. Whatever personal ideas we may hold about God, there seems to be little doubt that He must view much of our conduct with disgust and repulsion. As Creator of the universe, there seems to be no reason for doubting that He could destroy us all whenever He so wished. But if He were to destroy those persons of whose conduct He disapproves, He would put an end to human free will. Having once seen flames from Heaven burning up the wicked, we should be reduced to perpetual terror and be unable to develop into free personalities.

Nearer at hand are Christ's own words – 'He that is greatest among you, let him be as the younger, and he that is chief, as he that doth serve . . . I am among you as he that serveth.' These words seem to me to contain the secret of leadership.

I do not think that any relaxation of discipline is here suggested, for His personality towered over His followers. On the contrary, I believe that subordinates will be better disciplined and will render more ready obedience, precisely because they know that their leader is not inspired by personal motives, but solely by the desire to serve.

Peace can only be achieved by the general acceptance of higher moral standards. Such a general acceptance can only be based on religion. No two people are identical, and systems of ethics produced by human brains can only lead to more strife instead of to harmony.

Many brilliant brains have produced plans for the revival of

Britain, though their suggestions rarely agree. In reality, the prescription is much simpler. Britain will be revitalized as soon as her citizens abandon selfish materialism, and offer to her in simple sincerity the service of their lives.

Index

Notes

Figures in **bold type** indicate principal references. The Arabic definite article (Al) in names is printed in place but ignored for alphabetization. All tribes mentioned by name are indexed, in alphabetical order, under 'tribes and tribal groups'. 'Abu' means 'father of', 'Ibn' means 'son of'; 'Hajji' is a title given to those who have made the pilgrimage (Al Haj) to Mecca.